The US economy today

Manchester University Press

Politics Today

Series editor: Bill Jones

The US economy today

Edward Ashbee

Manchester University Press
Manchester and New York

distributed in the United States exclusively
by Palgrave Macmillan

Published by Manchester University Press
Oxford Road, Manchester M13 9NR, UK
and Room 400, 175 Fifth Avenue, New York, NY 10010, USA
www.manchesteruniversitypress.co.uk

Distributed in the United States exclusively by
Palgrave Macmillan, 175 Fifth Avenue, New York,
NY 10010, USA

Distributed in Canada exclusively by
UBC Press, University of British Columbia, 2029 West Mall,
Vancouver, BC, Canada V6T 1Z2

British Library Cataloguing-in-Publication Data
A catalogue record for this book is available from the British Library

Library of Congress Cataloging-in-Publication Data applied for

ISBN   978 0 7190 8234 4 hardback
ISBN   978 0 7190 8235 1 paperback

First published 2010

Typeset in 10/12pt Photina MT
by Graphicraft Limited, Hong Kong
Printed in Great Britain
by CPI Antony Rowe, Chippenham, Wiltshire

Contents

List of figures

List of tables

Preface and acknowledgements

The US Economy Today looks at the historical context to contemporary developments by surveying the evolution of the US economy from 1929 onwards. It
examines the experience of the New Deal, the causes and consequences of
the post-war boom, the troubled period of 'stagflation' and 'malaise' during the
1970s, the impact of 'Reaganomics', and the US economic record during the
Clinton and Bush years. Against this background, the book considers two of
the debates that sometimes hit the headlines. It assesses the different arguments
about inequality and economic mobility and also evaluates the rival claims of
those who talk of very different American or European approaches to economic
policymaking. *The US Economy Today* concludes by examining the initial
responses of the Obama White House to the recession that hit the US from
late 2007 onwards.

I am very grateful indeed to all those who have helped me with the book.
Many of the ideas and approaches have been 'road-tested' with successive
cohorts of students at Copenhagen Business School (CBS). Colleagues in the
International Center for Business and Politics and the Center for the Study of
the Americas at CBS may well recognise their own contributions to my thinking
or at least note that I have sought to anticipate their likely criticisms. I also
wish to express my thanks to Jurate Beniulyte for her meticulous work on the
tables, figures and index, the International Center for Business and Politics for
the provision of financial assistance and a supportive atmosphere, Iwan Morgan
(Institute for the Study of the Americas, University of London) for his very
helpful comments on the initial proposal, Alex Waddan (University of Leicester,
UK) for our work together on US political economy, Elena Labastida-Tovar
for permission to use two of her tables, Bill Jones, the Politics Today series
editor for his enthusiastic support, and Aase Thomasen for her scrupulous
proof-reading. I am also enormously grateful to Alison Kelly for her thoughtful
and dedicated work on the manuscript.

It goes without saying that the responsibility for errors, omissions and misrepresentations is mine alone.

Edward Ashbee
International Center for Business and Politics –
Copenhagen Business School, Denmark

For Eva and Thomas

1

Assessing the US economy

This is an introduction to the study of the US economy. The chapter outlines the concepts that will be used throughout the book. It looks at Gross Domestic Product (GDP) and the different components of GDP and, on the basis of this, considers the ways in which the 'health' of a country's economy can be evaluated through measures derived from GDP. The chapter also surveys the criticisms of these measures and the claims of those who argue that a country's overall welfare and progress should be assessed in other ways apart from GDP statistics. The second half of the chapter considers economic growth (the rate of change of GDP) more fully. It looks at the business cycle, recessions and the variables shaping long-term growth rates. The chapter concludes by assessing the claims of those who stress the difficulties associated with growth as well as 'pro-growth' arguments.

The US is often described as an economic giant or colossus. Those who talk in these terms are thinking, first and foremost, of the country's Gross Domestic Product (GDP).[1] This is the sum of all the goods and services produced, or total output, within a country over the course of a year. The GDP statistics for the US (Table 1.1) are published by the Bureau of Economic Analysis (BEA), a federal government agency based within the Department of Commerce and Trade. Table 1.1 shows the figures for 2000–8.

GDP and its components

What are the components of GDP?[2] In other words, what contributes to the totals listed in Table 1.1?

The figures reveal significant structural change. Agriculture now constitutes only about 1 per cent of output. In 2007, industrial output fell below 20 per cent of GDP.[3] Despite the adoption of new technology the process of

1

Table 1.1 *GDP in billions of current US dollars*

Year	GDP in current dollars (billions)
2000	9,817.0
2001	10,128.0
2002	10,469.6
2003	10,960.8
2004	11,685.9
2005	12,433.9
2006	13,194.7
2007	13,841.3
2008	14,264.6

Source: adapted from the Bureau of Economic Analysis (2009), *National Economic Accounts – Gross Domestic Product (GDP)*, <http://www.bea.gov>

deindustrialisation has, at in least in relative terms, continued apace.[4] Correspondingly, the service sector, (particularly real estate) healthcare provision, transportation and finance, have grown significantly and now constitute almost 80 per cent of GDP (Economist Intelligence Unit, 2008).[5]

GDP can however be measured in other ways apart from totalling the output of goods and services. It can also be gauged using the income and expenditure approaches. (The term 'national income' is often used to refer to all the totals.) The income method is based upon the total income generated through the production of goods and service (and excludes those forms of income that are simply transfers). The expenditure method is the sum of spending on goods and services produced within the country (consumer spending, investment (spending by firms), and government spending together with the value of exports minus the value of imports.)[6] Although there will be some statistical discrepancies, the output, income and expenditure methods should always amount to the same figure.[7]

Calculations based upon the expenditure method highlight important changes in the structural character of the US economy between 1930 and today. As Table 1.2 indicates, expenditure on services has increased from 31.7 per cent to 42.5 per cent. Investment levels have fluctuated. Foreign trade has grown in importance although it is still a smaller component of GDP than in many other countries. Most importantly of all, government (at federal, state and local level) has doubled in size.

Methodological difficulties

Table 1.1 showed the year-on-year rise in GDP between 2000 and 2008. There is an increase in every year although the size of the increase varies. However, methodological difficulties can occur when drawing direct comparisons between

Table 1.2 *United States – percentage shares of GDP, 1930–2008*

	1930	1940	1950	1960	1970	1980	1990	2000	2005	2008
Gross domestic product	100.0	100.0	100.0	100.0	100.0	100.0	100.0	100.0	100.0	100.0
Personal consumption expenditures	76.9	70.3	65.4	63.0	62.4	63.0	66.2	68.7	70.0	70.5
Durable goods	7.9	7.7	10.5	8.2	8.2	7.7	8.2	8.8	8.2	7.2
Nondurable goods	37.3	36.5	33.4	29.0	26.2	25.0	21.5	19.8	20.2	20.8
Services	31.7	26.1	21.5	25.8	28.1	30.4	36.5	40.0	41.5	42.5
Gross private domestic investment	11.8	13.5	18.4	15.0	14.7	17.2	14.8	17.7	16.8	14.0
Net exports of goods and services	0.8	1.5	0.3	0.8	0.4	–0.5	–1.3	–3.9	–5.7	–4.7
Government consumption expenditures and gross investment	10.9	14.8	15.9	21.2	22.5	20.3	20.3	17.5	19.0	20.2

Source: Bureau of Economic Analysis (2009), *National Economic Accounts: Table 1.1.10. Percentage Shares of Gross Domestic Product,* <http://www.bea.gov>

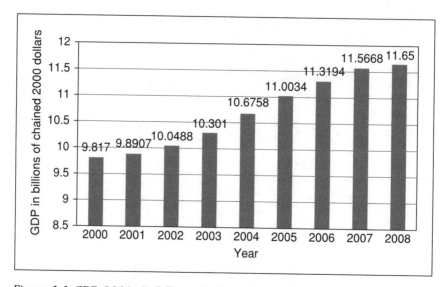

Figure 1.1 *GDP, 2000–7 (billions of chained 2000 dollars)*

Source: adapted from the Bureau of Economic Analysis (2008), *National Economic Accounts – Gross Domestic Product (GDP)*, <http://www.bea.gov>

different years because they are based on current prices (in other words, the prices prevailing during the year in question). This matters because although price rises have been modest in recent years when compared with some earlier decades (such as the 1970s), there has been *inflation*.[8] In other words, some of the increase in GDP in each of the years shown in the table has occurred simply because goods and services cost more. Therefore, the table exaggerates the extent to which GDP has, in reality, risen.

> If an accurate picture of GDP is to be obtained, the effects of price rises have to be factored in so as to allow the direct comparison of figures from different years. In the US, a 'chained-dollar' measure has been used since 1996. Figure 1.1 shows 'chained' prices from the year 2000. This is 'real' GDP. It can be seen that there is still a year-on-year rise in GDP but it is rather smaller than it initially appeared.

Using GDP statistics

GDP statistics can be used in a number of ways. First, they can be employed as a benchmark or yardstick so as to assess the economic strength of one country alongside another. Figure 1.2 shows the figures for some of the OECD

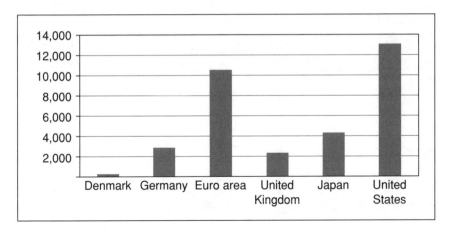

Figure 1.2 *GDP for selected OECD countries – at current prices and exchange rates, 2006 (US$bn)*

Source: adapted from OECD (2008), *Gross Domestic Product*, <http://www.oecd.org/dataoecd/48/4/37867909.pdf>

member countries.[9] Although there has been talk in recent years about American economic decline, the extent to which the US outranks the other OECD countries is immediately evident. It is not only small nations such as Denmark that are dwarfed. Even if all the countries using the euro are added together and regarded as a single country, the US is still far ahead in terms of the production and delivery of goods and services.

At this point, there are further methodological issues. There are often questions about the rates of exchange between currencies that are used when making comparisons such as these. These arise if there are frequent fluctuations in the exchange rate or if there are suggestions that a particular currency has been overvalued or undervalued by a government.[10]

Raw GDP statistics are however of only limited value. GDP figures, in themselves, say much about a country's size (as the difference between Denmark and the US indicates) and the extent to which there has been long-term industrialisation but do not readily reveal all that much about a country's current economic wellbeing. They do not, in other words, provide a useful economic 'snapshot'.

Economic growth

Because raw GDP figures say relatively little, the most usual way of assessing the state or 'health' of an economy and the direction in which a country is heading is to consider the rate of change of GDP.

Table 1.3 *US economic growth (% change in GDP), 2002–7*

	GDP % change based on current dollars	GDP % change based on chained 2000 dollars
2002	3.4	1.6
2003	4.7	2.5
2004	6.6	3.6
2005	6.4	3.1
2006	6.1	2.9
2007	4.9	2.2
2008	3.3	1.1

Source: adapted from the Bureau of Economic Analysis (2008), *National Economic Accounts – Percent Change from Preceding Period*, <http://www.bea.gov>

Like GDP statistics, growth figures are presented in different ways. They can be calculated on the basis of 'current' dollars (based upon the prices for goods and services that were charged at the time using the purchasing power of the dollar at the time the figures were collected and published) or in 'real' terms whereby an adjustment is made for price changes during the period under consideration. If there is a large difference between the two sets of figures, this indicates that the inflation rate has been relatively high. The 'real' figure based upon 'chained' dollars is always of much more use and relevance. Table 1.3 shows the US economic growth figures for 2002–7 in both 'current' and 'chained' dollars.

There are significant differences between countries when growth rates are examined. China has a very high growth rate. Its GDP in 2006 was 10.7 per cent above the 2005 figure. Despite some suspicions about the accuracy of the figures that have been published, commentators suggest that Chinese GDP, given these rates of growth, will overtake established industrial countries, including the US, within the coming decades. According to the *China Daily*, China's GDP overtook the United Kingdom in 2005 and moved towards comparability with Germany (Binglan, 2007). Goldman Sachs, the investment bank, predicts that China will have a larger GDP than the US by 2035 (Macartney and Duncan, 2005).[11]

The business or trade cycle

As many of the statistics cited above suggest, GDP does not grow evenly. Growth rates rise and fall. Although there are many trendless fluctuations and there is a long-term increase in GDP, there are also broad and periodic trends. Growth rates follow a cycle. As Figure 1.3 indicates, periods of boom (or expansion) tend to be followed by a downswing and recession (or contraction).

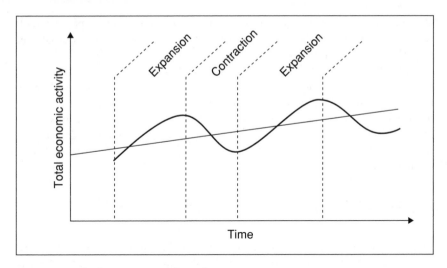

Figure 1.3 *The business or trade cycle*

Explaining the trade or business cycle

Why is there a business or trade cycle? For some, particularly those on the left, the swings between booms and recessions are an inevitable feature of an unregulated or unplanned economy. Capitalism, they assert, is inherently unstable and booms are invariably short-lived.

Other observers have stressed the part played by particular developments in triggering recessions. There is an emphasis on external events or processes rather than internal forces or pressures within the market economy itself. Such exogenous 'shocks' can have significant consequences. In 1973–4 the large increase in world oil prices added to inflation and contributed to a wage-price spiral as workers sought higher wages so as to keep pace with the increases in the price level. The US administration and European governments then responded by attempting to hold back wages, often through direct controls, and by dampening down demand levels. Faced by both falling consumption and instability, firms modified their production plans.

Other factors can also trigger a slowdown. Excess stockpiles will lead firms to scale back output. A high interest rate set by the Federal Reserve System (which controls US monetary policy) could also have *deflationary* consequences.[12] In other words, if firms and individuals find it costly to borrow funds (and mortgage payments increase) there will be a fall in both business expansion plans and consumer spending. As overall demand levels are reduced (or, at the least, the rate of growth of demand falls back) companies may face bankruptcy or be compelled to make redundancies and joblessness will increase. Conversely, an excessively low interest rate (allowing individuals and firms to borrow cheaply) could contribute to a 'bubble' driving up stock market prices which will at some point 'burst' leading to sharp falls in the price of assets (shares or perhaps houses) and a loss of investor confidence.

Some have suggested that a distinction should be drawn between the recessions that took place after 1945 but preceded the 1990s and those that have taken place in recent years. The earlier recessions were, for the most part, caused when the Federal Reserve adopted a tight monetary policy, raised interest rates, and restricted the supply of credit. More recent recessions have instead been triggered by the collapse of asset bubbles (Scheiber, 2009).

Recessions

In most countries the economy is defined as being in a recession when two consecutive quarters of negative growth take place. However, in the US the definition is looser and more subjective. The existence of an 'official' recession depends upon the judgement of the National Bureau of Economic Research's Business Cycle Dating Committee. There is a recession when, in its eyes, there is 'a significant decline in economic activity spread across the economy, lasting more than a few months' (quoted in Stelzer, 2008).[13]

In a 2002 report, the Congressional Research Service charted economic downturns and recessions (which it brings together as 'contractions') from the end of the Second World War onwards. These are listed in Table 1.4.

Table 1.4 *Economic contractions, 1945–99*

Period of contraction	Months of contraction	Contraction of GDP	Maximum unemployment rate
November 1948–October 1949	8	1.7	7.9
July 1953–May 1954	10	2.7	6.1
August 1957–April 1958	8	3.7	7.5
April 1960–February 1961	10	1.6	7.1
December 1969–November 1970	11	0.6	6.1
November 1973–March 1975	16	3.0	9.0
January–July 1980	6	2.2	7.8
July 1981–November 1982	16	2.9	10.8
July 1990–March 1991	9	1.5	7.8

Source: Marc Labonte and Gail Makinen (2002), *The Current Economic Recession: How Long, How Deep, and How Different From the Past?*, Congressional Research Service Report for Congress, 11, <http://www.fpc.state.gov/documents/organization/7962.pdf>

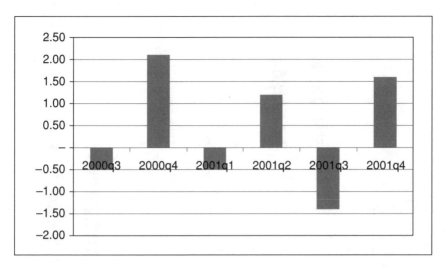

Figure 1.4 *Economic growth (GDP % change based on chained 2000 dollars), July 2000–December 2001*

Source: adapted from the Bureau of Economic Analysis (2008), *National Economic Accounts*, <http://www.bea.gov>

Despite impressive growth rates during the latter half of the 1990s which gave rise to talk of 'overcoming' the trade cycle, the US economy teetered on the edge of recession at the end of President Clinton's period of office and during President George W. Bush's first year in the White House (see Figure 1.4).

Then, in 2007–8, the 'credit crunch' took hold (see Chapter 5). Its effects spread from the financial sector to the wider 'real' economy and by late 2008 there was devastating fall in output levels (see Figure 1.5).

Consequences

In a recession, fewer goods and services are produced than in preceding periods. There are bankruptcies and lay-offs and unemployment inevitably rises. Investment, which may already have been cut back, will be reduced still further. Retail sales and consumer confidence fall. Personal bankruptcies increase and other indicators of hardship, such as evictions from homes (as individuals can no longer afford to repay loans), also rise.[14]

Recessions almost always have significant social and political, as well as economic, repercussions. Although the 1991 recession was relatively short and (if measured in terms of economic growth alone) confined to a six month period, it damaged President George H. W. Bush's standing and laid the basis for his defeat in the November 1992 election at the hands of Arkansas governor,

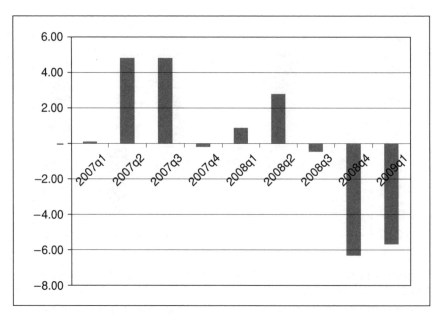

Figure 1.5 *Economic growth (GDP % change based on chained 2000 dollars),
January 2007–September 2008*

Source: adapted from the Bureau of Economic Analysis (2008), *National Economic Accounts*,
<http://www.bea.gov>

Bill Clinton. The recession contributed to the election of Senator Barack Obama
as US president in November 2008 and fuelled calls for increased regulation
as well as an enlarged role for government.

• Despite the hardships faced by those who are adversely affected, periods of
  recession serve a positive function when the long-term development of a
  nation's economy is considered. Not only are inflationary pressures eased
  but there is what Joseph Schumpeter, an influential economist and political
  scientist who lived during the first half of the twentieth century, dubbed
  'creative destruction'. Recessions add to and intensify the process of muta-
  tion by which old, less efficient industries are displaced by newer and more
  innovative forms of production.

Living standards

As well as providing a basis for economic growth statistics and a way of
charting the course of the business cycle, GDP figures can be used in another
way. Commentators often divide a country's GDP by its total population. This

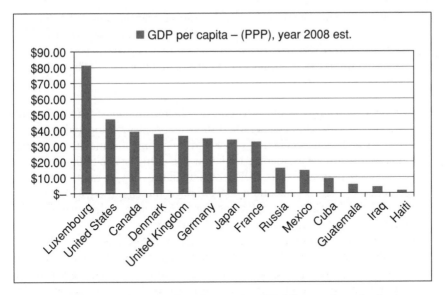

Figure 1.6 *GDP per capita – selected countries, US dollars and purchasing power parities*[15]

Source: adapted from Central Intelligence Agency (2009), *The World Factbook*, <https://www.cia.gov>

gives a 'snapshot' of average living standards. As Figure 1.6 suggests, these *GDP per capita* figures show that the US has a high average standard of living although it is exceeded by some other countries including Luxembourg.

Limitations

Although extensively used and widely cited, GDP figures, particularly if employed as a basis for estimates of living standards in a country (GDP per capita), have significant limitations.

- There are suggestions that the US GDP figures are methodologically flawed. As Kevin Phillips notes, the Bureau of Economic Analysis 'imputes' (or attributes) additional income to many individuals and households. This includes income for living in one's own home, the value of employer-provided health and life insurance premiums, and the benefits gained from the free current account facility offered by many banks. In 2007, imputed income represented about 15 per cent of GDP. This form of accounting, Phillips suggests, is a 'fiddle' that is pursued for political reasons. It leads to an overstatement of GDP and a consequent underestimation of recessions and their impact (Phillips, 2008: 46). According to John Williams:

> Upward growth biases built into GDP modeling since the early 1980s have rendered this important series nearly worthless...[T]he recessions of 1990/ 1991 and 2001 were much longer and deeper than currently reported [and] lesser downturns in 1986 and 1995 were missed completely. (Phillips, 2008: 46)

- GDP per capita figures suffer particular problems that go beyond those that affect GDP statistics more generally. If there is considerable inequality within a country and small numbers of people have very high incomes, the ordinary individual will have an income far below the GDP per capita figures listed by the OECD. In other words, GDP per capita figures can overstate individual wellbeing. In the US, inequality levels have increased since the 1970s (see Chapter 7). GDP per capita has therefore become a less useful guide to the wellbeing of the characteristic American.
- In practice, living standards also depend upon the level of income that the individual receives after deductions for income tax. GDP per capita statistics are generally based upon gross earnings. Taxation and levels of government provision are much higher in some countries (such as those in the Nordic region) than others. US taxation rates are lower than those in Europe and so disposable income is higher. However, Americans often have to pay for certain forms of provision such as health or higher education which are provided freely or at a subsidised rate in other countries. Having said that, in countries that offer extensive social provision, it is difficult to put an accurate market value on government services and there are debates about their quality and worth.
- Some countries have large hidden or 'underground' economies that evade the taxation system and may not be reported in the GDP statistics. Although cultural variables and the extent to which laws are enforced are important in shaping people's behaviour, high tax rates inevitably increase the incentive to evade the tax authorities. A study in Canada estimated that the underground economy represented 15–16 per cent of GDP (amounting to about 160 billion Canadian dollars in 2001) (Business Council of British Columbia, 2002). Other countries, where higher tax rates or where law enforcement procedures are lax, probably have even more sizeable hidden economies.
- Despite Kevin Phillips's claims that GDP statistics overestimate US output (see above), the statistics fail to record substantial amounts of unpaid labour. Because of this and the other criticisms of GDP as a measure, Redefining Progress (a voluntary organisation based in California) established the *Genuine Progress Indicator (GPI)* in 1995 so as to offer a fuller and more comprehensive picture of US economic 'health'. The GPI includes factors such as household work and parenting (which, because they are unpaid and unrecorded, are neglected by the GDP statistics), income distribution and inequality, the lifespan of consumer durables (such as dishwashers),

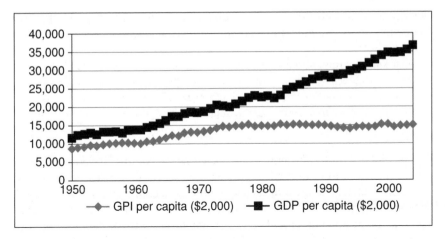

Figure 1.7 *GDP per capita and GPI, 1950–2004*
Source: adapted from Redefining Progress (2008), *Genuine Progress Indicator*,
<http://www.rprogress.org>

the costs of crime, the loss of leisure time as working hours have increased, the cost of commuting and the effects of pollution. Redefining Progress argues that, measured in this way, American economic growth has been 'stagnant' since the 1970s (see Figure 1.7). In other words, 'genuine progress' has been very much more limited than GDP per capita (Talberth, Cobb, and Slattery, 2007: 8–15).

Long-term economic development

Up to this point, the focus has been on relatively short-term economic growth. As has been noted, growth rates can in the short run be explained in terms of the point at which a country is on the business cycle (whether it is, for example, in a period of boom or recession) or the forms of monetary and fiscal policy that have been adopted.[16] Longer-term patterns of economic growth (or 'trend growth') need to be considered in a different way. They are generally understood by considering the different *factors of production*. These factors – land, labour and capital – facilitate the production of goods and services.[17]

'Land' refers to all natural resources, including, for example, mineral deposits. Few economic historians would question the importance of 'land' and geography as factors explaining patterns of economic development from the eighteenth century onwards. The industrial revolution was based in European countries and New England states which offered exploitable resources, a temperate climate and access to water. To an extent, natural resources still determine what and how much is produced. As the World Bank's Poverty Reduction and Economic Management Network has noted:

> A striking one third of the world's gross domestic product (GDP) is produced in the temperate ecological zones within 100 km of the world's navigable waterways; these zones amount to only 4 per cent of the world's landmass. Almost none of the industrialized countries are in the tropics or subtropics, or landlocked. (World Bank, 2005: 57)

'Land' alone is not sufficient, however. Growth requires a plentiful labour supply (provided in Britain during the eighteenth century by the enclosure of common land, which threw up a class of landless labourers who were in search of work). The process also depends upon capital. This refers to the capital goods (such as plant and equipment) that are employed in the production of consumption goods and the delivery of services. The British industrial revolution was tied to the adoption of new technology in the textile industries, advances in iron-making techniques and steam power.

Growth depends in part upon the quantity of factor inputs. An increase in the labour supply can, for example, contribute to growth. Increases in factor inputs are often limited, however. Although discoveries will be made, the supply of natural resources is by definition fixed. In practice, long-run growth depends upon the quality as well as the quantity of inputs. In other words, increases in *total factor productivity* also make an important contribution to long-term economic growth.[18] Advances in productivity depend, in part, upon physical capital and human capital (Elwell, 2006: 6).

Physical capital refers to the tools, equipment and plant used by workers in the productive process. Increases in physical capital require investment which is, in turn, dependent upon savings drawn from those within the country or foreign sources:

> In themselves capital goods do nothing to satisfy current wants and needs, but their use will expand the economy's capacity to produce goods in the future. A deferral of current consumption is the economic cost of increasing consumption in the future. The calculation that economic agents have made that warrants incurring this cost is that what is given up today is more than compensated for by what is gained tomorrow. (Elwell, 2006: 6)[19]

The process by which the amount of capital per worker increases is called *capital deepening*. Research in recent decades suggests that, in the US, capital deepening may account for almost 50 per cent of the recorded growth rate of output (Elwell, 2006: 8). This is, in part, because of the pace at which companies learn from each other and adopt advances in technology. Mass production techniques were pioneered by a handful of firms but then spread once the gains had become evident. During the 1990s, the IT revolution spread in a similar way. Furthermore, a particular technological advance may bring forth other innovations and developments.

'Human capital' refers to the defining attributes of an individual or social grouping that are economically productive. The term encompasses educational attainment, skills and the attitudes that an individual brings to the labour market. There is often a *complementarity* effect between advances in physical and human capital as the adoption of new forms of technology demands new and more advanced skills. Although those who emphasise the growth records of the Scandinavian nations point to the part played in their economic performance by human capital (extensive educational and social provision), there are measurement difficulties. While levels of educational attainment can be recorded, there are sometimes problems making direct comparisons between different nations. Furthermore, the concept of human capital includes imprecise and elusive notions such as levels of interpersonal 'trust' and 'connectedness'.

Other factors may also promote growth. Economic transactions are more likely to take place if a society is governed by the rule of law and if contracts are enforced through an ordered legal system. As a corollary, arbitrary rule or cultural patterns that impose additional transaction costs on those who seek to do business jeopardise growth. Entrenched class interests can stifle entrepreneurial initiatives by those on a lower rung of the ladder. Some commentators stress the extent to which a national economy is open to trade. Openness, they argue, allows a nation to specialise in producing the goods and delivering the services in which they have the greatest absolute and comparative advantage and then to trade with others (see pp. 151–2). Growth has been impeded in the countries that have erected barriers against others. Other analysts – and this is a dividing line between right and left – stress the importance of limiting government and minimising the tax burden. 'Big government', they assert, jeopardises entrepreneurship and growth.

The part played by variables other than land, labour and capital alone can be illustrated by a comparison between the US and Argentina. At times, both countries were at a similar level of development. Indeed, before the 1930s, Argentina was among the ten richest nations in the world (Beattie, 2009: 16). 'The countries were dealt quite similar hands but played them very differently. The similarities between the two in the second half of the 19th century and in fact up to 1939, were neither fictional nor superficial' (Beattie, 2009: 16–18). As Alan Beattie records, there were few opportunities to establish small farmsteads in Argentina because land ownership was highly concentrated. There was, furthermore, some early disdain for industry but the country later sought to catch up through import substitution industrialisation (ISI), a policy that sought to increase growth by excluding imports and diverting production towards the domestic market. During the early 1960s, tariffs averaged 84 per cent. Exports as well as imports were taxed. In place of growth, the policy of ISI led to depression and a 'lost decade' (Beattie, 2009: 20).

Negative externalities and strains

Although majority opinion regards economic growth as important, some fear the consequences of high growth rates and point to what they see as damaging consequences for the environment, particularly when growth draws upon non-renewable resources or places an excessive strain upon the infrastructure of a region. Those opposed to the North American Free Trade Agreement (NAFTA) argue that the rapid economic development it facilitated in the border region between the US and Mexico, particularly around cities such as El Paso, has caused pollution and 'a new strain on the border ecology as the pace of industrialization quickens and traffic increases from trucks hauling goods across the border' (Suro, 1991). The strain intensified with each successive year. As the US General Accounting Office recorded, nearly 4 million trucks (as well as 85 million passenger vehicles) entered the US from Mexico in fiscal year 1998 alone (US General Accounting Office, 1999: 2).

Gains from growth

Nonetheless, although some of these anxieties are vocally expressed, economic growth brings significant benefits.

- While some have questioned the character of the jobs that have been created in recent years, economic growth provides employment. Table 1.5 shows the number of (non-farm) jobs in the US between 1960 and 2007. Over the course of half a century, the US economy has grown so as to provide more than two-and-a-half times as many jobs as it did in 1960. Indeed, the relationship between growth and employment provision can be charted with some precision using 'Okun's law'. Despite the growth of new technology that many feared would displace jobs, for every percentage point that the economy grows above 2.5 per cent, the unemployment rate falls by half a percentage point (Krugman, 1996).[20]
- Growth also provides a growing array of goods and services and a basis for higher living standards. According to those who adopt a free market and 'pro-growth' perspective, growth has, together with technological change and free trade, brought about a cycle of progress 'that in the last two centuries enabled unprecedented improvements in every objective measurement of human well-being' (Cato Institute, 2008). The realities underpinning this claim are, it is said, seen most dramatically in countries such as India and China where many millions have over just a few decades been lifted out of hunger and malnutrition. However, the advantages of growth are also evident in the US. Although the rise in median household living standards was at times relatively slow and there were periods when there was a fall, there has been a long-term increase.[21] Table 1.6 shows this. The figures are

Table 1.5 *Numbers of employees on non-farm payrolls, 1960–2007 (000s)*

Year	Employees on non-farm payrolls
1960	54,296
1965	60,874
1970	71,006
1975	77,069
1980	90,528
1985	97,511
1990	109,487
1995	117,298
2000	131,785
2005	133,703
2007	137,623

Source: adapted from Bureau of Labor Statistics (2008), *B-1. Employees on Nonfarm Payrolls by Major Industry Sector, 1958 to Date*, <ftp://ftp.bls.gov>

Table 1.6 *Household income in constant (2005) US dollars, 1980–2005*

Year	Median household income (2005 dollars)
1967	35,379
1970	38,026
1975	37,736
1980	39,739
1985	40,868
1990	43,366
1995	43,346
2000	47,599
2001	46,569
2002	46,036
2003	45,970
2004	45,817
2005	46,326

Source: adapted from US Census Bureau (2008), *The 2008 Statistical Abstract – The National Data Book: Income, Expenditures, Poverty, & Wealth: Household Income*, <http://www.census.gov>

in constant (2005) dollars. In other words, they have been adjusted so as to take account of inflation. Increased income adds to consumer demand. Rising demand levels contribute to further investment in capital machinery by companies which, in turn, provides further growth, employment, and income. This process is dubbed the 'accelerator'.

• Growth also allows the reduction of absolute poverty. Absolute poverty is measured in terms of a family or individual's ability to meet basic needs such as food, shelter and healthcare. It is often distinguished from measures of relative poverty that define poverty in terms of living below a specified percentage of a country's median household income. According to an OECD study, if US poverty is calculated on a relative basis, at 50 per cent of median disposable income, there was a poverty rate of 16 per cent during the latter half of the 1990s. If it is set at 60 per cent of median disposable income, the figure was 24 per cent (Foerster and d'Ercole, 2005: 22). Relative poverty levels are therefore a measure of inequality in a particular society. Nonetheless, in practice, notions of absolute poverty have also shifted and the poverty line has been raised. Basic needs have been progressively redefined over time. As David Hamilton noted in 1962, the concept of a necessity is culturally shaped:

> items which were looked upon as luxuries initially force such changes in the way of life of a people that they eventually become necessities. The automobile is an excellent example of this effect. In American culture the automobile, shortly after its initial introduction, was viewed as a plaything for sons of the rich. But as the diffusion of the automobile proceeded it worked a change in the American way of life so that eventually what was a luxury became a technological necessity. (quoted in Fisher, 1995)

- Economic growth provides a 'fiscal dividend'. As incomes rise, more is paid to the government through direct taxes (including personal income and corporate taxes) and indirect tax (sales tax). This enables government to increase expenditure on social provision (such as healthcare and education) without raising the rate of taxation.
- Those who define themselves as 'pro-growth' argue that economic expansion allows countries to address environmental issues and take remedial action. More efficient production techniques can be adopted. They suggest that 'the early stages of development can indeed cause environmental problems, but additional development creates greater wealth allowing societies to create and afford cleaner technologies. Development becomes the solution rather than the problem' (Cato Institute, 2008).

Conclusion

Economic growth (the rate of change of GDP) is generally regarded as a key measure of a country's economic 'health'. Short-run growth is not, however, a steady process but takes a cyclical form. While there are booms (periods of high growth) there are also recessions. As the twentieth century progressed, economic and political debate was increasingly structured around ways of alleviating recessions and the toll that they take. Long-run growth depends on the ability of the economy to increase output. This is determined by the rate of growth of *productivity* of both labour and capital. Accounts based upon politics and cultural attitudes have been used to explain why north America prospered while many countries south of the Rio Grande continue to face economic difficulties.

Notes

1 Some texts refer to GNP (Gross National Product) rather than GDP. GNP includes 'net property income' from abroad. The American GNP statistics do not include goods and services produced by foreign firms within the US, but do include goods and services produced by American companies based overseas.

2 GDP calculations are based upon the market value of goods and services. Any taxes or subsidies must be factored in. It is important that only final products (rather than component parts) are included so that there is no double-counting. So as to do this, the calculations are based upon the value added at each stage of the production process. The output method is therefore sometimes also termed the 'value-added' method.

3 The industrial sector includes automobile production, aerospace, telecommunications, chemicals, electronics and information technology. Despite talk of 'deindustrialisation', US companies set the pace in the manufacture of computers, internet access, and software development. Some commentators suggest however that because industrial production and services are so interlinked, the manufacturing base, if defined in strict in strict terms, constitutes only about 12 per cent of GDP (Economist Intelligence Unit, 2008).

4 Despite the 'deindustrialisation' process, the US oil industry continues to be of pivotal importance. At the end of the 1990s, the US supplied more than a fifth of the world's refined petroleum. This more or less equalled the output of all the European countries taken together (Gale Encyclopedia of US Economic History, 2005).

5 Despite the US's economic strengths, some long-term economic strains were evident before the recession (see below) that began in late 2007. First, the US is becoming more dependent upon imports of foreign oil and the extraction costs of existing oil reserves in the US are increasing because the fields are scattered and small. This provoked many Republicans, including Governor Sarah Palin, the Party's 2008 vice-presidential nominee, to adopt 'Drill, Baby, Drill' as a campaign slogan. Secondly, the process of deindustrialisation has been tied to the use of new technology and the 'export' of many manufacturing jobs from the US to countries with lower wage costs. This has particularly affected 'rustbelt' states in the north-east such as Ohio and Pennsylvania and there have been frequent calls for action to curb 'offshoring' and 'outsourcing' (see Chapter 6). The adoption of new technology has, furthermore, contributed to the emergence of a 'two-tier' labour market. Those without education and training have fallen further and further behind in terms of wages and health coverage those with relevant and up-to-date skills. Indeed, household incomes have for the most part stagnated among lower socioeconomic groupings. Fourthly, the 'baby boom' generation is reaching retirement, adding to healthcare and Social Security (pension) costs (Central Intelligence Agency, 2009).

6 See Landefeld, Seskin and Fraumeni (2008) for a study of the methodological difficulties and problems associated with the collection of national income statistics.

7 The US began collecting comprehensive and detailed estimates of GDP in the mid-1930s. Before then, economic information was limited and fragmentary. As Richard Froyen notes: 'One reads with dismay of Presidents Hoover and then

Roosevelt designing policies to combat the Great Depression of the 1930s on the basis of such sketchy data as stock price indices, freight car loadings, and incomplete indices of industrial production. The fact was that comprehensive measures of national income and output did not exist at the time. The Depression, and with it the growing role of government in the economy, emphasized the need for such measures and led to the development of a comprehensive set of national income accounts' (quoted in Landefeld, Seskin and Fraumeni, 2008: 194).

8 Inflation refers to the generalised and sustained upward movement of prices for goods and services. Although there are different methods, it is often measured through *Consumer Price Indexes*. These track price rises by taking weighted 'baskets' of goods and services.

9 The OECD is the Organisation for Economic Cooperation and Development. It brings together many of the countries that are committed to 'democracy and the market economy' including the US, the United Kingdom, Denmark and Germany. Its membership does not at the time of writing include China or Russia.

10 There have been claims, often heard in Congress, that China undervalues the yuan so as to boost the country's exports. Economists often adjust comparative statistics on the basis of Purchasing Power Parity (PPP) so exchange rates between currencies are considered on the basis of their buying power.

11 Questions have however been asked about the accuracy of the Chinese statistics. (See, for example, Rawski, 2001.) Nonetheless, countries that are 'catching up' with more advanced nations often have very high growth rates. These slow down as a country approaches 'maturity'.

12 'Monetary policy' refers to the supply of money and its 'price' (the interest rate). In the US, the setting of the base interest rate (the target Federal Funds rate) and other forms of monetary policy are the responsibility of the Federal Reserve System. The 'Fed' was established in 1913 and although in some respects it is a federal government institution it also has some private components including twelve regionally based Federal Reserve Banks. While the chairman and the board of governors are nominated by the president and subject to confirmation by the Senate, the Federal Reserve makes its own day-to-day decisions. There have been suggestions (which may or may not be accurate) that President Ronald Reagan had reservations about the tight monetary policy (high interest rates) pursued by the Paul Volcker (who served as 'Fed' chairman between 1979 and 1987) and that President George H. W. Bush wanted interest rates cut more quickly in the early 1990s and felt that the Federal Reserve's policy of high interest rates contributed to his election defeat in November 1992. In 2009, against a background of recession, Ron Paul and over 250 other members of Congress backed a bill empowering the Government Accountability Office (the investigative arm of Congress) to 'audit' the Federal Reserve's decisions on interest rates. Critics charged that this threatened its independence (Bienkowski, 2006: 70 and Andrews, 2009).

13 Although its statements are assigned quasi-official status, the National Bureau of Economic Research (NBER) is a private organisation. The NBER considers some other indicators as well as economic growth statistics. These include unemployment, real personal income, industrial production as well as wholesale and retail sales. At the end of November 2008, the Bureau announced that the US had been in a recession from December 2007 onwards (Isidore, 2008).

14 Developments such as these are sometimes lagged behind the business cycle. Employers will not, for example, reduce the size of the workforce at the beginning of a downswing. Correspondingly, they will not recruit at the first signs of an upturn.

15 Purchasing power parity (PPP) refers to the use of an exchange rate based upon equivalent purchasing power in the countries under consideration. It consists of 'simply price relatives which show the ratio of the prices in national currencies of the same good or service in different countries' (OECD, 2007).

16 'Fiscal policy' refers to the use of taxation and government spending so as to influence the economy.

17 Some also include 'entrepreneurship' and 'human capital' as factors of production.

18 'Productivity' refers to economic efficiency. It measures the relationship between inputs and outputs. The productivity of labour can, for example, be measured as output per labour-hour.

19 The input of physical capital is however subject to the law of *diminishing returns*. Each addition to the stock of physical capital will bring forth a progressively reduced increase in the productivity of labour.

20 Lawrence Summers, appointed as director of the White House's National Economic Council by President Obama, has argued that the relationship between growth (or negative growth) and employment levels is not as straightforward as Okun's law seems to suggest. During the recession that began in late 2007, unemployment increased significantly faster (and the unemployment rate was about 1 to 1.5 percentage points higher) than the fall in GDP might have led observers to expect. In an economic downswing, productivity generally decreases as firms hold on to workers (because of the costs of hiring new employees) even as the amount of work for them to do declines. This, as Summers noted, was has not a feature of the post-2007 recession. Indeed, productivity increased (Summers, 2009).

21 The 'median' is one 'type of average, found by arranging the values in order and then selecting the one in the middle. If the total number of values in the sample is even, then the median is the mean of the two middle numbers. The median is a useful number in cases where the distribution has very large extreme values which would otherwise skew the data' <http://www.investorwords.com/3030/median.html>

References and further reading

Andrews, Edmund L. (2009), 'Bernanke's 2nd-term challenge will be to undo first-term steps', *New York Times*, August 26, A1–A4.

Beattie, Alan (2009), 'The Superpower that never was', *FT Weekend Magazine*, May 23–4, 16–21.

Bienkowski, Wojciech (2006), 'The economic policy of George W. Bush: a continuation of Reaghanomics?', in Wojciech Bienkowski, Josef C. Brada and Mariusz-Jan Radlo (2006), *Reaganomics Goes Global: What Can the EU, Russia and Transition Countries Learn from the USA?*, Basingstoke: Palgrave Macmillan, 69–79.

Binglan, Xu (2007), 'China's GDP grows 10.7% in 2006, fastest in 11 years', *China Daily*, January 26, <http://www.chinadaily.com>

Business Council of British Columbia (2002), 'How big is the "hidden" economy?', *Business Council of British Columbia – Policy Perspectives*, 9: 3, June, <http://www.bcbc.com/Documents/ppv9n3.pdf>

Cato Institute (2008), *Cato Store – Indur M. Goklany, The Improving State of the World: Why We're Living Longer, Healthier, More Comfortable Lives on a Cleaner Planet*, <http://www.catostore.org>

Central Intelligence Agency (2009), *The World Factbook*, Central Intelligence Agency, <http://www.cia.gov>

Economist Intelligence Unit (2008), *Country Profile – United States of America*, Business Source Complete, <http://search.ebscohost.com>

Elwell, Craig K. (2006), *Long-Term Growth of the U.S. Economy: Significance, Determinants, and Policy*, Congressional Research Service, <http://www.usembassy.it/pdf/other/RL32987.pdf>

Fisher, Gordon M. (1995), *Is There Such a Thing as an Absolute Poverty Line Over Time? Evidence from the United States, Britain, Canada, and Australia on the Income Elasticity of the Poverty Line*, US Census Bureau – Poverty Measurement Working Papers, <http://www.census.gov>

Foerster, Michael and Marco Mira d'Ercole (2005), *Income Distribution and Poverty in OECD Countries in the Second Half of the 1990s*, OECD Social, employment and migration working papers.

Gale Encyclopedia of US Economic History (2005), *Petroleum Industry*, <http://www.accessmylibrary.com>

Isidore, Chris (2008), *It's Official: Recession since Dec. '07*, CNNMoney.com, December 1, <http://money.cnn.com>

Krugman, Paul (1996), 'Stay on their backs', *New York Times Magazine*, February 4, <http://pages.stern.nyu.edu>

Landefeld, J. Steven, Eugene P. Seskin and Barbara M. Fraumeni (2008), 'Taking the pulse of the economy: measuring GDP', *Journal of Economic Perspectives*, 22: 2, Spring, 193–216.

Macartney, Jane and Gary Duncan (2005), 'China expected to overtake US within three decades', *The Times*, December 21, <http://business.timesonline.co.uk>

OECD (2007), *Glossary of Statistical Terms*, <http://stats.oecd.org>

Phillips, Kevin (2008), 'Numbers racket', *Harper's Magazine*, 316: 1896, May, 43.

Rawski, Thomas G. (2001), *What's Happening to China's GDP Statistics?*, University of Pittsburgh – Department of Economics, September 12, <http://www.pitt.edu/~tgrawski/papers2001/gdp912f.pdf>

Rowe, Jonathan (2008), 'Our phony economy', *Harper's Magazine*, 316: 1897, June.

Scheiber, Noam (2009), 'Larry Summers on jobs and stimulus', *New Republic* (The Stash), July 18, <http://blogs.tnr.com>

Stelzer, Irwin (2008), 'Don't make a recession out of a downturn', *Sunday Times*, Business, August 3, 4.

Summers, Lawrence H. (2009), *Rescuing and Rebuilding the US Economy: A Progress Report*, Peterson Institute for International Economics, July 17, <http://www.piie.com>

Suro, Roberto (1991), 'Pollution tests two neighbors: El Paso and Juarez', *New York Times*, December 22, <http://query.nytimes.com>

Talberth, John, Clifford Cobb and Noah Slattery (2007), *The Genuine Progress Indicator 2006: A Tool for Sustainable Development*, Redefining Progress, <http://www.rprogress.org/publications/2007/GPI%202006.pdf>

US General Accounting Office (1999), *Report to Congressional Requesters – Issues and Challenges Confronting the United States and Mexico*, 2, <http://archive.gao.gov/f0902b/162399.pdf>

World Bank (2005), *Economic Growth in the 1990s: Learning from a Decade of Reform*, World Bank, <http://www.worldbank.org>

World Bank Statistical Manual (2009), *GDP – Final Output*, <http://www.worldbank.org>

Appendix: America's largest companies

The Fortune 500 top twenty companies (2009)

Rank	Company	Industry
1	Exxon Mobil	Peroleum refining
2	Wal-Mart Stores	Retail
3	Chevron	Petroleum refining
4	ConocoPhillips	Petroleum refining
5	General Electric	Finance (diversified)
6	General Motors (GM)	Motor vehicles
7	Ford Motor	Motor vehicles
8	AT&T	Telecommunications
9	Hewlett-Packard	Computers/office equipment
10	Valero Energy	Petroleum refining
11	Bank of America Corp.	Banking/finance
12	Citigroup	Banking/finance
13	Berkshire Hathaway	Insurance/holdings
14	International Business Machines (IBM)	Information technology
15	McKesson	Pharmaceuticals distribution
16	J.P. Morgan Chase & Co.	Banking/finance
17	Verizon Communications	Telecommunications
18	Cardinal Health	Pharmaceuticals distribution
19	CVS Caremark	Drug and general retail
20	Procter & Gamble	Household and personal products

Note: The companies are ranked by their gross revenue.
Source: adapted from CNNMoney.com (2009), *Fortune 500 – And the winners are...*, <http://money.cnn.com>

2

The New Deal, the long boom, government and the economy

Chapter 2 considers the increasingly important economic role of the federal government. It looks at the impact of the Wall Street crash and the depression of the 1930s, and against this background, evaluates the strengths and weaknesses of the New Deal programmes. The chapter then surveys economic performance during the decades that followed the Second World War and assesses the part played by *demand management* and *Keynesian* economic thinking.

The first US president, George Washington, took office in 1789. For much of the period since then, government (particularly the federal government) played only a minimal role in the American economy and the lives of the country's citizens. Indeed, if the mobilisation of resources during the war with Britain (1812–15), the Civil War years (1861–65) and the Reconstruction period is disregarded, government spending constituted only 2–3 per cent of GDP until the beginning of the twentieth century (see Figure 2.1).

However, although the federal government had a minimal presence by today's standards, 'laissez-faire' never took a pure form.[1] From the beginning of the republic onwards, the federal government pursued a protectionist course and imposed tariffs upon imported goods so as to shelter and bolster domestic industries. The US Constitution (1787) assigned the provision of post offices to the federal government. The 1792 Coinage Act established the US dollar as a national currency based upon silver and gold. In the mid-nineteenth century, land grants and subsidies were extended to railroad companies. States also had powers. In 1876, in *Munn v. Illinois*, the US Supreme Court established that the individual states had the constitutional power to regulate businesses that operated within their jurisdiction and served the public interest (such as the railroads). Slavery and the segregation laws in the southern states segmented the labour market as well almost every other aspect of daily life. Nonetheless, the power of government was limited. This can partly be attributed to entrenched anti-authoritarian sentiments but there were other reasons.

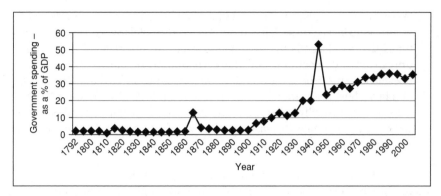

Figure 2.1 *US government spending as percentage of GDP, 1792–2005*
Source: adapted from USGovernmentSpending.com (2009), *US Government Spending as percent of GDP*, <http://www.usgovernmentspending.com>

- The provisions of the US Constitution were for a long period understood in narrowly defined and literal terms. Although Supreme Court rulings such as *McCulloch vs. Maryland* (1819) extended the implied powers assigned to the federal government and at least one clause (giving Congress the power to regulate trade 'among the several states') acquired growing significance with the passage of time, federal authority was largely limited to the specific, enumerated powers spelt out in Article I of the Constitution. Furthermore, these provisions were balanced by the Tenth Amendment. This assured the states and private individuals that they held the powers not assigned to the federal government under the Constitution.
- Prevailing economic theory rested upon free market principles. It followed the ideas established by Adam Smith in *The Wealth of Nations* (1776), which were then developed by later classical and neo-classical economists. From this perspective, individual self-interest served the interests of all by laying the basis for the ready supply of goods and services, a rational division of labour and a strong economy.[2] Prices, production and employment were to be regulated by the unfettered interplay of supply and demand. If there was excess production (a 'glut'), prices would fall. If however demand exceeded supply, prices would rise, thereby curbing demand and encouraging greater supply. The equilibrium price was the only point at which there was no pressure on prices to rise or fall. Although there was some acknow-ledgement of the case for the public provision of 'natural monopolies', government intervention was felt to distort market forces and have harmful consequences. For the most part, according to free market theory, the economy should be left to the 'invisible hand.'
- Towards the end of the nineteenth century, Social Darwinist ideas gained currency. Societies were represented in terms of the 'survival of the fittest'.

From this perspective, acumen, skill and ability allowed some to rise while others, who lacked these, fell behind. Although Social Darwinism was sometimes tied to ideas about the different races, it also seemed to legitimise unrestrained competition and the perpetuation of inequalities. John. D. Rockefeller, president of the Standard Oil Company, asserted that 'the growth of a large business is merely a survival of the fittest' (Ohio History Central, 2008). Paradoxically, however, many of the most prominent industrialists were generous philanthropists who spoke of the responsibilities that the wealthy owed to society.

By the end of the nineteenth and at the beginning of the twentieth centuries, there were, however, the beginnings of a shift although the US Supreme Court resisted expansionary notions of government and on the basis of 'due process of law', a phrase in both the Fifth and Fourteenth Amendments to the Constitution, struck down many efforts to regulate workplace conditions. In 1906, regulatory laws were passed requiring that foodstuffs were properly labelled and that meat was subject to inspection. In 1913, the Federal Reserve was established and assigned regulatory powers over the banking system. Nonetheless, as late as 1930, federal government outlays (or spending) represented just 3.4 per cent of US GDP and if state and local government spending are added in, the total only amounted to about 13 per cent (see Figure 2.1).

The Wall Street crash

After the recession at the beginning of the decade, the 1920s were a period of expansion. With each year that passed, production levels increased. Expansion was fuelled by the growth of the construction and the automobile industries, technological developments, the increased use of mass production and, on the demand side, the consumer spirit that often seemed to define the age. The spread of electricity, in particular, played a pivotal role. As Gene Smiley records:

> Electricity was the basis for a great many other new consumer products such as refrigerators, phonographs, electric irons, electric fans, electric lighting, toasters, vacuum cleaners, and other household appliances. (Smiley, 2002: 5)[3]

Although the incomes of working households only increased to a limited extent, economic growth encouraged a sense of wellbeing and optimism. The 1920s were, as countless documentaries have charted, an era popularly defined by 'speakeasies', the development of the radio and film industries, and jazz.

Against this background, the corporate shares that were bought and sold on the stock markets inevitably increased in value.[4] Optimism turned to speculation as people realised that the appreciation in stock prices enabled significant sums to be made by simply buying and then selling. Large numbers of people were caught up in the process. Although the rules governing the sale of shares were increasingly tightened so that full cash payments were required for lower value shares, they borrowed. Furthermore, shares were often bought 'on margin' so that the collateral for a loan was provided by the stocks themselves. As Smiley notes:

> Speculating investors used small amounts of their own cash and borrowed up to 70 or 80 percent of the purchase price. This allowed them to buy shares of a stock, wait for the stock's price to rise, sell the stock, repay the margin borrowing with interest, and reap significant capital gains on their small cash investment. (Smiley, 2002: 10)

Although there were warning signs such as the Florida property bubble, many of those who held shares were new to the markets and were easily swept away by the optimism of the late 1920s. Frederick Lewis Allen described the prevailing mood:

> The rich man's chauffeur drove with his ears laid back to catch the news of an impending move in Bethlehem Steel; he held fifty shares himself on a twenty-point margin. The window-cleaner at the broker's office paused to watch the ticker, for he was thinking of converting his laboriously accumulated savings into a few shares of Simmons. Edwin Lefevre (an articulate reporter...) told of a broker's valet who made nearly a quarter of a million in the market, of a trained nurse who cleaned up thirty thousand following the tips given her by grateful patients; and of a Wyoming cattleman, thirty miles from the nearest railroad, who bought or sold a thousand shares a day. (Galbraith, 1992: 101)[5]

Intensified demand added still further to the rise in share prices. Price levels increasingly bore no relation to the commercial prospects for a particular company. Although there were interruptions, there was what has often been described as an 'orgy' of trading and speculation. Indeed, by the autumn of 1928 it was commonplace for 5 million shares to be traded in a day.

Bubbles inevitably burst. In October 1929, a few companies reported lower profits than had been expected. Congress was considering the imposition of tariffs that would restrict trade. Margin requirements were being increased so that higher cash payments were required before shares could be purchased. There was a growing realisation that the period of speculative gains was probably coming to a close. All of this contributed to a change in sentiments. Furthermore, 'once confidence snapped, and investors sold rather than bought, investors who had borrowed or who bought on margin were anxious to sell as quickly as possible to minimise their losses' (Badger, 1989: 32). In October 1929 share prices began fall, at times dramatically. Although the crash was

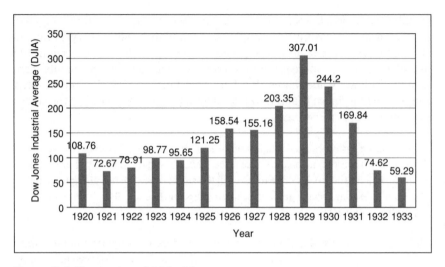

Figure 2.2 *Share prices, 1920–30*

Note: the figures are taken from the first day of trading in each year.
Source: adapted from Measuringworth (2009), *Daily Closing Value of the Dow Jones Average*,
<http://www.measuringworth.org>

Table 2.1 *Economic growth (rate of change of GDP) (%)*

Year	Growth (rate of change of GDP) (%)
1930	−8.6
1931	−6.4
1932	−13.0

Source: adapted from Bureau of Economic Analysis (2008), *Percent Change from Preceding Period*,
<http://www.bea.gov>

a process rather than a single event, entire fortunes were lost on 'Black Thursday' and 'Black Tuesday' (respectively October 24 and 29 1929).

The crash had consequences for the wider economy. In the years that followed, growth rates plummeted (see Table 2.1). (The data can be presented in another way. With negative growth rates such as these GDP was falling dramatically. Table 2.2 shows real GDP.[6])

Why did this happen? Table 2.3 shows the process by providing a breakdown of GDP into its component parts. The figures are in nominal dollars.[7] The table brings together spending by consumers (C), investment (in other words, business spending on, for example, machinery and equipment) (I), government spending (G), and the difference between exports and imports (X–M). As the table indicates, government spending rose as the depression took hold although not

Table 2.2 *Real GDP, 1928–33*

Year	Real GDP (billions of 2000 dollars)
1928	815.9
1929	865.2
1930	790.7
1931	739.9
1932	643.7
1933	635.5

Source: adapted from Louis D. Johnston and Samuel H. Williamson (2008), *What Was the U.S. GDP Then?*, <http://www.measuringworth.org>

Table 2.3 *GDP and its components, 1929–33 (US$bn)*

Year	GDP	Consumption (C)	Investment (I)	Government purchases (G)	Exports (X)	Imports (M)	Net exports (X–M)
1929	791	594	92.4	105	35.6	46.3	−10.7
1930	720	562	59.8	116	29.4	40.3	−10.9
1931	674	545	37.6	121	24.4	35.2	−10.8
1932	584	496	9.9	117	19.1	29.2	−10.1
1933	577	485	16.4	113	19.2	30.4	−11.2

Source: Thayer Watkins (n.d.), *The Depression of the 1930s and Its Origins*, <http://www.sjsu.edu>

markedly during the period of the Hoover administration.[8] Exports (X) fell away but spending on imports (M) also declined. The balance of payments deficit (X–M) therefore remained broadly constant although foreign trade represented only a very small proportion of GDP (see pp. 146–7). Spending by consumers on goods and services fell markedly. Savings based upon share holdings became worthless. Debts incurred by borrowing to buy shares or for other purchases could not be repaid and the banking system came under severe strain. There was widespread uncertainty about the future, leading to retrenchment by consumers. However, the most dramatic decline was in investment (I). In the wake of the crash, investment funds dried up and companies slashed spending on new plant and equipment.[9]

The impact of the depression was not confined to long-established industries such as mining and textiles but felt across the entire economy:

The Depression, however, was not confined to the 'sick' atomised industries of the 1920s. It was also marked by the collapse of the technologically advanced, consumer durable industries which had led the way to prosperity in that decade. Both the automobile and electrical manufacturing industries, dominated by a few large corporations, saw their sales shrink by over two-thirds between 1929 and 1932. (Badger, 1989: 20)

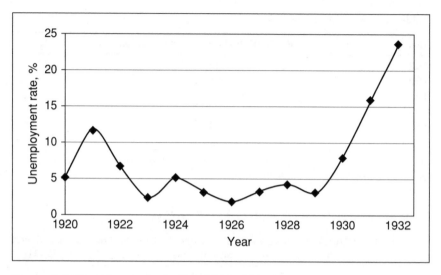

Figure 2.3 *Unemployment rate (%), 1920–32*

Source: adapted from the Proceedings of the Friesian School, Fourth Series (2009), *Historical Statistics and Analysis on Unemployment, Poverty, Urbanization, etc., in the United States,* <http://www.friesian.com>

Although increases in unemployment are invariably lagged behind the business cycle, the joblessness figures increased dramatically in the wake of falling GDP. As companies folded or scaled back production, they inevitably reduced the size of their workforce. By 1932, almost a quarter of the workforce was unemployed (Figure 2.3). There was also underemployment. One estimate suggested that by January 1932 half those with jobs were working part-time (Badger, 1989: 19). Although the depression hit almost every industry, both unemployment and underemployment had a disproportionate impact. More often than not, women employees lost their jobs before men (Badger, 1989: 24). African-Americans were overrepresented in industries such as construction that were most severely hit (Badger, 1989: 25).

Other developments

The Wall Street crash is not, in itself, a sufficient explanation of the depression that followed it. Private wealth was cut by about 10 per cent. For many individuals the relationship between assets and debt shifted so that they had rather more debt in relative terms (or, put another way, there was increased *leverage*) (Temin, 1994: 7–8). However, the depression should also be attributed to other developments:

- The Federal Reserve pursued deflationary policies.[10] Although the discount rate (the rate of interest charged by the Fed to the banks) was reduced over the two years that followed the Wall Street crash, the Fed allowed bank reserves to fall. Banks customarily operate on a fractional reserve basis. When funds are deposited, a large proportion will be lent out to individuals and firms but a certain amount (the fractional reserve) will be held back in case sudden withdrawals are made or in readiness for other contingencies. When reserves fall, there has to be a corresponding reduction in the availability of bank credit. This, and the fears that banks had about lending in a period of uncertainty, contributed to the contraction of economic activity after the Wall Street crash.[11]

- There was a major crisis in the financial sector. The impact of the Wall Street crash was magnified by the structural character of the banks. Many were small or medium sized and had only limited funds.[12] Because of the difficulties in agriculture, they had already been hit by bad debts. They were therefore overexposed by the late 1920s. The banks' difficulties intensified because many of the company securities that they held fell in price following the crash (and more were being issued as firms sought to raise funds).[13] As individuals began to lose their confidence in the banking sector they began to hold rather more of their wealth as cash and rather less as bank deposits.[14] Against this background, bank failures inevitably increased, particularly at the end of 1930. This fuelled the sense of panic still further. The banking crisis intensified in October 1931 when, under the strain of world economic crisis, countries abandoned the gold standard but looked to the US to exchange their dollar reserves for gold.[15] So as to stem the outflow of gold, the Federal Reserve raised interest rates. This added to deflationary pressures and also reduced bond prices.[16] All of this placed yet further pressure on the banks (which held bonds together with other securities) and many more had to close during late 1931 and early 1932. There was a further banking crisis at the end of 1932 caused by a loss of confidence in the dollar and a scramble to buy gold. Reserves were dramatically denuded. The succession of financial panics and bank failures had reverberations throughout the economy and contributed very significantly to the falls in investment and consumption that precipitated the depression.

- Despite reductions in prices (or 'deflation') after 1929, wage rates were slow to fall. There was, as conservative commentators have emphasised, nominal *wage rigidity* or *stickiness*. Indeed, real wages (wages measured in terms of their purchasing power) rose by 2.8 per cent in 1929–30, 7.2 per cent in 1930–1, 9.9 per cent in 1931–2, and 5.8 per cent in 1932–3 (Bordo, 2003: 1201). Why was this? Earlier literature emphasised the ways in which employers were tied into union contracts that had been negotiated in earlier years (Hanes, 2000: 1432). More recent research has pointed to company fears that wage cuts might prompt an employee to leave or slack off and the ways in which, formally and informally, incumbent employees are 'insiders' who can sway corporate decision-making. It also stresses the degree of variation across industries and the significance of particular variables:

> across industries relative rigidity in nominal wage rates has been associated with high earnings, capital intensity, and product-market concentration, but not with establishment size or profit per worker except to the degree those variables have been correlated with capital-intensity or product-market concentration. (Hanes, 2000: 1443)

Firms therefore had to cut the costs of production in other ways and they did this by cutting the size of their workforce. Unemployment rose rapidly. This and the falling value of assets led, despite the rise in real wages, to reductions in consumption levels.

- Those on the left point to the increasing gap between rich and poor that characterised American society during the 1920s. Because of these inequalities, large numbers of people had relatively low levels of purchasing power and overall demand for goods and services was insufficient. The core problem facing the US economy was therefore *underconsumption*. The fact that investment in housing fell (because disposable income was limited) before the process of industrial decline began seems to illustrate the argument. However, Peter Temin suggests that the effects of growing inequality had only a very limited impact on consumption levels (Temin, 1994: 4–5).
- Many economic commentators and many later historians have pointed to what they regard as policy failures by President Herbert Hoover and Congress.[17] Although overall government spending edged upwards during the Hoover years, and the administration brought forward federal building projects and encouraged state and local initiatives as well as voluntary efforts, there was a commitment to balanced budgets. Against a background of economic collapse, and a sharp decline in tax revenue, this meant tax rises. As President Hoover asserted, a balanced budget was indispensable to the restoration of confidence and to the very start of economic recovery: 'we cannot maintain public confidence nor stability of the Federal Government without undertaking some temporary tax increases' (quoted in Reynolds, 1995). From the perspective of some economists, however, such tax rises dampened down demand levels and thereby exacerbated the country's economic difficulties. The Hoover administration was also fearful of extending federal government power and usurping the prerogatives of the states. As Hoover said in a radio address:

> I am convinced that where Federal action is essential then in most cases it should limit its responsibilities to supplement the states and local communities, and that it should not assume the major role or the entire responsibility...To do otherwise threatens...the very basis of self-government. (Hoover, 1999: 184)[18]

- Although foreign trade constituted only a small proportion of US GDP, there were strong protectionist impulses. In 1930, the Smoot-Hawley Tariff Act was introduced, raising tariffs to 60 per cent on more than 3,200 products and materials imported into the US (see p. 148). In the short term, the Act appeared to work insofar as imports fell dramatically. In the two years following passage of the Act imports fell by more than 40 per cent (Shlaes, 2007: 112).[19] At the same time, however, the Act led to the imposition of retaliatory tariffs by about twenty-five other countries and contributed to a contraction in world trade that denied export opportunities to US companies (Nichols, 1995). Nonetheless, the impact of Smoot-Hawley should not be exaggerated. Temin suggests that the economic consequences of retaliation for Smoot-Hawley would have been small, given the relatively small size of the export sector and the boost to domestic demand provided by the tariff (Temin, 1994: 8).
- After a period of prosperity between 1900 and 1920 (and high levels of wartime demand), agriculture faced severe difficulties. Indeed, it has been said that the farming sector was in depression a decade ahead of the wider economy. The foreign markets that had opened up in the war were lost. Against this background, there was oversupply of agricultural products (a 'glut'), and prices stagnated. Many farmers were overextended through purchases of equipment and machinery (such as tractors and threshers) during the years of relative prosperity. As a consequence, real income fell and foreclosures were at a high level because mortgage payments could not be maintained.

The New Deal

Against this background, laissez-faire and individualist notions were increasingly questioned. Franklin Roosevelt was elected to the presidency in November 1932 and took office in March 1933. It was a 'realigning' election that changed the character of US politics. The Democratic ticket secured backing from a broad coalition of groupings including blue-collar workers, farmers, minorities, the white south and intellectuals.

Roosevelt followed up his inauguration (when he had declared in a celebrated phrase that 'the only thing we have to fear is fear itself') with 'a hundred days' of frenetic activity. He declared a four day 'bank holiday' during which banking transactions were barred. His administration then secured Congressional backing for measures such as the Emergency Banking Act that encouraged mergers and reorganisation and allowed banks to reopen if they could demonstrate that they were solvent. These actions largely restored confidence in the banking sector and some of the cash that had been withdrawn during the panics was returned to the banks (Smiley, 2002: 76). At the same time, the Roosevelt administration took steps that brought an end to the dollar's fixed

value against gold and allowed the currency to float downwards. The depreciation of the dollar reduced export prices.

There were also public works projects. The Reforestation Relief Act created
the Civilian Conservation Corps (CCC), which provided employment for about
a quarter of a million young men on public works schemes, including road
construction projects, reforestation and development of the national parks.
The Federal Emergency Relief Act provided grants-in-aid to the states for relief
projects. The Tennessee Valley Authority (TVA) was created and went on to
construct nine dams and develop hydroelectricity generation plants. The TVA
not only provided employment but transformed part of the rural south, traditionally one of the most economically backward regions of the US.

The National Industrial Recovery Act, which incorporated reforms addressing longstanding labour grievances by limiting the working week to forty
hours, establishing a minimum wage and prohibiting child labour, created the
Public Works Administration (PWA) and the National Recovery Administration
(NRA). The PWA provided further funding for public works programmes
including the construction of roads, dams and public buildings. The NRA
launched a campaign to secure the agreement of companies to maintain
employment and regulate production levels along with wages and prices. The
creation of the NRA was underpinned by the belief, shared by many on the
left, that the depression had been caused by underconsumption (workers lacked
the means to buy goods and services) and companies had therefore produced
too much ('overproduction') (Smiley, 2002: 87).

The plight of agriculture was also addressed. The 1933 Agricultural
Adjustment Act (AAA) offered assistance to farmers by providing subsidies if
the production of particular crops (including corn, cotton, dairy products,
hogs, rice, tobacco and wheat) was restricted and land left idle so as to push
up price levels. The subsidies were funded by a tax on the food processing
industry. In the three years that followed passage of the Act farm incomes rose
significantly but insofar as prices rose this owed much to the effects of droughts
and dust storms (Smiley, 2002: 85).

From 1935 onwards, according to some commentators, there was a 'second
New Deal' which has been described as more radical in character and more
labour-orientated than the reforms of 1933–4. The 1935 National Labor
Relations Act (or Wagner Act) guaranteed rights of workers to organise and
form unions, engage in collective bargaining and take strike action. The
National Labor Relations Board (NLRB) was empowered to investigate cases
where there were unfair labour practices and to hold ballots so that employees
in a company could decide whether they wished to have union representation.
Although the Supreme Court modified some elements within the Act it contributed, together with recovery and war, to a significant growth in labour
union membership (Table 2.4).

The Works Progress Administration (WPA) provided hundreds of thousands
of mainly blue-collar jobs for the unemployed. The Fair Labor Standards Act

Table 2.4 *Proportion of the workforce in labour unions, 1930–45*

Year	Percentage of labour force in unions
1930	11.6
1935	13.2
1940	26.9
1945	35.5

Source: adapted from David R. Kamerschen, Charles D. DeLorme, Jr., John M. Mangel and John E. Morgan, Jr (n.d.), *The Union Life Cycle within the Byproduct Theory of the Labor Movement*, <http://www.westga.edu>

drew upon the powers conferred upon the federal government by the Constitution's interstate commerce clause to establish a national minimum wage, guarantee higher pay levels for overtime and prohibit the employment of children.

At the same time, the US took its first steps towards some form of welfare state although provision was minimal when compared with that offered in many European countries, where labour movement pressures, traditionalist paternalism, Roman Catholicism and the protection of imperial interests had come together to create a basic safety net for those facing the most severe forms of disadvantage. The Social Security Act created pensions for the elderly, unemployment insurance and assistance for those on the lowest incomes (including women bringing up children alone, such as widows, who were assisted through Aid to Dependent Children). Nonetheless, important groupings, including agricultural labourers, those in domestic service, government employees and many white-collar workers, were excluded from the provisions of the Act. It was largely directed towards the white, male, manual worker. The racial implications of the Act were reinforced in many cases by the policies adopted at state level, given that some of the funding was distributed, through the states, as grants-in-aid. Furthermore, the programme was not redistributive as those on the left might have hoped. Instead of funding Social Security from general taxation, payments to those who were retired were funded by a payroll tax and employers' contributions.

One other development also requires consideration. Indeed, Robert J. Samuelson argues that it was the most important component of the New Deal. Shortly after assuming office, Roosevelt took the US off the gold standard.[20] Up until then, the Federal Reserve was required to ensure that every US dollar was backed by at least forty cents of gold and the 'Fed' had maintained relatively high interest rates so as to limit outflows of gold (Samuelson, 2008). Once the gold standard had been suspended, interest rates could fall. The 1934 Gold Reserve Act fixed the dollar against gold again but at a significantly lower parity.

Christina Romer, who was appointed as chair of the Council of Economic Advisers by President Obama in 2009, also points to the part played by the

US's gold standard policy during the 1930s. She has argued that although most accounts emphasise the importance of the New Deal spending pro- grammes, 'fiscal policy was not key in the recovery from the Great Depression' (Romer, 2009: 5). Instead, once the US had set a higher price for gold (thereby, in effect, devaluing the dollar) large amounts of gold flowed into the US Treasury from overseas. This continued as fears of war in Europe grew and investors sought the relative security of asset-holding in the US. As a consequence, the money supply expanded by almost 17 per cent annually between 1933 and 1936 (Romer, 2009: 6).

Although it did not trigger a fall in the interest rate (because it was already so low), the expansion of the money supply had an impact on the wider 'real' economy by limiting the price falls that had contributed to the loss of business confidence in the wake of the Wall Street crash:

> What it could do was break expectations of deflation. Prices had fallen 25 per cent between 1929 and 1933. People throughout the economy expected this deflation to continue. As a result, the real cost of borrowing and investing was exceedingly high...Devaluation followed by rapid monetary expansion broke this deflationary spiral. (Romer, 2009: 6)

This, together with the rebuilding of economic confidence through the New Deal programmes (even though fiscal policy had in itself a very limited effect), provided a basis for a rise in investment levels and recovery (Romer, 2009: 5).

The impact of the New Deal

There were periods of strong growth as the US recovered from the depression. This can be seen in Table 2.5.

Table 2.5 *Economic growth (rate of change of GDP), 1933–40*

Year	Growth (rate of change of GDP) (%)
1933	−1.3
1934	10.8
1935	8.9
1936	13.0
1937	5.1
1938	−3.4
1939	8.1
1940	8.8

Source: adapted from Bureau of Economic Analysis (2008), *Percent Change from Preceding Period*, <http://www.bea.gov>

Those who have backed the New Deal and large-scale government inter-ventionism argue that the free market had failed. Whereas advocates of laissez-faire claim that if market forces were left to operate freely, wages would fall to their market-clearing rate, employment levels would rise and investment would be brought forth, those who backed intervention believed that the market had settled at a point where factories lay idle and many millions were unemployed. They also point to the impact of the *multiplier* and the extent of *spillover* effects in regenerating the economy.[21] The concept of the multiplier suggests that an *injection*, such as an increase in government spending, will have a larger impact on GDP than the injection. This is because those who are employed on public works projects spend the wages that they are paid, thereby adding to overall demand. Companies will respond to this by increasing supply and taking on additional workers. They then spend their earnings, thereby adding still further to total demand. There is, in other words, a *virtuous circle.*[22] The spillover effect refers to the wider economic effects of public works projects. A new road will permit goods to be transported at a lower cost and more speedily and open up new regions or neighbourhoods to commercial investment. Furthermore, particular New Deal agencies directly reduced the unemployment statistics. Iwan Morgan points to the Works Progress Administration: 'the WPA provided maximum employment and spending in a minimum of time' (Morgan, 1995: 33).

Others have gone further and seen the New Deal in almost lyrical terms. It did not only transform the economy but restructured politics and society. Carl Degler, the distinguished historian, talked of the 'third American revolution'. Roosevelt's administration had ushered in 'a new conception of the good society'. The 1935 Social Security Act 'brought government into the lives of people as nothing had since the draft and the income tax'. The relationship between capital and labour had been fundamentally changed by mass union-isation which the administration had promoted (Radosh, 1972: 152).

Unemployment and recession

These claims should be set against the overall unemployment figures. Although joblessness fell from its peak in 1933 (24.9 per cent), unemployment remained at high levels throughout the 1930s. Indeed, as Table 2.6 shows, the joblessness numbers rose again during the latter half of the decade.

Furthermore, the process of recovery was interrupted by the recession of 1937–8 (see Table 2.5). Some see the recession of the late 1930s as the con-sequence of policy mistakes. According to Robert J. Samuelson, it was in large part a consequence of the decision by the Federal Reserve in 1936 and 1937 to raise the reserves that banks were required to hold either in their vaults or as deposits with the Federal Reserve itself. The increase in reserve requirements limited the funds that could be loaned to businesses and individuals (Samuelson,

Table 2.6 *Unemployment rate (%), 1934–44*

Year	Unemployment rate (%)
1934	21.7
1936	16.9
1938	19
1940	14.6
1942	4.7
1944	1.2

Source: adapted from Infoplease (2008), *Overall Unemployment Rate in the Civilian Labor Force, 1920–2006*, <http://www.infoplease.com>

2008). However, the deflationary character of the 1935 Social Security Act (which was based upon contributions and therefore reduced spending levels) and efforts to secure a balanced budget for Fiscal Year 1938 (FY1938) were also contributory factors (Morgan, 1995: 36).

The conservative critique

The failure of the New Deal to reduce unemployment to the levels seen before and after the 1930s is attributed by conservative commentators to 'big government'. This was partly because the federal government grew in size. While federal government spending had, in 1930, constituted just 3.4 per cent of GDP, the figure had tripled by the mid-1930s. Conservatives and free market advocates also, however, opposed the policies that were adopted which, they asserted, stifled market forces. In *FDR's Folly*, Jim Powell argues that Social Security, increased taxes and labour reforms increased unemployment by adding to wage costs (Powell, 2004). Amity Shlaes talks, in *The Forgotten Man*, of Roosevelt's 'war on business' (Shlaes, 2007: 392). Gene Smiley suggests that if manufacturing production is considered the recovery that was underway from Roosevelt's inauguration onwards (and the corresponding reduction in unemployment) stalled as early as September 1933 and did not resume until the late summer of 1935. He attributes much of this to overweening government. He points to the actions of the National Recovery Administration (NRA) in implementing industrial codes to regulate prices and production levels. However, for the NRA's critics, *cartelisation* restricts competition and hampers economic expansion:

> Producers were expected to increase prices and hold the line on or reduce production so as to restore profitability – exactly the opposite of what recovery required. Growing disagreements over the rules and growing noncompliance with them created uncertainty and confusion, discouraging firms from taking

Table 2.7 *Economic growth (rate of change of GDP) (%)*

Year	Growth (rate of change of GDP) (%)
1941	17.1
1942	18.5
1943	16.4
1944	8.1
1945	−1.1

Source: adapted from Bureau of Economic Analysis (2008), *Percent Change from Preceding Period*, <http://www.bea.gov>

actions that might have increased production or investments that might have given them competitive advantages. Thus during the life of the NRA, the recovery from the Great Depression largely stalled. (Smiley, 1994: 102)[23]

At the same time, the private sector faced other difficulties. The large-scale public works projects (such as the Tennessee Valley Authority) that came to define the New Deal 'crowded out' commercial investment. As Shlaes notes: 'lawmakers' preoccupation with public works got in the way of allowing productive businesses to expand and pull the rest forward...those who did have a job worked hard...But the government was taking all the air in the room' (Shlaes, 2007: 392–3). Public works not only squeezed the private sector and reduced investment opportunities but the forms of employment that they offered were short-term, usually lasting just a few months. Government direction was, furthermore, often structurally inefficient.

Full output and employment were only fully restored when, following the Japanese attack on Pearl Harbor in December 1941, the US was thrown into total war, requiring the optimal use of both physical and human resources. As men were serving in the armed forces women were employed in munitions production. Much was made of 'Rosie the Riveter'.[24] Plant and machinery were directed towards war needs and used to full capacity. As Table 2.7 suggests, there were unprecedented levels of growth. Much more was produced and delivered with each year that passed. Indeed, the war created boom conditions. Corporate profits jumped. Average wage levels (boosted by overtime) doubled, rising from almost $25 a week to $50 a week. Farm income increased 250 per cent (Gale Encyclopaedia of US Economic History, 2000).

For those on the conservative right the growing size of the federal government not only threatened economic recovery but also jeopardised individual liberty. Initially, Roosevelt's opponents hoped that the US Supreme Court would curtail what they saw as the federal government's excesses.[25] Some of its rulings gave them succour. While Article I of the Constitution assigned Congress the power to levy taxes and regulate businesses that crossed state lines (the interstate commerce clause) it did not, the Court asserted, extend unlimited powers to Washington and also required that taxation be used for the 'general welfare'. In 1935, the Court struck down sections of the National Industry Recovery Act (in *Schechter v. United States*, commonly known as the 'sick chicken' case) on this basis. In 1936 (*United States v. Butler*) the Supreme Court struck down the Agricultural Adjustment Act. The Act imposed taxes upon the food processing industry so as to provide subsidies for farmers who destroyed crop surpluses. The Court ruled that it was unconstitutional to impose a tax on one group so as to transfer the proceeds to another.

In response to these rulings and decisions that struck down other New Deal reforms, President Roosevelt put forward the 'court packing' plan (the Judiciary Reorganization Bill of 1937) which would have enlarged the Court's membership. The plan raised fears of bloated executive power and was abandoned. However, later appointments to the Court (and in some accounts a shift of opinion by its sitting members) changed its character and it became more sympathetic to looser readings of the Constitution that allowed a more expansive role for the federal government.

Criticism from the left

The New Deal was subject to other criticisms.[26] There were those who at the time sought more overtly Keynesian forms of policy. Untrammelled market forces, it was argued, could not bring down the mass unemployment of the 1930s. Indeed, the macro-economy seemed to be in a stable form of 'equilibrium' despite the underutilisation of capacity and chronic, widespread unemployment. Government intervention and large-scale spending were therefore required.[27] Furthermore, from this perspective, deficit budgets were required. A balanced budget would, at the most, be only mildly reflationary. Yet, while federal government spending increased significantly during the 1930s, deficit budgets never became an acknowledged policy goal. There were deficits but the administration sought to reduce them and at the time of the 1937–8 recession almost secured a balanced budget (Table 2.8). There was no notion of *pump-priming* (whereby the budget was used to boost overall demand levels) in the way that became an article of faith for many post-war Keynesians.

Furthermore, some of the policies pursued by the Roosevelt administration were *de*flationary rather than *re*flationary in character. The 1935 Social Security Act included the provision of old-age and unemployment insurance but the system was based upon contributory benefits which depressed purchasing power (Morgan, 1995: 31). Taxes were not regarded as an instrument by which demand levels could be raised:

> No effort was made to stimulate consumption through tax cuts. Instead New Deal taxes sucked purchasing power out of the economy and bore disproportionately on lower-income groups. (Morgan, 1995: 42)

Table 2.8 *US federal government budget (as a proportion of GDP), 1934–45*

Fiscal year	Deficit as a proportion of GDP
1934	−5.9
1935	−4.1
1936	−5.5
1937	−2.5
1938	−0.1
1939	−3.2
1940	−3.0
1941	−4.3
1942	−14.2
1943	−30.3
1944	−22.7
1945	−21.5

Note: Before 1976, 'fiscal years' began on July 1 and finished on June 30.
Source: adapted from Executive Office of the President (2008), *Budget of the United States Government – Fiscal Year 2009 – Historical Tables*, US Government Printing Office, 24, <http://www.gpoaccess.gov/USbudget/fy09/pdf/hist.pdf>

E. Cary Brown of the Massachusetts Institute of Technology (MIT) has also stressed the limited character of the fiscal policies that were pursued during the 1930s. Insofar as there was fiscal expansion it was not sustained. The budget deficit rose in FY1934 but fell again in FY1935. State governments sought surpluses. As Brown put it, fiscal policy failed to generate recovery 'not because it does not work, but because it was not tried' (quoted in Romer, 2009).

Those further to the left have criticised the structural character and purpose of the New Deal. New Deal programmes, they assert, sought to save capitalism from the uncertainties and irrationalities of the unfettered market. From this perspective, the liberalism that underpinned the New Deal served, though its rhetoric masked, the interests of business elites:

> the expansion of the role of the state was designed by corporate leaders and their allies to rationalize the economy and society. Rationalization encompasses all measures that stabilize economic and social conditions so that profits can be made on a predictable basis by the major corporations. (Skocpol, 1980: 161)[28]

In other words, the New Deal was driven by corporate interests. Indeed, some on the left (and on this point they are joined by sections of the right) draw parallels between the New Deal and fascism. Both, they argue, rested upon cartelisation and state direction (Radosh, 1972: 159). Insofar as workers and those in poverty secured gains, a different left-wing perspective suggests, it was in response to the labour movement. The reforms that constituted the 'second'

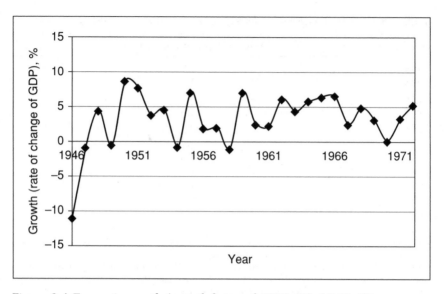

Figure 2.4 *Economic growth (rate of change of GDP) (%), 1946–72*
Source: adapted from Bureau of Economic Analysis (2008), *Percent Change from Preceding Period*,
<http://www.bea.gov>

New Deal, were, from this perspective, driven by growing labour militancy.
There were large-scale strikes and factory sit-ins in cities such as San Francisco,
Toledo and Minneapolis in 1934. Some more recent left-leaning commentators
have made a further point. They argue that the New Deal strengthened rather
than weakened existing class, gender and racial relationships. Housing provision
offered by the Tennessee Valley Authority and the Civilian Conservation Corps
was racially segregated. White power in the southern states was bolstered.

The long post-war boom

During the decades that followed the war there were some periods of recession
(in 1953–4 and 1958, as Figure 2.4 shows), but there were also sustained
periods of steady growth, particularly during the 1960s. Although there were
also boom conditions in western Europe (and there were frequent references
to the 'economic miracle' in West Germany), the US economy grew at a
sustained rate, laying the basis for claims that it was not only the biggest but
also the strongest and most resilient economy in the world.

    In sharp contrast to the 1930s, unemployment did periodically rise but was,
for the most part, minimal and levels fell again quite quickly. Indeed, many
economists suggested that at points, the unemployment figures were close
to the 'irreducible minimum'.[29] This created labour market pressures and

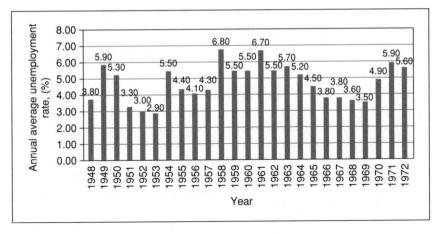

Figure 2.5 *Unemployment, 1948–72*

Source: adapted from Bureau of Labor Statistics (2009), *Labor Force Statistics from the Current Population Survey*, <http://www.bls.gov>

contributed to calls for immigration reform. From 1924 onwards, immigration had been severely restricted and through a quota system largely limited to the countries of northern Europe. In 1965, the Immigration and Nationality Act established family reunification as a criterion for admission and laid the basis for significantly increased levels of immigration from other regions of the world.

The long post-war boom transformed the US. There was renewed talk of the American dream.[30] Housing provision expanded dramatically, with one property developer, William Levitt, boasting that his company could build a new home in just sixteen minutes for only $7,000. Rising living standards created the basis for suburbanisation as people escaped both the farm and the city. The automobile became an essential feature of daily life, particularly as the gap widened between home and work. There were many more white-collar jobs. Youth cultures, which were expressed most visibly in music and fashion, emerged as young people secured real wage rises. Women, who had been cast out of the labour force after 1945, were drawn back into employment. Their wages began to change gender relationships. At the same time, the demands of the labour market and the logic of consumerism added to the other pressures that led to the dismantling of segregation in the southern states.

Despite Cold War tensions and the fear of nuclear war, the boom laid the basis for increasingly expansive ideas about the country's future. President John F. Kennedy spoke of the 'new frontier'. His successor, President Lyndon Johnson, talked of building a 'Great Society' and established the 'War on Poverty'. Social programmes were initiated to address poverty, inequality and deprivation through educational, health and urban reform. In particular,

Medicare (providing health coverage for senior citizens) and Medicaid (which in conjunction with the states offers provision for those in the lowest income groupings) were established.

Demand management

What, then, explains the long boom? For many at the time, the answer lay in government interventionism and the use of demand management. In 1965, Andrew Shonfield asked, 'What was it that converted capitalism from the cataclysmic failure which it appeared to be in the 1930s into the great engine of prosperity of the postwar Western world?' (Prasad, 2006: 1). His answer was Keynesianism and regulation.

In a loose sense at least, Keynesianism became economic orthodoxy even among those who distanced themselves from the term. A distinction should however be drawn between the forms of Keynesianism that were adopted during the decade-and-a-half that followed the Second World War and those employed from the beginning of the 1960s.[31] During the Truman and Eisenhower years (1945–61), federal policy took a relatively cautious form. In particular, policymakers were reluctant to run a budget deficit. Only about half of the federal government's budgets were in deficit between FY1947 and FY1961 (Morgan, 1995: 55). Indeed, as Table 2.9 shows, there were times (most notably 1948) when there were substantial surpluses.

They sought a balance between growth (which many at the time felt required high levels of government spending) and the fear of inflation which, it was felt, might be fuelled if spending levels were excessive. Nonetheless, having said this, despite the emphasis that was placed on the balancing of the budget, 'automatic stabilisers' were employed so as to modify the excesses of the business cycle. The term 'automatic stabilisers' refers to the part played by tax revenue and government spending in influencing the business cycle. During a downswing, tax revenues will 'automatically' fall (or at the least the rate of increase will be reduced) because less income tax will be paid and lower levels of sales will cut sales tax revenue from consumer purchases.[32] At the same time, even where government provision is limited or minimal, additional funds will have to be spent during a downturn or recession. This will happen even if decision-makers make no policy reforms simply because more people face difficulties. In other words, it is a 'non-discretionary' form of policy. Although such stabilisers will have a more restricted impact in the US than Europe (where government provision and levels of taxation are higher), there will still be an impact. The fall in tax revenue and the rise in government spending boost overall demand levels and are therefore reflationary. A recession may therefore be modified. Similarly, in a period of boom, automatic stabilisers may help reduce the danger of an economy 'overheating'. Tax revenue will rise and government spending may, without policy changes, fall or at least the rate

Table 2.9 *US federal government budget (as a proportion of GDP), 1946–60*

Fiscal year	Surplus (+) or deficit (−) as a proportion of GDP
1946	−7.2
1947	+1.7
1948	+4.6
1949	+0.2
1950	−1.1
1951	+1.9
1952	−0.4
1953	−1.7
1954	−0.3
1955	−0.8
1956	+0.9
1957	+0.8
1958	−0.6
1959	−2.6
1960	+0.1

Source: adapted from Executive Office of the President of the United States – GPO Access (2009), *Economic Report of the President: 2009 Report Spreadsheet Tables B-79. Federal receipts, outlays, surplus or deficit, and debt, as percent of gross domestic product, fiscal years 1934–2009*, <http://www.gpoaccess.gov>

of growth may tail off. The net effect of this is deflationary. Iwan Morgan has argued that the 1946 Employment Act, which declared that it was 'the continuing policy and responsibility of the Federal Government . . . to promote maximum employment, production, and purchasing power', not only established that the White House should take the lead in the making of economic policy but also rested on the use of such 'stabilisers' (sometimes dubbed 'compensatory finance').[33] The Act thereby laid the basis for fiscal policy during the 1950s:

> It institutionalized federal responsibility for combating recession and rising unemployment. In the absence of a compensatory spending commitment, the so-called automatic stabilizers – the automatic decrease of tax revenues and corollary increase of unemployment insurance payouts in a recession – would serve as the primary instruments to reverse economic decline. (Morgan, 1995: 78)

'New economics'

From 1961, however, a much more assertive form of Keynesian policy, which was dubbed 'new economics', was adopted. It stemmed in part from anxieties about the effects of 'fiscal drag'. As incomes rise over time, individuals move into higher tax brackets and pay a higher proportion of their income to the authorities. This is deflationary insofar as it holds back demand and impedes economic growth.

The 'new economics' were also a response to developments during the three years that preceded President John F. Kennedy's inauguration. In 1958, there had been a recession and unemployment rose dramatically in automobile-producing cities such as Detroit.[34] This suggested to some that more adventurous forms of policy should be employed. The Eisenhower administration resisted tax-cutting, which some said prolonged the recession, and then, in the subsequent upturn, reiterated its faith in the principle of a balanced budget. Despite a large deficit in 1959 the White House sought to balance the budget in FY 1960. This had deflationary consequences and, many held, contributed to a further recession in late 1960.[35] The upturn following the 1958 recession was, therefore, only the briefest of recoveries. As Iwan Morgan has recorded: 'In American history since 1945, only one expansionary cycle – that of 1980–1981 – has been briefer than the one that began in mid-1958' (Morgan, 1995: 84).

The adoption of 'new economics' and the shift in the character of economic thinking also corresponded with the spirit of the age. There was a stress on US dynamism and energy. The election of the country's youngest president seemed to symbolise this. The new mood was caught by President Kennedy's May 1961 commitment to put a man on the moon by the end of the decade, stressing the need to harness American abilities, the challenges of the 'new frontier' and the abandonment of past orthodoxies.

The 'new economics' rested on the belief that US economic growth had to be maximised. There was, it was said, a 'performance gap'. This was the gap between the country's current output and its potential output (or the full utilisation of the country's labour force and capital equipment). Paul Samuelson, who at that time was president of the American Economic Association, caught the optimism and ambition of the period when he told the Association: 'With proper fiscal and monetary policies, our economy can have full employment and whatever rate of ... growth it wants' (quoted in Wells, 2003: 54).

The 'new economics' adopted by the Kennedy administration (or at least the president's Council of Economic Advisers) at the beginning of the 1960s rested upon the use of deficit budgets as a way of fuelling demand and thereby increasing economic growth. Federal government spending would be set at the level at which the budget *would* balance (because tax receipts would be higher) if the economy were operating at full capacity. Walter Heller, chairman of the Council of Economic Advisers from 1961 to 1964, summed up the shift in approach that had taken place as the caution of earlier years was thrown aside: 'Gone is the countercyclical syndrome of the 1950s. Policy now centers on gap closing and growth, on realizing and enlarging the economy's non-inflationary potential' (quoted in Collins, 2000: 52).

These notions underpinned the 1964 Revenue Act. The Act was proposed by President Kennedy but enacted once Lyndon Johnson was in the White House. A significant income tax reduction could, it was said, kick-start the US economy. The highest marginal rate was cut from 91 to 70 per cent. The lowest rate fell from 20 per cent to 14 per cent. At the same time, corporate taxation was reduced from 52 per cent to 47 per cent (Berthoud, 2001). According to Samuel Rosenberg: 'It was the largest stimulative fiscal action taken by the federal government in relative peacetime, up to that point. Taxes were cut at a time when the federal budget was in deficit and federal expenditures were rising' (Rosenberg, 2003: 109).

Results

The initial results of the fiscal stimulus seemed promising. As Wyatt Wells has concluded:

> The New Economics yielded favourable results through 1965. Over five years, inflation registered less than 2 per cent a year, a level so low that many economists considered it synonymous with price stability. Production expanded by 27 per cent over these years, and joblessness fell from 6.7 to 4.5 per cent. (Wells, 2003: 59–60)

The faith in government action upon which the 'new economics' rested also informed President Lyndon Johnson's *Great Society* programmes. As Iwan Morgan has noted, they were 'interlinked' (Morgan, 1995: 101). The 1964 Economic Opportunity Act established the Office of Economic Opportunity (OEO) which created antipoverty programmes resting on education, job training and community development. As in the New Deal era, a plethora of agencies were formed. These included the Job Corps, VISTA (Volunteers in Service to America) and Head Start, which offered early years educational activities for poorer children. The 1965 Social Security Act established Medicare. In the following year Medicaid was created.

The Phillips curve

The Keynesian model was embraced because it seemed to 'fit' the economic realities of the period. Economic difficulties such as those in 1958 were attributed to mistakes made by successive administrations or Congress rather than systemic flaws. One conclusion certainly seemed to be beyond question. It appeared on the basis of the available evidence that unemployment and inflation were, as the Keynesian model suggested in its most simple form, opposites. If unemployment was high, it was because demand levels and output were relatively low. In the absence of demand, producers, distributors and retailers will be compelled to restrain price increases and inflation will be minimal. If, on the other hand, unemployment is low, wage demands are likely to rise and employers will have to pay more to secure skilled or experienced workers who may be in short supply. At the same time, these higher wages ensure that demand levels

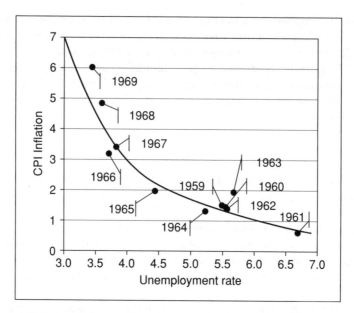

Figure 2.6 *Inflation and unemployment, 1959–69*

are buoyant, allowing producers, distributors and retailers to raise their prices, particularly if markets are not especially competitive.

The inverse character of the relationship between unemployment and inflation was charted in the Phillips curve.[36] In some versions, it considers unemployment and wage inflation. In other versions, such as that seen in Figure 2.6, it measures unemployment and the overall price index. Figure 2.6 charts the way in which inflation falls as unemployment rises between 1959 and 1969. The figures correspond very closely to the Phillips curve. There are shifts but they are, at least in broad terms, upwards and downwards along the curve. J. Bradford DeLong suggests that Democratic administrations and members of Congress tended to regard the reduction of unemployment as their principal objective. They accepted a degree of inflation as a necessary evil and the economy was therefore at the left end of the curve. Republican administration tended to be more concerned about inflation and the economy was therefore towards the right end of the curve. Slightly higher unemployment was a price that had to be paid (DeLong, 1997).

Criticisms

Many recent observers, particularly conservatives, are sceptical about the claims that were made at the time (particularly during the Kennedy and Johnson

years) for demand management and the Keynesian model. Government regulation, it was said, hindered rather than helped economic growth by strangling
initiative and entrepreneurship. They have argued, furthermore, that the levels
of government borrowing required to fund budget deficits have inflationary
consequences and displace private sector investment (a process known as
'crowding out', see p. 109).[37]

Amity Shlaes, author of *The Forgotten Man: A New History of the Great
Depression*, has suggested that the Eisenhower administration's building of the
interstate highway network and the emphasis upon government contributed
to a stifling of innovation during the 1950s (Shlaes, 2008). All too often,
public works projects were established by Congress to secure votes in a particular district or state rather than meet economic needs. Shlaes is particularly
critical of the Great Society programmes of the 1960s:

> The Great Society of that period was the ultimate Keynesian experiment, and it
> didn't work very well....The leaders of the 1970s and 1980S – Nixon, Ford, Carter,
> Reagan and Paul Volcker – were left to live with the Great Society aftermath.
> (Shlaes, 2008)[38]

The assumptions underpinning Keynesian economic remedies have also been
questioned. Some draw on Milton Friedman's *permanent-income hypothesis* and
suggest that tax rebates or other additions to consumer spending may only
have a limited impact. Individuals may not spend in the way that policymakers
hope because their spending decisions are not based upon their level of income
or mood at that particular moment. Instead, spending rests rather more upon
an individual's wealth or assets. These are both physical (such as a house) and
human (such as qualifications and experience). Others look to the *life-cycle
hypothesis*. This suggests that spending depends largely upon individual
estimates of future needs. People will, for example, incorporate the demands
associated with retirement when deciding upon spending during middle age.

While many on the left and many in the political mainstream argued that
'big government' was a positive development that constituted a defining feature
of modernity, the scope and scale of federal power was, the more resolute
conservatives argued, simply too large. Although the incorporate transition
to peace led to a dramatic reduction, federal government spending still represented 15 per cent of GDP in 1950 and had risen to almost 20 per cent in
1970 (see Table 2.10).

Brink Lindsey of the free market Cato Institute has offered a broader critique
of the post-war years. During the long boom, he argues, the US economy was
structured around cartels whereby relatively small numbers of firms controlled
markets. Entrepreneurs and companies faced controls and barriers to entry,
limiting access to particular markets. The progressive character of the tax
structure deterred initiative and growth. Immigration was severely restricted.
Discrimination against minorities and women was institutionalised in the

Table 2.10 *Federal government outlays as a percentage of GDP*

Year	Federal government outlays as % of GDP
1945	41.9
1950	15.6
1955	17.3
1960	17.8
1965	17.2
1970	19.3

Source: adapted from US Census Bureau (2008), *The 2008 Statistical Abstract – Federal Government–Receipts and Outlays*, <http://www.census.gov>

labour market and the provision of services. Individualism was suppressed. Whereas later decades were marked by an explosion of creativity, there were oppressive demands for conformity. Immigration was severely restricted, contributing to tight labour markets within which, from his perspective, the labour unions had a disproportionate hold. Progressive taxation deterred initiative:

> a progressive rate structure acts as a 'success tax' that reduces the upside of possible entrepreneurial ventures relative to the wages of continued employment. The result is to discourage possible entrepreneurs from striking out on their own. (Lindsey, 2009: 10)

Towards the end of the 1960s, the limits of 'new economics' and some of the difficulties associated with the application of Keynesian approaches became more visible. The federal government budget deficit swelled. As Table 2.11 suggests, although deficits were far less sizeable than those of later decades, they became an accepted and institutionalised feature of economic life from the beginning of the 1960s onwards. Indeed, by 1968, the budget deficit represented 2.9 per cent of GDP. It was the result of President Lyndon Johnson's commitment to the prosecution of the Vietnam War and the War on Poverty, in other words both 'guns <u>and</u> butter' (Rosenberg, 2003: 114–15).

Even before then, there had been growing fears about inflation levels (together with anxieties about the balance of payments deficit and foreign exchange holdings).[39] As Figure 2.7 shows, inflation began to rise from 1965 onwards and had, by the end of the decade, reached almost 6 per cent. Price rises were eroding real wage growth, reducing profits and threatening to trigger a crisis of confidence in the dollar (see pp. 00–00). Against this background, monetary policy was tightened in 1965–6 as inflationary fears grew but then loosened again as concerns about a prospect of a downturn came to the fore.[40]

Nonetheless, although there was uncertainty about the ways in which policy should be applied, policy the defining features of the Keynesian paradigm still held sway. As Iwan Morgan has recorded:

Table 2.11 *US federal government budget (as a proportion of GDP), 1961–73*

Fiscal year or period	Surplus (+) or deficit (–) as a proportion of GDP
1961	−0.6
1962	−1.3
1963	−0.8
1964	−0.9
1965	−0.2
1966	−0.5
1967	−1.1
1968	−2.9
1969	+0.3
1970	−0.3
1971	−2.1
1972	−2
1973	−1.1

Source: adapted from Executive Office of the President of the United States – GPO Access (2009), *Economic Report of the President: 2009 Report Spreadsheet Tables B-79. Federal receipts, outlays, surplus or deficit, and debt, as percent of gross domestic product, fiscal years 1934–2009*, <http://www.gpoaccess.gov>

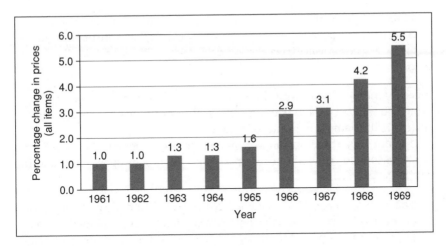

Figure 2.7 *US inflation rate (CPI-U) (%), 1961–9*
Source: adapted from US Census Bureau (2009), *The 2009 Statistical Abstract*, <http://www.census.gov>

The inclusion in the Johnson CEA's final economic report of a Phillips curve diagram based on annual inflation and unemployment data from 1954 to 1968 expressed the conventional Keynesian belief that movement up and down the curve was still possible. (Morgan, 2004: 1017)[41]

However, at the same time, the ambitions that had been tied to Keynesianism earlier in the 1960s and had underpinned the New Frontier, the Great Society and the War on Poverty were scaled down. As Lyndon Johnson completed his last year as president, there was no longer talk about the expansion of social programmes but instead of efforts to ensure that they were maintained: 'In 1968 growth liberalism came a cropper and the American Century came to an end' (Collins, 2000: 97).

Other explanations

For some, the problems that became evident at the end of the 1960s were triggered by the exigencies of the period, most notably the Vietnam War. Others argue that the causes had a more fundamental and systemic character. Free market commentators such as Brink Lindsey (see pp. 49–50) deny that demand management contributed to the post-war boom. Although he acknowledges is a correlation between the employment of Keynesian approaches and the boom, he stresses the distinction between correlation and causation. Demand management approaches may have been employed at the time but this does not necessarily mean that they caused the long boom:

> all things being equal, we should expect better economic policies to generate better economic performance. But in the real world, all things are seldom equal; thus strong performance is not always reliable evidence of good policies. (Lindsey, 2009: 23)

Indeed, Lindsey emphasises, there are policies that can generate economic growth for limited periods (such as large-scale government borrowing) but are economically damaging in the longer term.

It is not only those on the free market right who accept that there were other reasons for the long boom apart from Keynesian approaches and the role of government.

- The basis for a period of sustained growth was laid during the depression of the 1930s. The productive process was rationalised and modernised as less efficient companies went out of business. At the same time, the labour force became more pliant:

> The US economy took off during the wartime years between the end of the 1930s and the middle of the 1940s. The way was prepared for the new epoch of growth by the huge reductions in the costs of production that were achieved during the course of the depression – by way of the enormous shakeout of obsolete capital stock, the strong downward pressure on real wages that resulted from record levels of unemployment, and the build-up of a great backlog of unused innovations, as well as the containment of the dynamic

labour movement that had exploded onto the scene between 1934 and 1937. (Brenner, 2003: 10)

- At the end of the Second World War there was pent-up domestic demand for goods and services. Savings (through, for example, the purchase of war bonds) that had accumulated during the war were released. Pent-up demand thereby boosted the housing and automobile sectors as families sought a house in the suburbs. After 1945 at least a million houses were built a year. The construction industry stimulated the wider economy and brought forth increasing levels of investment which Wyatt Wells aptly describes as 'the foundation of prosperity' (Wells, 2003: 28).
- There was 'catch-up growth' in the south and to a greater extent in the south-western states which up until then had been relatively under-developed (Lindsey, 2009: 24). This was partly because, in backward regions or nations, productivity tends to be very low. Fairly small amounts of capital investment can lead to large increases in productivity. Furthermore, such regions or nations can take advantage of the technology, institutional structure and production methods that have been pioneered in more advanced areas or countries. They are not burdened by older or perhaps obsolete forms of production.[42]
- There were significant infrastructural advances, particularly in transportation (symbolised by the construction of the interstate highways which revolutionised freight haulage and opened up large parts of rural America to investment and development), communications and air conditioning. The building of interstate highways from the 1950s onwards laid the basis for sustained economic growth across a broad front and made a contribution to the productivity gains of the period. The new roads allowed journeys to be made over long distances at about 65 miles an hour, thereby lowering production and distribution costs. At the same time, the construction of the interstate highways facilitated economic development in neighbouring areas. There was a 30 per cent increase in manufacturing employment in counties in the Wisconsin I-43 Corridor and an 18 per cent increase in manufacturing employment between 1971 and 2000 in the Virginia I-81 Corridor (National Cooperative Highway Research Program, 2006: 51). Arguably, government spending (at federal, state and local level) fused together with private investment so as to create a significant stimulus during the latter half of the 1940s and 1950s:

> From the end of World War II to the New Frontier, no source of growth was stronger. Millions of new homes and factories – together with the supporting infrastructure of highways, roads, water and sewage treatment works, shopping centers, schools, and public buildings – had transformed the domestic aspect of America. (Hughes and Cain, 2003: 527)

- There were significant developments in terms of 'human capital' during the post-war years. In part, there were more consumers fuelling demand levels and, at a later stage, increasing numbers of workers. During the 'baby boom' years (1945–65), about 80 million babies were born. Alongside this, from the mid-1960s onwards, the process of desegregation brought America's minorities into the consumer market and liberalised the labour market by opening up white-collar occupations and the professions to African-Americans.

- 'Human capital' developed in another way as educational opportunities grew. The *GI Bill of Rights* (the 1944 Servicemen's Readjustment Act) offered college courses and vocational education to the soldiers returning from the Second World War. Although there were significant disparities between different ethnic and racial groupings, there were, in proportionate terms, fewer high school 'drop outs' as the post-war decades progressed. In 1940, just 25.5 per cent of adults aged 25 or over had a high school diploma. By 1970, the figure had reached 52.3 per cent. During the same period, the proportion of college graduates in the US population (those aged 25 or over with a bachelor's degree) more than doubled from 4.6 per cent to 10.7 per cent (US Census Bureau, 2007).

- There were significant productivity gains as a result of technological developments. The Second World War sparked the growth of new industries such as electronics, television, aviation, and chemical and metallurgical processing (Gale Encyclopaedia of US Economic History, 2000). Later productivity advances were symbolised by the rapid development of the aerospace industries and, most visibly, US space exploration. In May 1961, after many delays, the US sent Colonel Alan Shepard into space but only for a few minutes. *Friendship 7* was launched from Cape Canaveral in Florida but landed in the sea only fifteen minutes later. In contrast to these limited efforts, the Soviet Union was far ahead in the space race. Just eight years later, however, the US sent Apollo XI to the moon. Having said this, however, a caveat should be entered. Despite the spectacular character of developments in the space race, productivity levels do not grow on the basis of sudden leaps. Between 1870 and 1910, the railroads reduced their costs (thereby increasing productivity) because of small, gradual and incremental changes in the design of freight cars and locomotives. Nonetheless, there was, with only periodic fluctuations, solid productivity growth (measured in terms of output per hour) up until about 1973.

- Although the labour unions may seem, when considered from the vantage point of today, to have been relatively well-organised and self-confident, the labour market was fairly pliant. Despite low levels of unemployment, wage demands (and therefore the labour costs imposed upon employers) generally remained moderate. Why was this? The answer may lie in the fragmented and relatively apolitical character of the US unions. In contrast with many union movements in western Europe (particularly Italy and France), they accepted the logic of a market economy, eschewed militancy and rejected doctrines drawn from socialism and Marxism. The industrial working class

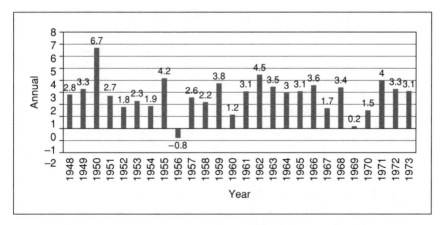

Figure 2.8 *Percentage annual change in output per hour (non-farm business), 1948–73*

Source: adapted from Bureau of Labor Statistics (2009), *Percentage Annual Change in Output Per Hour (Nonfarm Business), 1948–1973*, <http://data.bls.gov>

was, furthermore, fragmented by race, ethnicity, gender and geography. Having said this, the unions had gained a hold in some industries during the Second World War and in the wake of reforms such as the Wagner Act. This proved to be temporary. They lost ground following the passage of the Taft-Hartley Act in 1947. This Act was a response to the strike wave of 1945–6 and a belief that labour had acquired excessive rights during the New Deal era. It limited the circumstances in which strike action could take place, made it difficult for Communists, who were often among the most effective labour organisers, to hold office, and allowed the states to pass 'right-to-work' legislation. This outlawed agreements between the unions and employers that would make membership or payment of union dues a condition of employment. It may also be that the labour force was growing, thereby forcing workers to accept a measure of wage restraint. Those who have considered the post-war development of western Europe suggest that the drawing in of underemployed labour from rural areas and from countries such as Yugoslavia and Turkey led to a moderation of wage demands. A comparable process may have been at work within the US as geographical mobility increased and former agricultural workers, women and African-Americans were incorporated within the mainstream labour force. There may also be other reasons for the relative passivity of organised labour. At the same time, post-war Republicanism often took a moderate form (symbolised by President Dwight Eisenhower's presidency), accepted the reforms of the New Deal era and did little to challenge the earlier gains secured by the labour unions.

- During the period following the war, US exports were boosted because so much of European and Asian industry had been destroyed. Nonetheless, in the twenty years that followed the end of the war, the economies of these regions were rebuilt. Indeed, commentators spoke of the West German *Wirtschaftswunder* (or 'economic miracle') and increasingly sought to learn from and emulate Japanese business practices. Nonetheless, there were growing export opportunities for the US.[43] This can be attributed at least in part to the changes in the international trading regime that followed the Second World War. Exchange rates were fixed and the dollar assumed the role that gold had played during the years of the gold standard. The dollar thereby became the world's principal reserve currency. The Bretton Woods system of exchange rates (which was agreed in 1944) pegged the US dollar at $35 an ounce of gold and dollars could be exchanged for gold.[44] In turn, other currencies were fixed against the dollar although they were allowed a 1 per cent fluctuation from their 'par value' (Collins, 2000: 70) (see p. 69). This provided world trade with a stable basis and contributed, along with the tariff reductions negotiated through the General Agreement on Tariffs and Trade (GATT), to an increase in the volume of trade between nations. It may also have contributed to increasing competitiveness because there may have been a generalised understanding among businesses and governments that if wages and other costs rose to a disproportionate extent then this might price firms and nations out of the world market. Fixed exchange rate systems do not allow the option of depreciation so as to compensate for large rises in the costs of production.[45] It also largely eliminated opportunities for currency speculation. At the same time, the creation of institutions such as the General Agreement on Tariffs and Trade (GATT), the World Bank and the International Monetary Fund (IMF) helped open up access to markets in colonial and newly independent countries and, together with the Marshall Plan, assisted the process of European reconstruction so that the nations of western Europe offered openings to US companies (Gale Encyclopaedia of US Economic History, 2000).
- Radical and Marxist commentators have pointed to the ways in which countervailing forces ameliorated the contradictions that they would assert are inherent within the capitalist economic order. Paul Baran and Paul Sweezy's classic study, *Monopoly Capital: An Essay on the American Economic and Social Order,* was first published in 1966. The book considered the displacement of earlier, more competitive, forms of capitalism by the growth of monopoly corporations. Furthermore, the surplus that they generated was tending to rise. At the same, however, there were relatively few outlets for this surplus. This, Sweezy and Baran argued, was leading to economic stagnation. Indeed, the drift towards stagnation was, from this perspective, 'the *normal* state' (Foster and Magdoff, 2009: 66). Nonetheless, some developments were creating 'surplus absorbers' that softened or postponed

all of this and offer an explanation of relative economic stability during the 1950s and 1960s. Government spending and military build-ups played a role. However, as explained by two later commentators drawn from the framework of thought that Baran and Sweezy established, there were limits upon their capacity to absorb the surplus and there would again be recession and crisis:

> there was a lack of symmetry between stagnation and those factors combating it. While the stagnation tendency was deeply rooted, powerful and persistent, the countervailing tendencies were more superficial, weaker and self-limiting. (Foster and Magdoff, 2009: 65–6)[46]

Others from within the Marxist tradition talk of the 'permanent arms economy'. They argue that the high level of military expenditure during the arms race between the west and the Soviet bloc constituted a form of 'military Keynesianism' insofar as it provided a stimulus for other sectors of the economy and postponed the crises that, according to Marxist thinking, generally characterise capitalist economies.[47] Others have however questioned whether military spending was as economically important as these accounts suggest. Although military expenditure was at a high level, it was falling as a proportion of GDP. Much of the military budget was financed by taxation and injections were therefore for the most part balanced out by leakages from national income. And although companies such as Boeing used military technologies as a basis for the development of civilian-oriented production, military research also absorbed resources, including personnel, that could have been employed within the private sector (Wells, 2003: 34–5).[48]

Conclusion

This chapter has charted the increasing emphasis placed upon the role of government in managing the US economy. In loose and broad terms, Keynesian notions won acceptance and federal agencies secured extensive regulatory powers. Having said that, the degree to which the US economy *could* be 'managed' or 'regulated' should not perhaps be exaggerated. Whereas there was a significant public sector (and many core industries and public utilities were nationalised) in most of the countries of western Europe, providing a degree of leverage for government in shaping the wider economy, in the US much more remained in private hands. Furthermore, public attitudes were different. According to opinion polling, Americans saw government, particularly the federal government, in more minimalist terms. They stressed the importance of individual responsibility to a much greater extent than Europeans. At the same time, a president and his administration have only limited authority over fiscal and monetary policy. Tax rates and levels of government spending have to be negotiated with Congress.[49] Lastly, and this defines the approaches adopted by the Austrian School, economic processes are often beyond the control of planners. Fiscal and monetary policy has only a limited and lagged impact on economic trends, which are instead determined by the iron logic of market forces. Therefore, although the decades following the Second World War are often described in terms of economic 'management' or 'direction', terms such as these should be regarded with some caution.

Notes

1 'Laissez-faire' refers to the belief that government should play only a minimal role and economic decisions should be left to market forces.
2 Smith was not, perhaps, committed to pure forms of free market principles in the way that his later backers have suggested. As David Leonhardt argues, the phrase 'invisible hand' with which Smith is associated is only used once in *The Wealth of Nations*. He was sympathetic to regulation that benefited the worker (Leonhardt, 2009).
3 Agriculture was excluded from the boom. Farm produce prices, especially those for grain, were falling (partly because mechanisation led to overproduction) and there was strong competition from other countries once the European nations had recovered from the war. African-American sharecroppers and farm labourers were particularly affected. The coal industry also faced difficulties caused by falling demand levels and overcapacity, (Smiley, 2002: 8).
4 There was, in other words, a 'bull market'.
5 John Kenneth Galbraith notes that the picture offered by Frederick Lewis Allen should be qualified. Large numbers of people were not caught up in the speculative wave. For them, 'the stock market was a remote and vaguely ominous thing' (Galbraith, 1992: 102).
6 Prices were falling significantly at this time and the statistics ('real' GDP) have therefore been adjusted to allow for this.
7 In other words, these are the prices prevailing at the time; they have not been subsequently adjusted for inflation. They therefore overstate the impact of the depression.
8 President Herbert Hoover (Republican) served between 1929 and 1933.
9 The fall in investment levels may be tied to expectations about consumption: 'Businesses failed to invest in production for a simple reason: they suddenly lacked customers to buy their products' (Garfinkle, 2006: 101).
10 Deflationary policies (such as a rise in interest rates) tend to dampen down economic activity and can lead to a fall in prices.
11 The argument that the shrinking of the money stock turned a downturn into a deep and prolonged depression was put forward by Milton Friedman and Anna Schwartz in *A Monetary History of the United States, 1867–1960*. They refer to 'the Great Contraction' and point out that the money supply fell by 35 per cent (Parker, 2007: 13). They argue that the Federal Reserve should have used open market operations (the buying of securities) so as to curtail banking panics, swell the money supply, ensure liquidity and prevent monetary collapse. Randall Parker has put the argument succinctly:

As banks were failing in waves, was the Federal Reserve attempting to contain the panics by aggressively lending to banks scrambling for liquidity? The unfortunate answer is 'no'. When the panics were occurring, was there discussion of suspending deposit convertibility or suspension of the gold standard, both of which had been successfully employed in the past? Again the unfortunate answer is 'no'. Did the Federal Reserve consider the fact that it had an abundant supply of free gold, and therefore that monetary expansion was feasible? Once again the unfortunate answer is 'no'. (Parker, 2007: 13)

12 The development of the banking sector may also have been shaped by the unit banking laws that had been passed in many states. These prevented banks from opening branches and thereby protected the small-town banks from competition by the big-city banks (Powell, 2004: 31). In a different account of the Great Depression, Ben Bernanke, who became chairman of the Federal Reserve in 2006, has attributed much of it to a collapse in lending (Romer, 2009).

13 'Securities' is a broad term referring to bonds (see below) and other financial instruments such as stocks issued by companies.

14 Large-scale and rapid withdrawals of funds from bank deposits are often described as 'runs' on a bank.

15 The gold standard was, at least in theory, a self-regulating system that had governed world trade before the First World War. Gold would flow out of countries with a trade deficit, forcing them to reduce their prices and thereby regain their competitiveness. The gold standard was suspended by the belligerents during the war, but they sought to return to it afterwards. Some did this, despite wartime inflation at pre-war parity. This demanded the adoption of deflationary policies.

16 Bonds are issued by companies or governments so as to borrow funds. Interest rates and bond prices are inversely related.

17 John Maynard Keynes (1883–1946) was an English economist whose books, including *The General Theory of Employment, Interest and Money*, shifted thinking towards macroeconomic concerns such as unemployment and aggregate output. Keynesian theory suggested that laissez-faire approaches did not necessarily lead to full employment and that government intervention was required.

18 Some commentators argue that the customarily harsh judgements of President Hoover's record are unfair. They point out that some forms of interventionism were adopted well before Roosevelt took office. In 1930 Congress cut tax rates and increased public works appropriations. In January 1932, the Reconstruction Finance Corporation was created to provide loans to banks. Although there was a commitment to a balanced budget, few were advocating such a course. Indeed, during the 1932 election campaign, Roosevelt criticised the deficits that had been incurred. Furthermore, as Iwan Morgan notes: 'Only in FY 1934 and 1936 were the full-employment deficits of the New Deal budgets substantively higher than those in Hoover's budgets, and these were insufficient to boost recovery' (Morgan, 1995: 25).

19 The fall in imports may however have been due to falling US consumption levels rather than the tariffs.

20 During this period, the use of gold as a form of legal tender ended and most private holdings of gold were prohibited. The 'Austrian School' argues that because during this period the dollar became a 'fiat currency', resting on government policy rather

than being tied to a physical commodity such as gold, this opened the way for successive administrations to inflate or 'debase' the currency.

21   The multiplier is closely associated with Keynesian economics (see pp. 00–00). Although the Roosevelt administration did not formally embrace Keynesian thinking, the New Deal has been hailed by many later Keynesians.

22   The value of the multiplier depends upon the extent to which there are *leakages*. These are (in a 'four-sector' model of the economy) savings, taxation, and spending on imports. These weaken spending power and thereby limit the effectiveness of any injection.

23   A cartel (or 'trust') is where a group of firms seek to restrict competition by colluding together to set prices or regulate output.

24   'Rosie the Riveter' has come to symbolise the wartime employment of women. The human issues involved are explored in the 1981 film, *The Life and Times of Rosie the Riveter*.

25   The US Supreme Court interprets the Constitution and can, on the basis of this, strike down federal and state laws if it finds them unconstitutional.

26   The Roosevelt administration's relative economic caution can be attributed to both a reluctance to break with prevailing economic orthodoxy and the political constraints that it faced. Many Democrats were conservatives and the Republicans made gains in the 1938 mid-term elections.

27   Some New Dealers made another argument for government interventionism. They adopted a long-term historical perspective and asserted that the settling of the American continent and the slowing rate of population growth had led to a decline in private investment opportunities (Wells, 2003: 8–9). Government investment was therefore required.

28   The claim that the New Deal served corporate interests also formed the basis for populist opposition to Roosevelt and was taken up by, for example, Louisiana governor (and senator) Huey Long.

29   There will always be some *frictional* unemployment as workers have gaps or shift between jobs.

30   At the same time, however, some feared the pressures to conform associated with the American dream, the drive to secure a higher income, anti-communism and seemingly happy families.

31   Samuel Rosenberg distinguishes between the 1950s and 1960s by talking in terms of 'passive' and 'active' Keynesianism (Rosenberg, 2003: 55).

32   Sales taxes are levied by states and local governments in the US, not the federal government.

33   The 1946 Employment Act was a modified version of the original 1945 bill which had more overtly Keynesian goals. The bill had stated that 'All Americans…are entitled to an opportunity for useful, remunerative, and full-time employment' (Santoni, 1966: 12).

34   There had also been a recession in 1953–4 triggered by the restrictive monetary policies that were imposed as inflation rates rose in the wake of the Korean War.

35   Those who advocated a change of course also noted that 'fiscal drag' (whereby tax brackets do not keep pace with rising incomes, thereby taking individuals into higher brackets and increasing tax revenue) was having a deflationary impact on the US economy (Wells, 2003: 50).

36   The Phillips curve was originally drawn up by Professor Alban Phillips in an article first published in 1958. In its original form, it depicted the inverse relationship between changes in money wages and unemployment rates in Britain.

37   Many conservative economists have argued in recent years that government budget deficits are not inflationary and do not 'crowd out' private investment if there is an independent central bank that will set an interest rate designed to keep inflation at minimal levels and an open capital market that will provide large-scale investment funds from both foreign and domestic sources (Bienkowski, Brada and Radlo, 2006: xii).

38   Paul Krugman, however, vehemently denies that that the 'Great Society' was tied to Keynesianism. He offers a perhaps circumscribed definition of Keynesianism by restricting it to the use of deficit spending in times of depression. The 1960s were a period of growth and the Great Society was a programme of social reform: 'It was social engineering; we can talk about how well or badly it worked, but it had nothing whatsoever to do with Keynesian economics' (Krugman, 2008).

39   By the late 1960s, the Bretton Woods system looked increasingly shaky. The US trade deficit and the federal government budget deficit (which had been fuelled by the Vietnam War) imposed strains. Furthermore, inflation led to the overvaluation of the dollar in terms of the Bretton Woods price for gold ($35 an ounce). As doubt and uncertainty about the future of the system grew, other countries sought to cash in their dollars for gold. Indeed, France withdrew from the Bretton Woods agreement in 1965 (Hughes and Cain, 2003: 604).

40   At the same time, there was an increasingly vocal critique of the Johnson administration from the New Left. From this perspective, Vietnam was a brutal imperialist venture. Despite the rhetoric of the Great Society, there had been no transfer of wealth to the poor but instead transfers were largely within middle-income groupings. Indeed, there had a decline in real median family income.

41   The 'CEA' refers to the Council of Economic Advisers. This is based in the White House and offers advice and policy recommendations to the president.

42   The 'catch-up effect' has been used to explain high levels of growth in Asian countries and countries such as Japan and West Germany that were largely destroyed during the Second World War.

43   Nonetheless, the part played by foreign trade in the long boom should not be exaggerated. Net exports constituted a smaller proportion of GDP than in many other countries (see pp. 146–7).

44   At the end of the Second World War, the US held about 60 per cent of the world's gold reserves.

45   In the Bretton Woods regime, depreciation and devaluation were only allowed in very limited circumstances.

46   Foster and Magdoff have more recently explored the ways in which the growth of the financial sector provided a degree, albeit temporary, of stabilisation or a reprieve from stagnation (Foster and Magdoff, 2009: 66–7).

47   Some other reasons for the post-war boom should also be considered. There was widespread saving during the war and this boosted consumption levels once the war was over. The 'baby boom' added further to consumer demand while returning soldiers, suburbanisation, the widespread ownership of automobiles and changing family structures provided a basis for new forms of growth. Companies

gained *economies of scale* through a process of consolidation and mergers. Local enterprise gave way to national brands either through the emergence of the industrial giant or through franchising.

48 Wells, however, emphasises that there is no way of calculating the numbers that could have found work with private companies and argues that the Cold War drew some towards engineering and science (Wells, 2003: 34–5).

49 President Richard Nixon (1969–74) sought to circumvent Congressional prerogatives through a process of 'impoundment' by which funding assignment by Congress for a particular purpose was held back by the administration. The 1974 Congressional Budget and Impoundment Control Act sought to limit a president's ability to do this (see Ashbee, 2004: 120).

References and further reading

Ashbee, Edward (2004), *US Politics Today*, Manchester: Manchester University Press.

Badger, Anthony J. (1989), *The New Deal: The Depression Years, 1933–40*, Basingstoke: Macmillan.

Baran, Paul and Paul Sweezy (1966), *Monopoly Capital: An Essay on the American Economic and Social Order*, New York: Monthly Review Press.

Berthoud, John (2001), *Ten Facts about the Kennedy-Johnson Tax Cuts*, National Taxpayers Union, March 13, <http://www.ntu.org>

Bienkowski, Wojciech, Josef C. Brada and Mariusz-Jan Radlo (2006), *Reaganomics Goes Global: What Can the EU, Russia and Transition Countries Learn from the USA?*, Basingstoke: Palgrave Macmillan.

Bordo, Michael D. (2003), 'Comment on "The Great Depression and the Friedman-Schwartz Hypothesis" by Lawrence Christiano, Roberto Motto, and Massimo Rostagno', *Journal of Money, Credit, and Banking*, 35:6, December, 1200–3.

Brenner, Robert (2003), *The Boom and the Bubble: The US in the World Economy*, London: Verso.

Collins, Robert M. (2000), *More: The Politics of Economic Growth*, Oxford: Oxford University Press.

DeLong, J. Bradford (1997), *Slouching Towards Utopia?: The Economic History of the Twentieth Century -XX. The Great Keynesian Boom: 'Thirty Glorious Years'*, <http://www.j-bradford-delong.net>

Foster, John Bellamy and Fred Magdoff (2009), *The Great Financial Crisis: Causes and Consequences*, New York: Monthly Review Press.

Friedman, Milton and Anna Schwartz (1971), *A Monetary History of the United States, 1867–1960*, Princeton: Princeton University Press.

Galbraith, John Kenneth (1992), *The Great Crash 1929*, Harmondsworth: Penguin.

Gale Encyclopaedia of US Economic History (2000), *Postwar Boom*, <http://www.accessmylibrary.com/coms2/summary_0193-13366_ITM>

Garfinkle, Norton (2006), *The American Dream vs. The Gospel of Wealth: The Fight for a Productive Middle-Class Economy*, New Haven: Yale University Press.

Hanes, Christopher (2000), 'Nominal wage rigidity and industry characteristics in the downturns of 1893, 1929, and 1981', *American Economic Review*, 90: 5, December, 1432–46.

Hoover, Herbert (1999), 'Herbert Hoover reassures the nation', in Colin Gordon (ed.), *Major Problems in American History 1920–1945*, Boston: Houghton Mifflin, 183–5.

Hughes, Jonathan and Louis P. Cain (2003), *American Economic History*, Reading, MA: Addison Wesley.

Krugman, Paul (2008), 'Amity Shlaes strikes again', *New York Times – The Conscience of a Liberal*, November 19, <http://krugman.blogs.nytimes.com>

Leonhardt, David (2009), 'Theory and morality in the new economy', *New York Times Book Review*, August 23, 23.

Lindsey, Brink (2009), *Paul Krugman's Nostalgianomics: Economic Policies, Social Norms, and Income Inequality*, Cato Institute, February 9, 9–10, <http://www.cato.org/pubs/wtpapers/Nostalgianomics.pdf>

Morgan, Iwan W. (1995), *Deficit Government: Taxing and Spending in Modern America*, Chicago: Ivan R. Dee.

Morgan, Iwan W. (2004), 'Jimmy Caster, Bill Clinton and the New Democratic economics', *Historical Journal*, 47: 4, December, 1017.

National Cooperative Highway Research Program (2006), *Technical Memorandum Task 2: The Economic Impact of the Interstate Highway System*, <http://www.interstate50th.org/docs/techmemo2.pdf>

Nichols, Jeffrey D. (1995), *Reed Smoot and the Smoot-Hawley Tariff, 1930*, Utah History to Go, <http://historytogo.utah.gov>

Ohio History Central (2008), *Social Darwinism*, Ohio History Society, <http://www.ohiohistorycentral.org>

Parker, Randall E. (2007), *The Economics of the Great Depression: A Twenty-First Century Look Back at the Economics of the Interwar Era*, Cheltenham: Edward Elgar.

Powell, Jim (2004), *FDR's Folly: How Roosevelt and His New Deal Prolonged the Great Depression*, New York: Three Rivers Press.

Prasad, Monica (2006), *The Politics of Free Markets: The Rise of Neoliberal Economic Policies in Britain, France, Germany, and the United States*, Chicago: University of Chicago Press.

Radosh, Ronald (1972), 'The myth of the New Deal', in Ronald Radosh and Murray N. Rothbard, *A New History of Leviathan: Essays on the Rise of the American Corporate State*, New York: E.P. Dutton and Co., 146–87.

Reynolds, Alan (1995), 'Unbalanced amendment: balanced budget amendment, R.I.P.', *Reason*, June, <http://www.reason.com>

Romer, Christina D. (2009), *Lessons from the Great Depression for Economic Recovery in 2009*, The Brookings Institution, March 9, <http://www.brookings.edu/~/media/Files/events/2009/0309_lessons/0309_lessons_romer.pdf>

Rosenberg, Samuel (2003), *American Economic Development since 1945*, Basingstoke: Palgrave Macmillan.

Samuelson, Robert J. (2008), 'Great Depression', *The Concise Encyclopaedia of Economics*, <http://www.econlib.org>

Santoni, G. J. (1966), *The Employment Act of 1946: Some History Notes*, Federal Reserve Bank of St Louis, <http://research.stlouisfed.org/publications/review/86/11/Employment_Nov1986.pdf>

Shlaes, Amity (2007), *The Forgotten Man: A New History of the Great Depression*, New York: Harper Perennial.

Shlaes, Amity (2008), *Obama Will Take Us Backward By Channeling Keynes*, Bloomberg. com, November 19, <http://www.bloomberg.com>

Skocpol, Theda (1980), 'Political response to capitalist crisis: Neo-Marxist theories of the state and the case of the New Deal', *Politics and Society*, 10, 155–201.

Smiley, Gene (2002), *Rethinking the Great Depression*, Chicago: Ivan R. Dee.

Smiley, Gene (2004), *The American Economy in the Twentieth Century*, Cincinnati: South-Western Publishing.

Smiley, Gene (2008), *The US Economy in the 1920s*, EH.Net Encyclopaedia, ed. Robert Whaples, March 26, <http://eh.net>

Temin, Peter (1994), *The Great Depression*, National Bureau of Economic Research, Historical Paper #62.

US Census Bureau (2007), *A Half-Century of Learning: Historical Statistics on Educational Attainment in the United States, 1940 to 2000: Table 1. Percent of the Population 25 Years and Over with a High School Diploma or Higher by Sex and Age, for the United States: 1940 to 2000*, US Census Bureau, <http://www.census.gov>

Wells, Wyatt (2003), *American Capitalism, 1945–2000*, Chicago: Ivan R. Dee.

3

Curtailing the role of government

Chapter 3 considers the reaction against government economic interventionism. It surveys the critique of Keynesianism offered by conservative economists such as Milton Friedman and looks at the economic crises of the 1970s and the ways in which 'stagflation' contributed to an economic and political counter-revolution. It looks at the displacement of Keynesianism by approaches associated with monetarism and supply-side economics. Against this background, the chapter evaluates the economic record of the Reagan administration and the extent to which a 'counter-revolution' was wrought.

The nine most terrifying words in the English language are, 'I'm from the government and I'm here to help'
> (President Ronald Reagan, quoted in US Department of Labor – Occupational Safety and Health Administration, 2006)

Although most post-war economists and politicians were committed (either openly or in a more unconscious way) to notions associated with Keynesianism and the concept of a managed economy, there were always dissidents who challenged what they saw as the new economic orthodoxy. Some drew on Friedrich von Hayek's 1944 book, *The Road to Serfdom*. Hayek, who was associated with the Austrian school of economics and saw himself as a classical liberal rather than a conservative, argued that central economic planning and government direction inevitably leads to tyranny.[1] At the least, it is from this perspective a 'fatal conceit' to believe that a government can control or 'manage' economic forces (Hayward, 2006: 53). Modern economies rest upon a multitude of complex day-to-day micro-level transactions and government planners simply cannot have the knowledge or understanding required to coordinate these processes.

From the perspective of the Austrian school, government frustration and disagreement about policy options will inevitably lead governments to fall back upon increasingly authoritarian methods. Such authoritarianism would win public backing because of discontent with the inability of economic planning to deliver the promised results. Government economic interventionism thereby set nations on the 'road to serfdom'.

Professor Milton Friedman of the University of Chicago was another 'dissident' classical liberal. Although there were some differences between Friedman's thinking and the Austrian school he, like almost all other conservatives or 'classical liberals, shared the Austrians' hostility to government economic interventionism. Indeed, Friedman later held up the free market order in Hong Kong as a model economy. In a celebrated comment, he once remarked that 'if you put the federal government in charge of the Sahara desert...in five years there'd be a shortage of sand' (quoted in *Economist*, 2008). Writing in 1948, Friedman distinguished himself from what he saw as mainstream or Keynesian economics by reasserting the pivotal role of a free market allowing the unhindered interplay of supply and demand:

> The basic long-run objectives, shared, I am sure by most economists, are political freedom, economic efficiency and substantial equality of economic power...I believe – and at this stage agreement will be far less widespread – that all three objectives can best be realized by relying, as far as possible, on a market mechanism within a 'competitive order' to organize the utilization of economic resources. (Friedman, 1953: 134)

Friedman revived, redefined and promoted 'monetarist' theory and the *quantity theory of money*. From a monetarist perspective, changes in the price level (inflation or deflation) were directly tied to changes in the supply of money: 'inflation is always and everywhere a monetary phenomenon' (Milton Friedman, quoted in Wells, 2003: 76). The Federal Reserve had a responsibility, therefore, to control the money supply.[2] Furthermore, when the Federal Reserve misjudged the rate of monetary growth that was required, it could have catastrophic consequences for the wider economy. Writing with Anna Schwarz, Friedman argued that the depression of the 1930s had been caused by the contraction of the money supply (by about a third) between 1929 and 1933.[3] In other words, it was a consequence of errors by the Federal Reserve Board, which had mistakenly pursued a policy of monetary restraint from 1928 onwards. This had been compounded by further reductions in the money supply during the years that followed:

> The Fed, having no experience of the sort of financial crash it had inadvertently helped to set in train, responded to the collapsing economy, not by easing monetary policy and injecting liquidity, but by a further contraction...Had the Fed been pursuing a pre-arranged growth path for the money stock – money rules – the Great Depression would at best never have happened at all, and at worst would have been confined to a short-lived downturn, quickly reversed. (Smith, 1987: 21–2)

Similarly Friedman argued that the inflation of the 1970s had been the consequence of errors. The Federal Reserve had allowed the money supply to grow excessively. In arguing this, he dismissed other, more widely accepted, explanations of inflation, which attributed it to cost-push factors such as the oil price rise or labour union militancy.

Why was inflation so important? It results in an inefficient allocation of resources and disrupts investment plans, thereby curtailing expansion and development. By preventing inflation (or a falling price level), the Federal Reserve would, it was said, provide a solid and secure framework for investment and other economic activity, thereby fuelling growth.[4] Beryl Sprinkel, an economic adviser in the Reagan White House, put it in succinct terms when he said: 'Control the money supply and everything else falls into place. Thank you and good night' (Martin, 2009).

Figures such as Friedman and Hayek were for the most part isolated voices. Indeed, the historian Eric Hobsbawm described Hayek at the time as a 'prophet in the wilderness' (Prasad, 2006: 2). Their isolation was seemingly reinforced by the outcome of the 1964 presidential election. Senator Barry Goldwater, the Republicans' nominee, drew on the economics and philosophy of classical liberalism. In contrast with many other Republicans, he broke with the centre-ground, consensus politics of the period. Goldwater attacked the dangers posed by government social provision (or 'welfarism' as he dubbed it), and called for the privatisation of Social Security, the ending of farm subsidies and the privatisation of the Tennessee Valley Authority (Bjerre-Poulsen, 2002: 244–5). In the book that he used to define his politics, *The Conscience of a Conservative* (1960), Goldwater stressed the need for laissez-faire and limited government. Government expenditure and the taxation required to pay for it threatened livelihoods. Regulation placed liberty and economic growth in jeopardy.

Federal spending is now approaching a hundred billion dollars a year (compared with three and one-half billion less than three decades ago)...nearly a third of earnings are taken every year in the form of taxes...The farmer is told how much wheat he can grow. The wage earner is at the mercy of national union leaders whose great power is a direct consequence of federal labor legislation. The businessman is hampered by a maze of government regulations, and often by direct government competition. The government takes six per cent of most payrolls in Social Security Taxes and thus compels millions of individuals to postpone until later years the enjoyment of wealth they might otherwise enjoy today. Increasingly, the federal government sets standards of education, health and safety. (Goldwater, 1974: 20–1)

Senator Goldwater was, however, crushed by the incumbent president Lyndon Johnson in the 1964 election and his defeat was widely seen as testimony to the futility of the abrasive and uncompromisingly conservative message that he offered. Nearly all economists and policymakers remained wedded to the defining features of Keynesianism.

The Nixon administration, 1969–74

President Richard Nixon, who took office in January 1969, was instinctively drawn to free markets. His administration was concerned about inflation levels (which as Figure 3.1 indicates rose significantly during his first two years in office) and opposed to the Great Society programmes that his predecessor, President Lyndon Johnson, had pursued. Nonetheless, his administration followed a pragmatic and increasingly interventionist course.

At the time, the alternatives lacked credibility. Government direction seemed to many on both the left and right the only course of action. Some looked beyond the US and drew inspiration from the *dirigisme* (faith in central planning and government economic direction) of successive French governments and the role of MITI (Ministry of International Trade and Industry) in guiding the development of Japanese industry during the post-war years (Morris, 2008: 16).

In his State of the Union Address at the beginning of 1971, Nixon stressed the importance of using fiscal policy to secure full employment. He told Congress:

> I will submit an expansionary budget this year – one that will help stimulate the economy and thereby open up new job opportunities for millions of Americans. It will be a full employment budget…By spending as if we were at full employment, we will help bring about full employment. (quoted in Stein, 1984: 172–3)

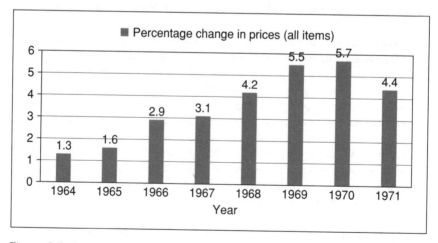

Figure 3.1 *Consumer price index, 1964–71*

Source: adapted from US Census Bureau (2009), *The 2009 Statistical Abstract*, <http://www.census.gov>

Against this background, Nixon proclaimed in a celebrated phrase, 'Now I am a Keynesian' (Stein, 1984: 135).

Faith in Keynesianism and a fear that reflationary fiscal policies might lead to increased inflation led the Nixon administration towards direct controls over the economy and the daily lives of individuals. In mid-August 1971, the administration adopted the 'New Economic Policy'. Citing powers extended to him under the Economic Stabilization Act of 1970, Nixon issued an executive order imposing a 90-day freeze on wage and price increases and a 10 per cent import surcharge (which was dropped at the end of the year). For his part, Milton Friedman denounced such interference with market forces and called Nixon 'the most socialist president' in American history (Parker, 2005).[5] The freeze was followed by 'Phase II' and 'Phase III' but inflation levels rose at a rapid rate. Between January and May 1973, food prices alone rose by 8.7 per cent (or over 22 per cent if the figures are considered on an annualised basis) (Rosenberg, 2003: 186). The administration responded by changing tack and pursuing an increasingly deflationary course.

The end of Bretton Woods

Having said this, the Nixon administration was not entirely wedded to interventionism. Circumstances compelled the White House to make a shift that despite its initial intentions took the US and other nations towards free market economics.

From the end of the Second World War onwards, exchange rates had been regulated by the *Bretton Woods* system. So as to provide a stable and secure basis for world trade, the world's major currencies were fixed against the US dollar. It was the world's reserve currency. Although countries could, in certain circumstances, revalue or devalue their currencies, these fixed rates survived for long periods. Between 1949 and 1969, the British pound sterling was fixed at $2.80. During the same years, there were 6.91 Danish kroner to the dollar. So as to ensure absolute solidity, the dollar was fixed against gold at $35 an ounce.

By the beginning of the 1970s, the system was under severe strain. The US had been running balance of payments' deficits and, as a consequence, foreign treasuries and central banks had accumulated dollars. These far exceeded the US's holdings of gold if the dollar was valued at $35 an ounce. Indeed, by August 1971, foreign holdings of dollars amounted to more than three times the US gold reserves. As Herbert Stein, chairman of the Council of Economic Advisers under both Nixon and Ford, later recalled:

> Everyone knew that if the foreign holders presented their dollars for conversion there wouldn't be enough gold to go around. So there was a tacit understanding among foreign treasuries and central banks not to ask for gold less doing so precipitate a run. But the situation was unstable. Every country had to be

concerned that some other one would get to the gold window first and draw out the gold while it lasted – or while the United States remained willing to keep the window open. (Stein, 1984: 164)

In a step that proved the point, in the second week of August 1971, against a background of economic uncertainty, the British ambassador asked the US Treasury Department to convert holdings of $3 billion into gold.

In response, the Nixon administration 'closed the gold window', ending the dollar's convertibility with gold. At the end of 1971, there was a short-lived effort to revive fixed rates. The Smithsonian Agreement was based around a dollar that had been devalued against gold ($38 an ounce) and allowed some flexibility for currencies (they could devalue by 2.25 per cent from the agreed exchange rates) but it could not be maintained and gave way to a floating exchange rate regime.

Many free market theorists, most notably Milton Friedman, welcomed these developments. Exchange rates were now determined, like commodities or services, by supply and demand rather than government manipulation. Others on the right were much less sanguine. Once detached from the security and stability of fixed rates, governments would be unrestrained. So as to secure political gains or accommodate powerful lobbies, government spending would be increased, interest rates would be maintained at artificially low levels and paper or 'fiat' money would be created. According Murray Rothbard of the Ludwig von Mises Institute: 'Since the U.S. went completely off gold...the United States and the world have suffered the most intense and most sustained bout of peacetime inflation in the history of the world' (Rothbard, 1980).

'Stagflation' and malaise

Commentators have passed different verdicts on the Nixon administration's economic record. In the short term, its policies were widely applauded. Perhaps surprisingly, business interests were enthusiastic about controls. There was also a temporary economic upturn. The 1972 economic growth was 5.3 per cent:

Nixon's New Economy Policy produced a booming economy in 1972, with real income growth ranging from 4.5 per cent for working poor families to 6.6 per cent for families at the 95th percentile of the income distribution. This robust growth contributed significantly to Nixon's landslide re-election. (Bartels 2008: 45)

However, as Larry Bartels has noted, the boom was short-lived and had petered out by 1973–4. The years that followed were beset with problems. Indeed, the mid and late 1970s have become synonymous with a sense of malaise. There were repeated crises that tied together with fears of long-term national decline.[6] As Edward S. Greenberg has recorded: 'phrases like "limits", "zero-sum choices", and "diminishing expectations" became the watchwords of the 1970s' (Greenberg, 1991: 109).

For David I. Fand, writing in 1977, much of the responsibility for this lay with the Nixon administration and the New Economic Policy (NEP) that it had adopted in August 1971:

> That the NEP and its descendants represent a failure of substantial proportions is…beyond discussion. The U.S. is now completing a decade of inflation. The succession of inflation, recession, and high unemployment, of capacity shortages, and idle plant and equipment, and of inventory accumulation and liquidation is sapping the strength of the American economy – a deterioration that is manifest in the decline of the dollar in the past decade. (Fand, 1977: 362)

As Fand suggests in his graphic description, different economic difficulties came together during the 1970s. Inflation rose dramatically in 1974–5 and again at the end of the decade, (see Figure 3.2). It also remained high (above 5 per cent) between the peaks.

Why did inflation levels rise? Despite Fand's focus on White House policy, many observers have pointed to the part played by external 'shocks' and 'cost-push' factors. In particular, in 1973–4, the Organization of Petroleum Exporting Countries (OPEC) limited the supply of oil and raised its price. The real price

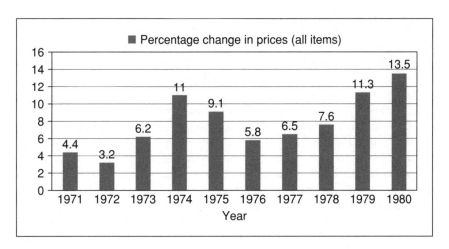

Figure 3.2 *Consumer price index, 1971–80*

Source: adapted from US Census Bureau (2009), *The 2009 Statistical Abstract*, <http://www.census.gov>

of oil rose by 140 per cent during the course of 1974. The crisis was intensified by US price controls which removed some stocks of oil from the market. A bizarre form of rationing was introduced so that those who drove vehicles with license plates having an odd number as the last digit could purchase gasoline on odd-numbered days of the month. Those who drove vehicles with even-numbered license plates bought fuel only on even-numbered days. The increase in oil prices added to the costs borne by industry, which in turn increased prices and laid the basis for a wage-price spiral as workers sought wage rises to compensate for the effects of a higher price level. Although the US labour movement was much weaker than its west European counterparts, there were still growing numbers of strikes. A 1971 report in *Time* magazine captures the prevailing mood:

> a steel strike was averted at the last moment, but inevitably at an inflationary cost. Within 24 hours after the wage settlement was announced, most of the big steel producers posted a price hike. After 18 disruptive days, the nationwide rail strike was brought to an end. Though many featherbedding work rules were finally eliminated, the United Transportation Union extracted a 42 per cent pay increase spread out over 42 months. (*Time*, 1971)

However, the rise in inflation may also be attributable to longer-term structural processes.[7] From the early 1970s onwards, the rate of productivity growth slowed markedly. The failure to recognise this as it was happening led to policy errors because policymakers overestimated the capacities of the economy and the extent to which demand levels could be raised before inflation took hold (Morgan, 2004: 1022–3).[8]

Inflation was not, however, the only concern. Unemployment levels also rose. As Figure 3.3 shows, there was a particularly marked increase in 1974–5 and numbers rose again at the beginning of the new decade. In other words, there were high levels of inflation and unemployment at the same time. Media commentaries quickly dubbed this 'stagnation' (because there was both inflation and low economic growth or 'stagnation').

The simultaneous rise in both inflation and unemployment had significant consequences and contributed to a paradigm shift among both economists and politicians. In other words, they had to think again about their most basic assumptions. Although Keynes himself was a more nuanced writer than his later followers, Keynesianism had represented unemployment and inflation as opposites (see Chapter 2). High inflation occurred when demand grew at an excessive rate. Unemployment rose when demand, or the rate of growth of demand, was relatively low. There was therefore an inverse relationship between the two variables that was charted in the Phillips curve (see Figure 2.6, p. 46). By the late 1970s, it was evident that unemployment and inflation were no longer opposites.

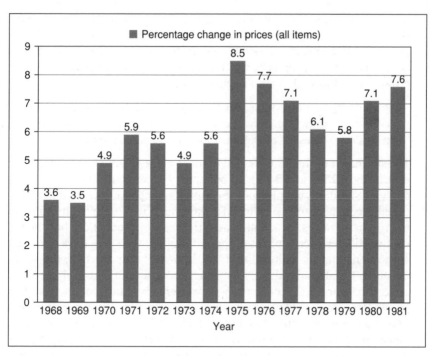

Figure 3.3 *Unemployment rate (percentage), 1968–81*
Source: adapted from Bureau of Labor Statistics (2009), *Labor Force Statistics from the Current Population Survey*, <http://www.bls.gov>

Longer-term problems

The crises of the 1970s were tied to, and underpinned by, longer-term economic strains.

- Although foreign trade contributed only a relatively small share of America's GDP, the US was losing its former place in the world market as other countries, most notably Japan and the countries of western Europe, grew at a rapid rate. The US's share of manufactured exports across the globe halved between 1950 and 1970 (from 33 per cent to 16 per cent) (Glyn, 2007: 9).
- Productivity growth rates slowed down in the US and other countries after 1973 (Glyn, 2007: 13). Productivity – or efficiency – is a measure of the relationship between a particular input (labour or capital) and overall output. An increase in productivity through, for example, the adoption of new technology or an expansion of the production process so as to secure *economies of scale*, allows for the production of the same level of output

with fewer inputs. If fewer workers are used to produce the same amount then there has been productivity growth. Although some talk of *multifactor* productivity, the most common form of measurement is to consider output per worker over a given period of time. A country's productivity rate is of pivotal importance. As Paul Krugman notes:

> 'Productivity isn't everything, but in the long run it is almost everything. A country's ability to improve its standard of living depends almost entirely on its ability to raise its output per worker' (Krugman, 1998: 11).

The slowdown in the US (rates fell from an average annual rate of 2.8 per cent in the 1950s and 1960s to only about 1 per cent) had implications for living standards but also for the country's competitiveness and its ability to sell products overseas. Why did it happen? It was initially attributed to the rise in oil prices, which increased the costs of production, but the fall continued after energy prices dropped in the 1980s. There have also been suggestions that the cultural shifts of the 1960s (in particular, the youth 'rebellion') had consequences for educational attainment and the work ethic. Others argue that companies were less ready to take commercial risks by modernising.[9] This was partly because of political uncertainties and growing economic anxieties brought about by inflation. In his book, *Capitalism Unleashed*, Andrew Glyn suggests that the 'Fordist' system of mass assembly-line production was approaching its limits. As mass production expanded and grew, there were increasingly *diseconomies of scale*. For example, there was an erosion of managerial control and workplace discipline in many of the larger factories (Glyn, 2007: 14–15). At the same time, the growth of the service sector, which has a lower level of productivity growth than manufacturing, also played a part. As the service sector came to constitute a larger share of the US economy, overall productivity growth levels inevitably fell. Other explanations have also been put forward. Some point to the low level of public investment in infrastructural development such as rail and roads. Left-leaning commentators such as Robert Reich (who served in the Clinton administration) and Lester Thurow have suggested that the market does not always generate the type of investment that serves the overall interests of the economy and have called upon government to play a more proactive role. The public education system is said to have failed many students, particularly those from lower-income backgrounds. For their part, conservatives point to what they regard as excessive and intrusive forms of government regulation that, they assert, have hampered enterprise and development.

- Alongside these anxieties, the 1970s were marked by rising concern about, and often hostility towards, 'big government'. The criticisms of federal power that Senator Barry Goldwater had raised during the early 1960s seemed to have been confirmed by subsequent developments. The size and scale of government (taking federal, state and local government together) had

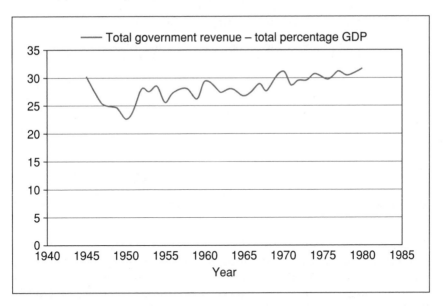

Figure 3.4 *Federal, state and local government revenue, FY 1945–80 (%)*

Source: adapted from usgovernmentrevenue.com (2008), *Time Series Chart of Total Revenue*, <http://www.usgovernmentrevenue.com>

continued to grow. As Figure 3.4 indicates, the share of GDP taken by government reached record levels in the 1970s. Indeed, from 1969 onwards the government took a greater share of GDP than it had during the Second World War.

Paradigm shift

The claims made by the commentators who talk of 'stagflation' or 'malaise' are sometimes exaggerated. If the economic growth figures for the 1970s are considered there was recession during 1974–5 and again during the last year of President Jimmy Carter's term of office, but there was a period of strong growth between 1976 and 1979 (see Table 3.1). Indeed, as Dan Clawson notes: 'the economy had one of its longest sustained boom periods; 1980 brought recession' (Clawson, 1982: 615).

Nonetheless, images and perceptions sometimes outweigh realities.[10] There was a deeply rooted belief that the US economy was in decline and that Keynesianism no longer explained economic realities. Paul Volcker, who became chairman of the Federal Reserve in 1979 and later served as chairman of President Barack Obama's Economic Recovery Advisory Board, acknowledged that Keynes had left an important legacy but also said to a journalist: 'if you

Table 3.1 *Economic growth (rate of change of GDP) (%), 1973–80*

Year	% change in GDP (chained 2000 dollars)
1973	5.8
1974	−0.5
1975	−0.2
1976	5.3
1977	4.6
1978	5.6
1979	3.2
1980	−0.2

Source: adapted from Bureau of Economic Analysis (2008), *Percent Change from Preceding Period*, <http://www.bea.gov>

mean that we've got to pump up the economy, that all these relationships are pretty clear and simple, that this gives us a tool for eternal prosperity if we do it right, that's all bullshit' (Collins, 2006: 63). Against this background, the economic 'dissidents' of earlier years such as Friedrich von Hayek and Milton Friedman began to gain a wider hearing.

For their part, Friedman and the Chicago school offered a critique of Keynesianism and the proposition that there was an inverse relationship or *trade-off* between unemployment and inflation. From a Keynesian perspective, as noted above, when unemployment rates fell, inflation would rise. Conversely, a rise in unemployment would lead to a fall in the inflation rate. The negative relationship between the two variables had been charted in the *Phillips curve*. Friedman accepted the initial logic of the Phillips curve. Governments, he asserted, often pursued reflationary policies so as to reduce unemployment. They accepted increased inflation as a necessary evil. And, Friedman accepted, unemployment would fall. However, at this point he parted company with the Keynesian mainstream. Workers would, he argued, recognise that inflation was reducing the buying power of wages and they would, over time, adjust their behaviour accordingly. There would be a reluctance to take the lowest-paid jobs at the bottom end of the labour market. Other options, particularly if government social provision could be secured, would prove more attractive and some workers would therefore drop out of the labour market. As a consequence, unemployment would rise again while, at the same time, inflation remained at a higher rate. Governments, often lured by political expediency, would again be driven to adopt reflationary policies. Unemployment would temporarily fall but inflation would again rise. Again workers would adjust their behaviour and the entire cycle would be repeated. Unemployment would keep returning to its natural rate (the 'long-run Phillips curve') which was set by government policy, the structural character of the labour market and cultural variables. Friedman depicted the process in the *expectations-augmented Phillips curve* (Figure 3.5).

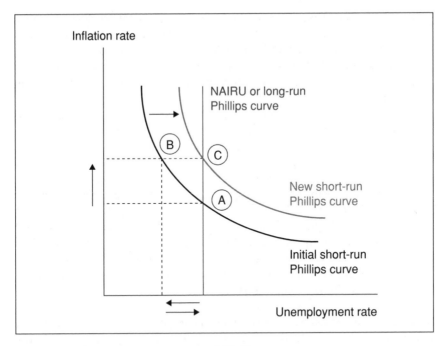

Figure 3.5 *The expectations-augmented Phillips curve*

Economists associated with the 'rational expectations' (RE) school have built upon Friedman's critique. Employees, they argue, will recognise the inflationary implications of reflationary fiscal and monetary policies with little delay and adjust their behaviour immediately. There is therefore no short-run reduction in unemployment. Instead, unemployment remains at its long-term level while inflation levels rise. More generally, the rational expectations school suggested that all forms of government economic interventionism were counterproductive because both capital and labour would expect that intervention and adjust their behaviour ahead of it. In other words, they knew that government would accommodate wage rises or uncompetitive forms of production. RE theorists 'argued that predictable government intervention was destined to be futile and ineffectual because economic actors would anticipate it. Thus, government activism of any sort was suspect' (Collins, 2006: 62).

Friedman and his co-thinkers did not, however, only offer a critique of the Phillips curve and the forms of public policy that flowed from it. The expectations-augmented Phillips curve and the arguments put forward by the Chicago school were tied to broader propositions.

• First, the curve was associated with the Chicago school's claim that inflation (rather than unemployment) was 'public enemy number one'. Inflation, it was said, eroded the value of both savings and debts (leading to rather arbitrary forms of redistribution) and threatened the competitiveness of US exports. Most importantly of all, it created instability, disrupting investment and business planning. From this perspective, the reduction of inflation would lay a basis for stable long-term economic growth and, with it, rising employment levels.

- Secondly, the Chicago school, along with others on the right, helped popularise laissez-faire notions and the belief that government intervention necessarily impedes growth and prosperity. Even the most carefully crafted and well-intentioned policies have unintended consequences. Instead, it was said, the process of production should be guided by the free interplay of supply and demand. There was in other words a paradigm shift: the framework of ideas and assumptions that structured policy choices about the economy changed in character. The new thinking has been assigned different labels. Some talk about 'neo-liberalism'. Others refer to the ideas of the 'new right' or conservatism. The terms 'free market' or 'laissez-faire' economics are also applied. And, in anticipation of the 1980s, the word 'Reaganomics' has often been used.[11]

Monetarist economics were controversial. Some saw its prescriptions as a form of class warfare. The reduction of unemployment, they argued, should be the foremost goal of economic policy because it hit those who were most vulnerable. Inflation was a secondary concern. There were also more specific criticisms of monetarist thinking. Friedman's proposition that inflation was always caused by the excessive growth of the money supply led monetarists to assert that governments and central banks should curb inflation by targeting the money supply. Interest rates, they argued, should be raised or lowered on the basis of changes in the rate of growth of the money supply. However, as many commentators noted, there is no single measure of the money supply. Indeed, in a modern economy characterised by different forms of bank accounts, widespread share holdings, and asset ownership, the question arises, 'what is money?' Economic strategists could target 'narrow money' which is the notes and coins in circulation together with funds held in checking accounts or 'broader' monetary aggregates that include savings accounts and deposits of 'Eurodollars'. The problem for a strategy based upon the money supply is, as some commentators observed, that these monetary aggregates grow at markedly different rates.

Ford, Carter and the economic crisis

Gerald Ford's brief presidency (August 1974–January 1977) was characterised by a continuing faith in the use of fiscal and monetary tools and by the adoption of contradictory approaches to economic management. Initially, the

White House responded to the oil crisis by emphasising the dangers posed by inflation and pursuing a deflationary course. Then, in January 1975, Ford proposed a one-year tax rebate that was subsequently expanded and broadened by Congress (Bartels, 2008: 45).

The shift towards a new paradigm based around the ideas of the Chicago school and free market economics began to become evident during Jimmy Carter's presidency (1977–81). Later observers have often stressed the differences between the Carter administration and the Reagan years that followed. They point to antitrust actions in the courts, which many conservatives saw as an attack on business and free enterprise, the administration's faith in direct controls and Carter's energy plan, which incorporated a windfall tax on the oil companies, redistributive measures and government direction. Carter also signed legislation that greatly increased the payroll tax for Social Security, the system that provided for those in old age.

Nonetheless, some of Carter's policies anticipated the strategies that would be adopted by the Reagan administration during the 1980s.[12] President Carter signed the Depository Institutions Deregulation and Monetary Control Act which phased out ceilings on interest rates. The 1978 Revenue Act reduced income and corporate taxes and allowed more people to escape capital gains tax. Carter's January 1980 Economic Report rested upon deflationary measures so as to curb demand-pull inflation. Although rendered impossible by entrenched expenditure commitments, renewed Cold War tensions and economic downturn, the reduction of the budget deficit became, as it was for many later 'deficit hawks', a primary goal of public policy:

> In the eyes of the president and his advisers, budget deficits had become harbingers of inflation that drive up interest rates, aggravated demand pressures at a time of productivity decline, and served as a bad example of public excess when business and labour were being asked to practise price and wage restraint. (Morgan, 2004: 1024)[13]

The shift towards a more conservative form of economic policy was also signalled by Carter's appointment of Paul Volcker as chairman of the Federal Reserve. Volcker was a figure in whom investors and those in the financial sector had faith and he served from August 1979 until 1987. Although Bruce Bartlett, formerly associated with the National Center for Policy Analysis, a conservative thinktank, suggests that Volcker was constrained in terms of policy options until Reagan entered the White House, he clearly established that the Fed's principal goal was the reduction of inflation and that other policy goals, such as a fall in the unemployment rolls, were subordinate. Furthermore, from October 1979, the Federal Reserve Board began to follow monetarist precepts (which asserted that inflation was caused by the excessive growth of the money supply) and adopted monetary targeting. This 'entailed controlling the aggregate quantity of money and reserves…This…put the

Table 3.2 *US Interest rates (the Federal Funds effective rate), 1970–80*

Year	Federal funds – effective rate (%)
1970	7.17
1975	5.82
1980	13.35

Source: adapted from US Census Bureau (2008), *The 2008 Statistical Abstract – Federal Government – Money Market Interest Rates and Mortgage Rates: 1980 to 2006*, <http://www.census.gov>

onus on banks and financial markets to raise interest rates' (Morgan, 2004: 1027).[14]

The rise in interest rates, which began well before Reagan took the oath of office, limited borrowing and encouraged savings. Although the economy was in recession for half the year, the 'prime rate', the rate of interest used for many corporate loans, reached 21.5 per cent, the highest rate in US history, in December 1980. The Federal Funds rate reached double digits (Table 3.2).

There was also a process, promoted by the White House and accepted by Congress, of deregulation so as to encourage competition and the free interplay of market forces. Some market sectors were subject to extensive regulation that imposed barriers to entry, limiting the admission of newcomers and restricting the competitive process. This, from the perspective of those who advocated deregulation, kept prices artificially high and had consequences for the quality of service. Steven F. Hayward has described the airline industry before the reforms of 1978:

> Prior to 1978, the federal government dictated routes and fares to any airline that flew interstate, which covered all airlines except a couple of small carriers which operated only in California and Texas. The Civil Aeronautics Board (CAB), the regulatory agency that oversaw the airline industry, sometimes took several years to approve an airline's request to begin service on a new route. (Hayward, 2006: 57)

The Airline Deregulation Act phased out the regulatory powers of the Civil Aeronautics Board and opened up airlines to competition and the market. There were other deregulatory moves. Although he argued for a 'Windfall Profits Tax' on the oil industry, Carter also announced a phased decontrol of oil prices and the phasing out of the government allocation system. Despite opposition from the Teamsters Union, the Motor Carrier Act of 1980 curtailed the authority of the Interstate Commerce Commission (ICC) over the trucking industry. The Act made it easier to enter the industry and ended restrictions on the commodities that could be carried and the regions which truckers could serve. The deregulation process led, as its backers had hoped, to a reduction of process. 'Between 1977, the year before the ICC started to decontrol the industry, and 1982, rates for truckload-size shipments fell about 25 per cent in real, inflation-adjusted terms' (Gale Moore, 2002).

Table 3.3 *US interest rates (the Federal Funds effective rate), 1981–9*

Year	Federal funds – effective rate (%)
1981	16.39
1982	12.24
1983	9.09
1984	10.23
1985	8.1
1986	6.8
1987	6.66
1988	7.57
1989	9.21

Source: adapted from US Census Bureau (2008), *1166 – Money Market Interest Rates and Mortgage Rates: 1980 to 2006*, <http://www.census.gov>

'Reaganomics'

President Reagan's administration built upon the policies pursued by the Carter administration. However, although sometimes more pragmatic than commentaries suggest, the Reagan White House was, if compared with the Carter administration, much more vigorous in its embrace of the ideas that defined the 'new right'.[15]

For the first eighteen months or so, administration policy emphasised monetarist priorities and strategies. If inflation fell, it was said, investor confidence would grow, the economy would expand again and unemployment would begin to fall. Inflation was attributed to the excessive growth of the money supply (see p. 66). Money supply targets were therefore established and policy was directed towards a reduction in its rate of growth. So as to facilitate this, interest rates were maintained at a high level. Indeed, as Table 3.3 shows, the Federal Funds rate reached over 16 per cent in 1981.

However, as Grahame Thompson notes, the monetarist experiment was only pursued for a limited period. None of the targets for the growth of the money supply were achieved and policy increasingly fell back upon interest rate targeting instead (Thompson, 1990: 76). Indeed, the monetary aggregates which had been set as targets often fluctuated. For example, M1, which measures 'narrow money', shifted fairly erratically during 1981 and 1982 (Smith, 1987: 134–5). Paul Volcker, whom Reagan reappointed as chairman of the Federal Reserve in 1983, has recalled the way in which the policy switch was made:

> Then in October (1982), or whenever it was, the money supply (by some measures) was increasing again rather rapidly. We had a tough explanation to make, but I thought we had come to the point that we were getting boxed in by money supply data that was, in any event, strongly distorted by regulatory changes and

bank behavior. We came to the conclusion that it was not very reliable to put so much weight on the money supply any more, so we backed off that approach. (Paul Volcker, quoted in Econbrowser, 2007)[16]

- Alongside monetarism, the Reagan administration emphasised supply-side issues. There were, in particular, dramatic tax cuts.[17] The 1981 Economic Recovery Tax Act (or 'Kemp-Roth' as it is known after the names of its Congressional sponsors, although they had initially hoped for more drastic reductions) cut tax rates by about 30 per cent across the board. The bottom rate would be reduced from 14 per cent to 11 per cent and the top rate from 70 per cent to 50 per cent.[18] The Act was, in part, driven by the rise in federal income tax rates over preceding decades. Because of inflation during the 1960s and 1970s, people moved into higher tax brackets. A worker on the median income who had kept $0.83 out of every $1 saw the amount reduced to $0.78 when his or her pay increased (Bartlett, 2002). These sentiments tied together with propositions drawn from conservative economic theory. Arthur Laffer, a supply-side economist who served on Reagan's Economic Policy Advisory Board, made a powerful case for tax cuts. In particular, he addressed the anxieties of 'deficit hawks', many of whom were in the ranks of the conservative movement, who feared that tax reductions would simply add to the federal government budget deficit. The 'Laffer curve' (Figure 3.6) suggested that tax rates could be cut and this, by encouraging people to take on additional work or start their own businesses, would lead to increased economic growth. As a consequence, more would be paid in incomes taxes, corporate taxation and sales tax.[19] Government revenue would therefore increase rather than fall. Laffer himself asserted that 'each of the 10 per cent reductions in tax rates would, in terms of overall tax revenues, be self-financing in less than two years' (Hayward, 2006: 60).

Those who backed the 1981 Economic Recovery Tax Act drew heavily on the Laffer curve. The proposed tax cut would, they asserted, increase economic growth, allow the US to escape the economic difficulties of the 1970s and, over time, raise rather than reduce government revenue.[20]

Many on the right, and those who subscribed to supply-side economics, were also deeply critical of what they regarded as the excessive powers of the labour unions. Union activity, it was said, placed upward pressure on wage levels so that they were often above the market rate and therefore made businesses less competitive. Against this background, in August 1981, the Professional Air Traffic Controllers Organization (PATCO) took strike action in pursuit of improved working conditions, increased pay and a 32-hour working week. Although this was in violation of federal law, other government employees had taken action without penalties being imposed. The Reagan administration responded by declaring the strike a 'peril to national safety'. Citing the 1947

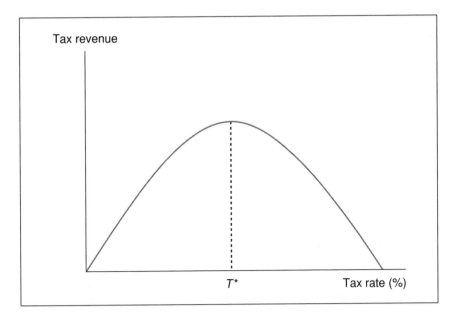

Figure 3.6 *The Laffer curve*

Note: T^* is the optimum tax rate. At this point tax revenue is maximised. Once the tax rate is set to the right of T^*, it deters individuals and businesses from engaging in legitimate economic activity. Economists had customarily argued that T^* was at a very high rate of tax. Laffer placed it much further to the left.

Taft-Hartley Act, it ordered them back to work. Only 1,500 returned to work. In response, Reagan then dismissed the 11,345 strikers who had ignored the order. They were also banned from federal employment for three years although this was later rescinded. The defeat of the PATCO strikers had repercussions across the US labour market. Although the number of annual work stoppages is a crude measure of workplace protests, the statistics in Table 3.4 show the decline during the Reagan years.

- 'Small government' and free market economics were articles of faith for the conservative movement and the Reagan administration. On taking office Reagan took action to limit federal regulations. There were to be no new rules for thirty days and an executive order was issued prohibiting federal government agencies from issuing regulations without authorisation from the Office of Management and Budget (OMB). The OMB is within the Executive Office of the president and is directly accountable to him.
- Some also talk of a revolution in antitrust policy that stemmed from the Reagan White House's commitment to small government. Although progressives and reformers have always hoped for stricter forms of enforcement, the federal government has, from the 1890 Sherman Act onwards, seen

Table 3.4 *Number of work stoppages (involving 1,000 or more workers),
1960–89*

Year	Number of work stoppages
1960	222
1965	268
1970	381
1975	235
1980	187
1981	145
1982	96
1983	81
1984	62
1985	54
1986	69
1987	46
1988	40
1989	51

Source: adapted from Bureau of Labor Statistics (2008),*Work Stoppages Involving 1,000 or More Workers, 1947–2007*, <http://www.bls.gov>

the regulation of monopolies and cartels as important so as to ensure that markets remain reasonably open and competitive. Under the Reagan administration, actions against AT&T and IBM by the Antitrust Division of the Department of Justice were abandoned and large-scale mergers in oil, transportation and other industries were allowed. As Marc Allen Eisner and Kenneth J. Meier record:

> Many traditional antitrust violations were considered as being without merit and thus no longer subject to prosecution. The Antitrust Division presented specific guidelines with respect to mergers and vertical restraints, treating them as competitively benign if not efficiency promoting. As a result, few horizontal merger cases were filed, and no vertical or conglomerate mergers were challenged from 1981 to 1984. The vast majority of cases were brought against price-fixing arrangements, one of the few antitrust areas supported by the Chicago school. (Eisner and Meier, 1990: 274)[21]

Assessing 'Reaganomics'

The overall impact of a particular president and his administration should not be overstated. Although commentators talk in terms of 'Reaganomics' there were significant limits on President Reagan and his ability to shape economic policy. The passage of legislation is a prerogative of Congress. The Democrats had a majority in the House of Representatives throughout Reagan's two terms

Table 3.5 *Consumer price index, 1981–9*

Year	Percentage change in prices (all items)
1981	10.3
1982	6.2
1983	3.2
1984	4.3
1985	3.6
1986	1.9
1987	3.6
1988	4.1
1989	4.8

Source: adapted from US Census Bureau (2009), *The 2009 Statistical Abstract*,
<http://www.census.gov>

of office and controlled the Senate during his last two years in the White House. Members of Congress are sensitive to the interests and wishes of influential lobbies as well as corporate interests. Furthermore, government has only limited leverage over the economy. Economic changes are lagged behind policy shifts and there are often unintended consequences. Nonetheless some conclusions can be drawn about 'Reaganomics'.

For its supporters, the application of 'Reaganomics' at the beginning of the 1980s laid the basis for a prolonged boom that (disregarding the 1990–1 recession) lasted for almost two decades. The stock market began a long rise from 1,000 in 1982 to 7,000 in March 1997, a sevenfold increase (Anderson, 1997). Furthermore, according to this school of thought, 'Reaganomics' left a lasting legacy. Subsequent presidents and members of Congress accepted the broad economic paradigm established by the Reagan administration. In a remark that defined his presidency, Bill Clinton accepted that the era of 'big government' was over. 'New Democrats' such as Clinton stressed the importance of supply-side reforms rather than the 'tax and spend' policies traditionally associated with the Democratic Party. The result in terms of inflation levels appeared to vindicate the strategy that the Reagan administration had adopted. Despite the large tax cuts of 1981, which some predicted would fuel consumer demand and add to inflationary pressures, inflation fell from 12.5 per cent in 1980, to 8.9 per cent in 1981, and 3.8 per cent in 1982. Table 3.5 tracks the fall in the inflation rate.

All in all, from the perspective of its advocates, 'Reaganomics' led to significant economic gains:

The economy expanded for a record 92 months from 1982–90: real GDP grew by 31 per cent – an amount larger than the entire economy of then-West Germany. Over 20 million new jobs were generated – twice the number as in Europe and Japan combined. Real after-tax per capita income grew by 15.5 per cent, and

Table 3.6 *Economic growth and unemployment, 1981–3*

Year	% rate of change in GDP – chained 2000 dollars	Unemployment (January)
1981	2.5	7.5
1982	−1.9	8.6
1983	4.5	10.4

Sources: adapted from Bureau of Economic Analysis (2008), *Gross Domestic Product – Percent Change from Preceding Period*, <http://www.bea.gov> and Bureau of Labor Statistics (2008), *Unemployment Rate*, <http://data.bls.gov>

> median real after-tax income grew by 12.5 per cent, giving the lie to the charge that only the wealthy benefited from the economic growth of the 1980s. (Hayward, 2006: 61)

Furthermore, ethnic and racial minorities made significant socioeconomic progress during the 1980s although this may have been a lagged consequence of reforms in earlier decades. In particular, the number of African-Americans employed in mid-level white-collar jobs grew markedly (Kaufman, 2008).

Nonetheless, there have been significant criticisms of the Reagan years. The reduction in inflation levels was tied to recession (see Table 3.6). There had been a recession between January and July 1980, Jimmy Carter's last year in the White House. It turned out to be a 'double dipper'. There was a further recession between July 1981 and November 1982 (Labonte and Makinen, 2002: 11). Output levels fell and the 'rustbelt' states in the north-east were severely hit. Long-established capital-intensive industries closed or contracted. As a consequence, unemployment rose to over one in ten of the working population. In rustbelt states such as Michigan and Ohio unemployment was between 12 and 16 per cent. Although new jobs were created, many of these were in the service sector and lacked the earnings or security that employment in manufacturing had offered (Thompson, 1990: 79).

- The US became more unequal. The Gini coefficient, which records the degree of economic inequality, increased markedly during the 1980s (after having fallen during the 1950s and 1960s) (see pp. 180–1). Furthermore, despite the progress that minorities made, there was also a substantial urban underclass that seemed 'locked' into endemic joblessness and poverty. For conservative commentators such as Charles Murray the underclass is based upon those who are 'unsocialised'. He writes in terms that many moderates and liberals would resent:

> images show us the face of the hard problem: those of the looters and thugs, and those of inert women doing nothing to help themselves or their children. They are the underclass. (Murray, 2005: 1)

- Commentators looking back a quarter of a century later (from the vantage point of the financial crisis of 2008–9) have emphasised the extent to which the deregulatory process (to which they ascribe the severity of the downturn) began during the Reagan years. The savings and loan industry ('S&Ls' lend funds – mortgages – for the buying of homes) had, over the years, made funds available at relatively low interest rates but until 1980 (when the Depository Institutions Deregulation and Monetary Control Act was passed) had been limited from paying competitive rates of interest to savers. The Garn-St. Germain Depository Institutions Act of 1982 (which secured bipartisan backing) deregulated the S&Ls and allowed them to diversify their investments. Accounting rules were relaxed and supervision remained loose. According to the *New York Times*, the consequences at the end of the decade were: 'wild speculation and outright plundering. Signs of trouble arose right away, but the Reagan Administration and Congress did nothing' (*New York Times*, 1989). Some 745 S&Ls failed during the latter half of the 1980s and the early 1990s. The federal government bailout cost the taxpayer about $124.6 billion. Nonetheless, the deregulatory mood that began during the Reagan era continued. At the same time the standards that governed lending and borrowing were relaxed. Paul Krugman has spelt out what he regards as Reagan's legacy:

> The increase in public debt was, however, dwarfed by the rise in private debt, made possible by financial deregulation. The change in America's financial rules was Reagan's biggest legacy. And it's the gift that keeps on taking...Reagan-era legislative changes essentially ended New Deal restrictions on mortgage lending – restrictions that, in particular, limited the ability of families to buy homes without putting a significant amount of money down...It was only after the Reagan deregulation that thrift gradually disappeared from the American way of life. (Krugman, 2009)

- Although President Reagan structured much of his rhetoric around calls for 'small government', government retained its place within the US economy throughout the 1980s. Indeed, the number of federal employees rose by 61,000 during Reagan's presidency (Green, 2003).
- Despite the hopes of those who embraced the Laffer curve, the federal government budget deficit grew at a rapid pace until Reagan's last two years in office (Table 3.7).

As the 1980s progressed, the deficit was increasingly seen as a major economic problem and came to dominate political discourse. Even in the administration's second year, David Stockman, director of the Office of Management and Budget, later described the fiscal situation as 'an utter, mind-numbing catastrophe' (Collins, 2006: 75). Against this background, the Reagan administration used the closing of 'loopholes' to increase taxation levels, imposed a gasoline tax

Table 3.7 *US federal government budget deficit, 1960–89*

Fiscal year	Surplus or deficit (US$bn)
1960	+0.3
1965	−1.4
1970	−2.8
1975	−53.2
1980	−73.8
1981	−79.0
1982	−128
1983	−207.8
1984	−185.4
1985	−212.3
1986	−221.2
1987	−149.7
1988	−155.2
1989	−152.6

Note: The 'fiscal year' used by the federal government for budgetary purposes starts on October 1 and finishes at the end of September the following year. The number assigned to the fiscal year is the second of the two calendar years. The figures are not inflation-adjusted.
Source: adapted from US Census Bureau (2008), *The 2008 Statistical Abstract – Federal Budget – Receipts and Outlays: 1960 to 2007*, <http://www.census.gov>

and made Social Security benefits liable for taxation (Green, 2003). As Bruce Bartlett, a conservative critic of fiscal 'irresponsibility' records:

> In 1982 alone, he signed into law not one but two major tax increases. The Tax Equity and Fiscal Responsibility Act (TEFRA) raised taxes by $37.5 billion per year and the Highway Revenue Act raised the gasoline tax by another $3.3 billion...In 1983, Reagan signed legislation raising the Social Security tax rate....The year 1988 appears to be the only year of the Reagan presidency, other than the first, in which taxes were not raised legislatively. (Bartlett, 2003)

Grahame Thompson suggests that if the increases in Social Security contributions are factored in, the 'average American' was as 'highly taxed at the end of the Reagan administration as he was at the beginning' (Thompson, 1990: 79).

As well as these sometimes hidden tax increases, there were also attempts to secure large-scale expenditure reductions. There were efforts to cut spending on, for example, employment training projects, food stamps and welfare provision (Aid to Families with Dependent Children). Left-leaning critics of the Reagan administration argued that the cuts constituted a form of class war against the poor:

The very area the administration claims to be protecting, the 'essential safety net' of programs for the 'truly needy', in fact bears the brunt of the attack. Basic urban services and environmental programs are being cut as well, while functions valued by business are continuing to thrive. The 'New Federalism' proposals and the move toward block grants, cloaked in rhetoric about states' rights and decentralization, are actually attempts to shift the responsibility for painful cutbacks away from Washington and onto state and local governments. (Ackerman, 1982: 81)

Despite moves such as these, the deficit increased. This was in part because the economy failed to grow at the pace hoped for by those who had accepted supply-side arguments. However, there were other reasons.[22] During the period of renewed Cold War tensions, defence spending rose as a share of GDP from 4.9 per cent in 1980 to 6.1 per cent in 1985. At the same time, despite the hopes of those on the radical right, spending on social programmes (Social Security, Medicare and Medicaid) also rose as a share of GDP, from 6.0 per cent in 1980 to 6.7 per cent in 1985 and to 6.9 per cent in 1990 (Congressional Budget Office, 2002). Those who hoped to reduce the benefits offered by these *entitlement* programmes faced intractable political difficulties.

There was also resistance to budget-cutting from some parts of government. Attempts to cut expenditure on roads and mass transit were not only opposed by state and local officials, unions and contractors but also by members of Congress and the Transportation Secretary (Collins, 2006: 75). The fall in inflation levels also played its part. During the 1970s, increasing wages, which rose along with other prices, pushed individuals into higher tax brackets. As a consequence, federal tax revenue rose automatically. However, the lower inflation of the 1980s brought 'bracket creep' to an end.

- Paradoxically, although the increased budget deficit was seen as a defining economic problem, it may have had an unintended consequence. Keynesians, particularly during the depression years of the 1930s, had called for deficit budgets. By adding to overall demand levels, they would have a reflationary impact, and boost output and employment. Borrowing could then be repaid during the boom years so that the budget balanced on a long-term basis over the business cycle. Given this, the *Economist* referred to the budget deficits of the Reagan years as 'turbo-charged Keynesianism'. The deficits, the magazine was suggesting, had given the US economy a stimulus, leading to sustained growth during the years that followed the recession of the early 1980s (Parker, 2005). Conservatives would, however, attribute the growth record (Table 3.8) to the supply-side measures pursued by the Reagan administration (and, some grudgingly accept, during Carter's presidency.) Others are less generous to the White House. Economic growth, they assert, can be tied to demographic shifts. During the 1980s, the baby boomers hit their thirties and forties:

Table 3.8 *Economic growth and unemployment, 1984–9*

Year	Rate of growth (%)	Unemployment rate (%)
1984	7.2	8.0
1985	4.1	7.3
1986	3.5	6.7
1987	3.4	6.6
1988	4.1	5.7
1989	3.5	5.4

Sources: adapted from Bureau of Economic Analysis (2008), *Gross Domestic Product – Percent Change from Preceding Period*, <http://www.bea.gov> and Bureau of Labor Statistics (2008), *Unemployment Rate*, <http://data.bls.gov>

> They helped drive forward the demand for housing and commercial construction…When this demand exploded, it provided a boost in housing and throughout the economy. Baby boomers bought not only houses, but also everything to furnish them. During this time, consumers more than doubled their debt, and the spending spree of the 1980s was great enough to revive the economy throughout the decade. (Kamery, 2004: 62)

Whatever the causes, even by 1984 there was a sense that the US was well on the road to economic recovery. Reagan won re-election by a landslide with a campaign structured around the slogan, 'it's morning again in America'. Increasingly, despite the difficulties facing those in the 'rustbelt', commentators pointed to growth rates in the 'sunbelt' states of the south and west.[23] The sunbelt grew because businesses were attracted by lower wage rates and energy costs. Domestic energy sources were being developed. The western states looked towards the Asian markets. State governments pursued free market policies. The divide between the 'sunbelt' and the 'rustbelt' was at times so marked that there were references to 'two nations'.

> During the 1970s, the white South at long last accepted defeat in the Civil War. In the wake of the Civil Rights Revolution and the postwar economic boom, the region no longer clung to the traditional 'southern way of life.' But like Germany and Japan after World War II, this 'loser' reaped the spoils of victory. The Sunbelt South prospered while the old industrial heartland faced seemingly catastrophic decline. Regional conflict once again captured national attention; *Business Week* even ran a cover story on 'The Second War Between the States'. (Schulman, 1993: 340)

There were growing concerns about the balance of payments deficit. The current account deficit grew (Table 3.9) as the US recovered from the recession (when consumer spending and thereby demand for imports tends to fall). The 'deindustrialisation' of the north-east added to these anxieties and by the end

Table 3.9 *Current account balance, 1980–9*

1980	1981	1982	1983	1984	1985	1986	1987	1988	1989
2,317	5,030	−5,536	−38,691	−94,344	−118,155	−147,177	−160,655	−121,153	−99,486

Source: adapted from Bureau of Economic Analysis (2008), *U.S. International Transactions, 1960–Present*, <http://www.bea.gov>

of the decade many commentators asserted that Japan posed a significant threat to US economic interests through its capturing of markets, the volume of its exports and its direct investment in the US.

- The balance of payments and the federal government budget deficit were, in many accounts, tied together. Indeed, the phrase 'twin deficits' was often employed. The budget deficit was funded by government borrowing. This put upward pressure on interest rates (which were already high because of the commitment to curb inflation). Given this, overseas buyers sought interest-bearing assets in the US. The dollar was in demand and the exchange rate rose. Exports became relatively expensive and imports became relatively cheap. Consumer demand for imports rose and US companies had less of an incentive to seek out export markets for their products. Demand was fuelled still further by growing prosperity as the US recovered from the recession at the beginning of the decade.[24]
- Many people have seen the mid and late 1980s as a period of economic growth, laying the basis for a 'bull run' on the stock markets as share prices rose, and the acquisition of hitherto unforeseen wealth. Nonetheless, the US and many other countries were shaken by 'Black Monday' on October 19, 1987 when stock markets crashed. There had already been share price falls and then, in a single day, the Dow Jones Industrial Average, the principal index used to measure changes in US share prices, dropped by 22 per cent. The reasons for Black Monday are unclear but insofar as developments in the US played a role may have included fears about the economic consequences of both the budget deficit and the trade deficit and the impact of computerisation on the selling of shares. However, the markets recovered by mid-1988 and the crash had little overall impact.

Despite an increase in manufacturing, overall productivity growth levels remained low when compared with earlier decades, contributing to the fears that Japan might overtake the US as the world's leading economic power. Whereas labour productivity had grown at about 2.6 per cent during the 1960s, it fell to 1.1 per cent in the 1970s and then remained at about the same level during the 1980s (1.3 per cent) (Roubini, 1998).

Arguably, some of the economic difficulties that emerged during the Reagan years may have cost his successor, President George H. W. Bush, a second term in the White House. In particular, there have been suggestions that the S&L crisis contributed to the 1991 recession that led to a dramatic fall in support for Bush. Furthermore, the federal government budget deficit provided a platform for H. Ross Perot, the Texas billionaire who stood as an independent candidate. He portrayed the deficit as the cause of almost all other economic problems and, on this basis, compelled other candidates to address the issue and captured 19 per cent of the popular vote. Had Perot not stood, many of these voters would almost certainly have backed Bush. Their defection to Perot allowed Arkansas governor Bill Clinton to capture the White House.

Conclusion

Commentators have challenged claims that there was a 'counter-revolution' during the Reagan era so far as economic policy is concerned. They emphasise the failure to rein in the federal government, the growth of the budget deficit and the partial retreat from radical tax-cutting. In reality, the picture was mixed. Although hardline conservatives were disappointed, and while there was far more continuity with earlier years than is often acknowledged, the free market flourished in the new industrial sectors (such as mobile phones and personal computers) that began to emerge during the Reagan years. Furthermore, the economic agenda shifted during the late 1970s and 1980s. Ideas of a long-term 'social compact' between employers and workers were finally abandoned. Tax increases and the imposition of regulatory measures became much more politically dangerous. The reduction of unemployment became subordinate, as a public policy goal, to the fight against inflation. Socioeconomic inequality became more widely accepted (see Chapter 7).[25] Writing in bitter terms, Michael Meeropol described the changes that had been wrought in economic thinking:

> a new social structure of accumulation is being built, one in which the capital-labor accord is nonexistent; the social safety net is restricted to the elderly; and the most important thing that governments can do with the taxpayers' money is to finance the defense department and a growing police and prison industry. (Meeropol, 1998: 257)

Just as importantly, although some have suggested that the deficit and military expenditure constituted a form of 'unconscious Keynesianism', the use of discretionary fiscal policy lost much of the importance that it had had during the three decades that followed the Second World War. Instead, the manipulation of interest rates and other forms of monetary policy – the responsibility of the Federal Reserve – became paramount. This remained true until the financial and economic crises of 2007–8.

Notes

1 The meaning of 'liberalism' has dramatically shifted over the past century and a half. Classical or nineteenth-century liberalism (sometimes resurrected as 'neo-liberalism') rests upon laissez-faire economics and limited government. Contemporary 'left-leaning' liberalism emerged at the end of the nineteenth century and is tied to government interventionism. In recent decades, liberalism has also become associated with 'identity politics' and cultural progressivism.

2 The 'money supply' is, as the critics of monetarism note, difficult to define or measure, let alone control. See pp. 00–00.

3 Other recessions, such as 1875–8, 1892–4, 1906–8 and 1920–1, were also preceded, as Friedman and Schwarz emphasise, by a fall in the money supply (Smith, 1987: 22).

4 Friedman's name later became linked to the economic reforms in Chile that followed the coup d'état of September 1973. The Pinochet regime and economists who became known as the 'Chicago Boys' pursued policies based around the dismantling and privatisation of industries in the nationalised sector, the ending of inflation and monetary stability, and the extension of market forces so that businesses had to become more competitive. Trade barriers, for example, were removed.

5 Those on the free market right who saw the Nixon administration as 'socialist' could draw on other examples of government interventionism. The Penn Central Railroad was nationalised and Amtrak was established. Loan guarantees were extended to Lockheed, the aerospace company, in 1971 (Wells, 2003: 79).

6 Subsequent representations of the mid and late 1970s have focused almost entirely on stagnation. Arguably these accounts obscure some positive economic developments. For example, real incomes grew by over 5 per cent in 1978 (Bartels, 2008: 45).

7 Monetarists see the causes of inflation differently and assert that rises in the price level are invariably the consequence of excessive increases in the money supply. See p. 66.

8 See p. 54.

9 However, Paul Krugman observes that investment levels (as a share of GDP) did not fall during the 1970s (Krugman, 1998: 18).

10 This account of the move away from Keynesianism and towards 'Reaganomics' emphasises changes in economic ideas and the ways in which these ideas shifted because of the economic realities of the 1970s. There are, nonetheless, other accounts. Some stress the efforts of business groupings to maintain returns to capital. Others look at the role of grassroots 'tax revolts' during the latter half of the 1970s or emphasise the pressures of international competition or the ideology of competitive individualism which is said to define the US. For a discussion of competing explanations see Prasad, 2006: 15–42.

11 The New Public Finance school joined in the attack on Keynesian principles. It argued that the taxation system and structures distorted saving and investment, particularly because there had been a process of *fiscal drag*. Individuals and companies were drifting into higher tax brackets because of the higher nominal wages that inflation produced (Collins, 2006: 62–3).

12   The Carter administration was often pulled between the reduction of inflation
     and the lowering of unemployment. Its economic policy thereby appears, as
     Iwan Morgan notes, 'confused and vacillating' (Morgan, 2004: 1020).

13   Despite the rhetoric and to the concern of many within the conservative
     movement, the budget deficit rose during the Reagan years. See p. 89.

14   There is however a case for describing Volcker as a pragmatic monetarist. Arguably,
     there were few other ways of determining the level at which the interest rate
     should be set. As Volcker later recalled:

> There are decades, hundreds of years, of economic thinking relating the money
> supply to inflation, and people to some extent have that in their bones...It was also
> true that we had no other good benchmark for how much to raise interest rates in the
> midst of a volatile inflationary situation. (Paul Volcker, quoted in Econbrowser, 2007)

15   Although conservatives and Republicans took Ronald Reagan to their heart
     there was some resistance to the new economic thinking. Some (who came
     to known as 'deficit hawks') feared that tax cuts would simply increase the
     federal government deficit and the national debt. During the Republican primaries,
     George H. W. Bush, who became the vice-presidential nominee after seeking the
     presidential nomination himself, referred in a celebrated comment to 'voodoo
     economics'.

16   Along with other critics of monetarism, Dan Clawson has pointed to the difficulties
     inherent in efforts to control the growth of the money supply: 'Since the vast
     majority of the "money" in the economy is not paper bills but checking accounts
     and the like, even when the "Fed" does try to shrink the money supply, financial
     institutions simply create new forms of money – for example, credit cards and
     money market funds' (Clawson, 1982: 615).

17   There were tensions between supply-siders, who stressed the important of sweeping
     tax cuts, and monetarists, who emphasised the need for a stable monetary
     framework within which inflation was minimal (Smith, 1987: 133–4).

18   There were further tax reductions in 1986 when the top rate was reduced from
     50 per cent to 28 per cent (Hayward, 2006: 61).

19   Furthermore, if tax rates were reduced, individuals with high levels of income
     and wealth would be less likely to engage in tax avoidance (for example, by placing
     funds in overseas tax shelters) (Hayward, 2006: 59).

20   Some among the 'deficit hawks' as well as other critics of radical tax-cutting
     pointed to the 'income effect'. Whereas the 'substitution effect', upon which the
     Laffer curve rested, suggests that a tax cut – and the consequential increase in
     net hourly pay levels – will lead people to work harder and take entrepreneurial
     risks, the 'income effect' works in a very different way. Increased net income may
     instead lead some people to work fewer hours and increase their leisure time
     (Ackerman, 1982: 46). Furthermore, there is evidence to suggest that business
     investment decisions are influenced to a much greater extent by market considera-
     tions than by tax rates (Ackerman, 1982: 53).

21   Eisner and Meier do not, however, regard these developments as a consequence
     of 'Reaganomics'. They instead argue that the Antitrust Division was moving in
     this direction well before Reagan took office. They stress the logic of bureaucratic
     evolution (Eisner and Meier, 1990: 284).

22   Some have seen the federal government budget deficit as an attempt to 'starve the beast'. In other words, it was designed to ensure that lawmakers were subsequently compelled to reduce federal government expenditure.

23   The levels of growth and prosperity in the sunbelt should, nonetheless, not be exaggerated. Poverty continued and both Texas and California suffered economic difficulties during the 1980s. Growth also posed problems including congestion, pollution and sprawl.

24   The notion of 'twin deficits' has, however, been challenged. Some suggest that there is, in practice, little connection (Thompson, 1990: 86).

25   If a longer-term perspective is adopted, and the period between the 1980s and the inauguration of President Obama is considered, some of the changes wrought by 'Reaganomics' become clearer. The tax system became less progressive. Regulatory laws may have remained on the statute books but were less rigorously interpreted or enforced. The minimum wage shrank in real terms. Unemployment insurance and job training were restricted (Smith, 2007: 5–7).

References and further reading

Ackerman, Frank (1982), *Reaganomics: Rhetoric vs. Reality*, London: Pluto Press.

Anderson, Martin (1997), *The Ten Causes of the Reagan Boom: 1982–1997*, Hoover Institution, <http://www.hoover.org>

Bartels, Larry M. (2008), *Unequal Democracy: The Political Economy of the New Gilded Age*, Princeton: Russell Sage Foundation – Princeton University Press.

Bartlett, Bruce (2002), 'Hail, Kemp-Roth: on the 25th anniversary of an historic tax-policy measure', *National Review Online*, July 15, <http://www.nationalreview.com>

Bartlett, Bruce (2003), 'A taxing experience: the stars are aligning for a tax increase', *National Review Online*, <http://www.nationalreview.com>

Bjerre-Poulsen, Niels (2002), *Right Face: Organizing the American Conservative Movement 1945–65*, Copenhagen: University of Copenhagen – Museum Tusculanum Press.

Clawson, Dan (1982), 'Review: end of an era? Reagan and the 1980s', *Contemporary Sociology*, 11:6, November, 614–16.

Collins, Robert M. (2006), *Transforming America: Politics and Culture During the Reagan Years*, New York: Columbia University Press.

Congressional Budget Office (2002), *A 125-Year Picture of the Federal Government's Share of the Economy, 1950 to 2075*, <http://www.cbo.gov>

Econbrowser (2007), *How Paul Volcker Became a Practical Monetarist*, Econbrowser, February 11, <http://www.econbrowser.com>

Economist (2008), 'The trouble with Friedman', *Economist* (European edn), 388: 8592, August 9, 42.

Eisner, Marc Allen and Kenneth J. Meier (1990), 'Presidential control versus bureaucratic power: explaining the Reagan revolution in antitrust', *American Journal of Political Science*, 34:1 (February), 269–87.

Fand, David I. (1977), 'Review – expectations and inflation: Nixon, politics, and economics by Rodney J. Morrison', *American Political Science Review*, 71:1 (March), 362–3, <http://www.jstor.org/stable/pdfplus/1957015.pdf>

Friedman, Milton (1953), *Essays in Positive Economics*, Chicago: University of Chicago Press.

Gale Moore, Thomas (2002), 'Trucking deregulation', *The Concise Encyclopedia of Economics*, <http://www.econlib.org>

Glyn, Andrew (2007), *Capitalism Unleashed: Finance, Globalization, and Welfare*, Oxford: Oxford University Press.

Goldwater, Barry ([1960] 1974), *The Conscience of a Conservative*, New York: Manor Books.

Green, Joshua (2003), 'Reagan's liberal legacy: what the new literature on the Gipper won't tell you', *Washington Monthly*, January/February, <http://www.washingtonmonthly.com>

Greenberg, Edward S. (1991), 'Reaganism as corporate liberalism: implications for the American future', *Policy Studies Review*, 10:1, 103–25.

Hayward, Steven F. (2006), 'The evolution of US economic policy in the 1980s', in Wojciech Bienkowski, Josef C. Brada and Mariusz-Jan Radlo (2006), *Reaganomics Goes Global: What Can the EU, Russia and Transition Countries Learn from the USA?*, Basingstoke: Palgrave Macmillan, 53–63.

Kamery, Rob H. (2004), 'A brief review of the recession of 1990–1991', *Proceedings of the Academy of Legal, Ethical and Regulatory Issues*, 8:2, <http://www.sbaer.uca.edu/research/allied/2004_maui/legal_ethical_regulatory_issues/14.pdf>

Kaufman, Jonathan (2008), 'Rethinking racial progress', *Wall Street Journal*, August 28, A10.

Krugman, Paul (1998), *The Age of Diminished Expectations*, Cambridge, MA: MIT Press.

Krugman, Paul (2009), 'Reagan did It', *New York Times*, May 31, <http://www.nytimes.com>

Labonte, Marc and Gail Makinen (2002), *The Current Economic Recession: How Long, How Deep, and How Different From the Past?*, Congressional Research Service Report for Congress, <http://www.fpc.state.gov/documents/organization/7962.pdf>

Martin, Douglas (2009), 'Beryl Sprinkel, Reagan economic adviser, dies at 85', *New York Times*, September 2, A17.

Morgan, Iwan W. (2004), 'Jimmy Carter, Bill Clinton and the New Democratic economics', *Historical Journal*, 47, December, 1015–39.

Morris, Charles R. (2008), *The Two Trillion Dollar Meltdown: Easy Money, High Rollers, and the Great Credit Crash*, New York: Public Affairs.

Murray, Charles (2005), *Rediscovering the Underclass*, American Enterprise Institute for Public Policy and Research, October, <http://www.aei.org/docLib/20051007_Murrayg.pdf>

New York Times (1989), 'The S&L scandal's cruel truths', *New York Times*, November 21, <http://www.nytimes.com>

Parker, Richard (2005), 'The pragmatist and the utopian', *Boston Globe*, February 6, <http://www.boston.com>

Prasad, Monica (2006), *The Politics of Free Markets: The Rise of Neoliberal Economic Policies in Britain, France, Germany, and the United States*, Chicago: University of Chicago Press.

Rosenberg, Samuel (2003), *American Economic Development since 1945*, Basingstoke: Palgrave Macmillan.

Rothbard, Murray N. (1980), *What has Government Done to our Money?*, Luwig von Mises Institute, <http://mises.org>

Roubini, Nouriel (1998), *Productivity Growth, Its Slowdown in the 1973–90 Period and its Resurgence in the 1990s: Truth or a Statistical Fluke? The Productivity Debate of 1996–97*, <http://pages.stern.nyu.edu>

Schulman, Bruce J. (1993), 'Review: the sunbelt south: old times forgotten (*Searching for the Sunbelt: Historical Perspectives on a Region Politics in the New South: Republicanism, Race, and Leadership in the Twentieth Century*, Raymond A. Mohl and Richard K. Scher)', *Reviews in American History*, 21:2, June, 340.

Smith, David (1987), *The Rise and Fall of Monetarism*, London: Pelican.

Smith, Mark A. (2007), *The Right Talk: How Conservatives Transformed the Great Society into the Economic Society*, Princeton: Princeton University Press.

Stein, Herbert (1984), *Presidential Economics: The Making of Economic Policy from Roosevelt to Reagan and Beyond*, New York: Simon and Schuster.

Thompson, Grahame (1990), *The Political Economy of the New Right*, London: Pinter.

Time (1971), 'The economic blues', *Time*, August 16, <http://www.time.com>

US Department of Labor – Occupational Safety and Health Administration (2006), *Speeches – American Industrial Hygiene Conference & Expo*, <http://www.osha.gov>

Wells, Wyatt (2003), *American Capitalism, 1945–2000: Continuity and Change from Mass Production to the Information Society*, Chicago: Ivan R. Dee.

4

The 'new economy'

Chapter 4 considers developments during the 1990s. Although these years began with a sharp recession that contributed to President George H.W. Bush's failure to secure re-election in 1992, there was a period of sustained economic growth for the remainder of the decade. Unemployment was low but inflation remained minimal. This led some commentators to talk of a 'new economy'. The chapter explores the reasons for economic growth in the 1990s but also examines the socioeconomic problems that marked the Clinton years.

During the 1988 presidential election campaign and in the early days of his presidency, George H.W. Bush, who had served as Ronald Reagan's vice-president for eight years, sought to distance himself from Reagan by committing himself to the building of 'a kinder and gentler nation' (George H.W. Bush, quoted in Johnson, 1989). The use of the phrase and the calls that Bush made for community-based volunteering were an implicit attempt to win across those who had anxieties or reservations about the harsh realities of the free market and the seeming abrasiveness of the Reagan administration's record.

The Bush presidency is remembered above all else, however, for the recession of 1990–1. Although the Cold War came to a close and the US secured a quick military victory in the Gulf War, the Bush administration often seemed indifferent to the country's economic ills. The White House conveyed aloofness. Indeed, there was a moment in the 1992 presidential election campaign when Bush appeared unfamiliar with a price scanner in a supermarket. The incident seemed to capture his lack of understanding of everyday realities for middle and lower-income workers, particularly at a time of recession. The Clinton team was quick to capitalise on this. There was a celebrated notice in the campaign 'war room' that came to define the election. The notice read, 'It's the economy, stupid'.

The 1991–2 recession

As Figure 4.1 suggests, the recession at the beginning of the 1990s was relatively short-lived. If defined in strict terms (as a fall in GDP), it lasted from July 1990 until the end of March 1991. GDP fell in total by 1.5 per cent. Furthermore, unemployment (which reached a peak of 7.8 per cent in June 1992) was low compared with the rates in many European nations (Figure 4.2).[1]

Nonetheless, the impact of the recession was widely felt. This was partly because the overall unemployment rate masks the degree of 'labour-churning'. This is the process by which workers lose jobs and then at some point secure new forms of employment. During 1991 and 1992, 5.4 million workers lost their jobs. Furthermore, when the labour market is considered, recovery from the recession was slow compared to earlier periods of recovery. Although new jobs were becoming available, job losses continued. Even in 1993–4, when labour market conditions were improving markedly, 2.4 million long-tenured employees lost their jobs (US Department of Labor, 1999: 89).

Why was there a recession at the beginning of the 1990s?

• Fearing increased inflation, the Federal Reserve raised interest rates between February 1988 and May 1989. (The federal funds rate was increased from approximately 6.5 per cent to 9.75 per cent.) While monertary policy had

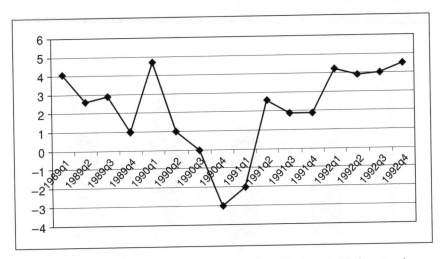

Figure 4.1 *Economic growth (rate of change of GDP), 1989–92 (quarters)*
Note: the percentage figures for each quarter are annualised. In other words, they show the change in GDP if the trends evident in the three month period under consideration had extended across a year.
Source: adapted from Bureau of Economic Analysis (2008), *Gross Domestic Product – Per cent Change from Preceding Period*, <http://www.bea.gov>

to some extent been loosened again by the time the recession began, this was too late to prevent a downturn (Labonte and Makinen, 2002: 12). Furthermore, there were continuing limits on interest rate reductions. Inflation remained a threat until it fell to tolerable levels during the first half of 1991.

- There were, at the same time, other changes in the financial system that may have contributed to a squeeze on investment. As Robert E. Hall notes: 'During the relevant period, bank regulators imposed higher capital requirements, more rigorous valuation standards for assets, and higher deposit insurance rates...both fixed investment and inventory investment fell during the recession; the "credit crunch" may have been a factor' (Hall, 1993: 277).
- There were other forms of disruption in the financial markets. In particular, as noted in Chapter 3, there were growing difficulties among Savings and Loan institutions ('S&Ls').[2] Many had become over-extended in terms of the loans they had made and regulation had been slack. Furthermore, the subsequent taxpayer 'bailout' (the Financial Institutions Reform, Recovery, and Enforcement Act of 1989), which rescued 743 institutions at a cost of approximately $150 billion between 1989 and 1993, added to the federal government budget deficit and increased the need for deflationary measures (Labonte and Makinen, 2002: 13).
- Iraq's invasion of neighbouring Kuwait in August 1990 increased oil prices. Crude oil prices rose from an average in June 1990 of $15 a barrel to $33 a barrel in October 1990. External economic 'shocks' can often have

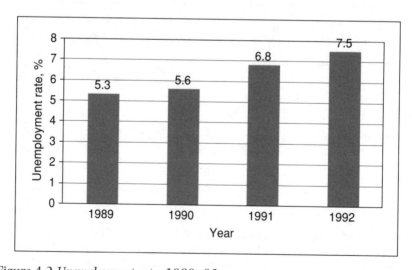

Figure 4.2 *Unemployment rate, 1989–92*

Source: adapted from Bureau of Labor Statistics (2009), *Labor Force Statistics from the Current Population Survey*, <http://www.bls.gov>

deflationary consequences both by increasing the costs of production and adding to pressure for interest rate rises as central banks seek to dampen down the inflationary results of oil price rises. Rob Kamery notes that the economic slowdown that eventually led to recession began in the first three months of 1989 (Kamery, 2004: 61). However, the oil shock may have played a part in a more generalised way by undermining business and consumer confidence and thereby leading to spending reductions.

The 'new economy'

The recession came to end as oil prices fell and interest rates were eventually lowered. The Federal Funds rate (the 'base' interest rate), which had been approximately 9.75 per cent in May 1989, was only about 3 per cent at the end of 1992 (Labonte and Makinen, 2002: 14).

Despite the slow rate at which the joblessness figures fell, the mid and late 1990s are now associated in the popular mind with economic expansion and talk of a 'new economy'. As Table 4.1 shows, real growth rates from 1992 through to the beginning of the new century were relatively high and stable. At the end of Bill Clinton's terms of office, the White House boasted with some justice that it had presided over 'the longest economic expansion in US history' (*On the Issues*, 2008).

The term 'new economy' was used in different ways. It was often only applied to the most technologically advanced sectors of the economy. A contrast was drawn with the 'old economy', which rested on the industrial corporations and was said to be represented by the Dow Jones Industrial Average (DJIA), the long-established index of share prices based upon weighted average of thirty stocks. The 'new economy' was represented on NASDAQ (National

Table 4.1 *Real economic growth, 1992–2007*

Year	Economic growth (GDP % change) based on chained 2000 US dollars
1992	3.3
1993	2.7
1994	4.0
1995	2.5
1996	3.7
1997	4.5
1998	4.2
1999	4.5
2000	3.7

Source: adapted from Bureau of Economic Analysis (2009), *National Economic Accounts: Gross Domestic Product (GDP) – Percent Change from Preceding Period*, <http://www.bea.gov>

Association of Securities Dealers Automated Quotation), a computerised trading system that gave more of a weighting to 'dot.com' companies. In the second half of the 1990s, the 'new economy' expanded rapidly. Between 1996 and 2000, the number of companies traded through NASDAQ grew from 600 to 5,000 and there were more and more share offerings for the 'dot.coms'.

Sometimes, however, the term 'new economy' was used in a more expansive way and seemed to be applied to the entire economy. The US economy had, it was said, been transformed beyond recognition. What was the basis for claims such as this?[3] The arguments used, and the forms of reasoning that were employed, varied but there were some common threads. First, it was said, business operations and markets had become increasingly globalised. Many of the barriers to free market capitalism had been removed or at least lowered. At the same time, the collapse of the communist bloc and the transformation of China provided new markets. Only a handful of nations, such as Cuba and North Korea, seemed to be holding out against the inevitable logic and dynamic of the market order: 'Simply put, capitalism is spreading around the world – if not full-blown capitalism, at least the introduction of market forces, freer trade, and widespread deregulation' (Shepard, 1997).

Secondly, the 'new economy' rested on the adoption of new technology. Alan Greenspan, chairman of the Federal Reserve, talked in wide-ranging and expansive terms:

> When historians look back at the latter half of the 1990s...I suspect that they will conclude we are now living through a pivotal period in American economic history. New technologies that evolved from the cumulative innovations of the past half-century have now begun to bring about dramatic changes in the way goods and services are produced and in the way they are distributed to final users. Those innovations, exemplified most recently by the multiplying uses of the Internet, have brought on a flood of start-up firms, many of which claim to offer the chance to revolutionize and dominate large shares of the nation's production and distribution system. (quoted in Fleckenstein, 2008: 96)

Writing in *Business Week*, Stephen Shepard shared the sense of wonderment that at times seemed to colour economic and political discourse:

> the revolution in information technology...is all around us – fax machines, cellular phones, personal computers, modems, the Internet. But it's more than that. It's the digitization of all information – words, pictures, data, and so on. This digital technology is creating new companies and new industries before our eyes. (Shepard, 1997)

Thirdly, and perhaps most significantly, it was argued that the laws that had traditionally governed the functioning of the economy had been superseded. Despite the economic traumas of the 1970s, unemployment and inflation still often appeared to be opposites. A tight labour market where unemployment was at a very low level would, it was felt, necessarily lead to increased wage demands. Indeed, if unemployment falls below the point known as NAIRU (the 'non-accelerating inflation rate of unemployment'), a tight labour market may create difficulties so that some job vacancies can only be filled if higher wages are offered. At the same time, well-organised groups of workers will make higher wage demands.[4] Alongside these processes, the boom conditions that gave rise to low unemployment would be tied to an upsurge in consumer demand. This would encourage retail outlets and suppliers to raise their prices still further thereby stoking the inflationary fires.

In the mid and late 1990s, however, all of this seemed to have been refuted by the inflation and unemployment statistics. Unemployment fell more or less continuously (see Figure 4.3). Indeed, the 4 per cent figure that unemployment reached at the beginning of the new century is close to the point that many economists regard as the 'irreducible minimum' below which unemployment cannot fall.

At the same time, inflation rates also fell (Figure 4.4). They dropped markedly (from over 6 per cent to about 3 per cent) during the recession. They remained at about that level until the beginning of 1997. At this point inflation fell to almost zero until early 1999.

The combination of economic growth, low unemployment and low inflation gave rise to profound optimism. Alongside all the talk of a 'new economy' there were increasing references to the 'Goldilocks economy'. The US economy was, it was said, akin to the porridge in the children's story insofar as it was

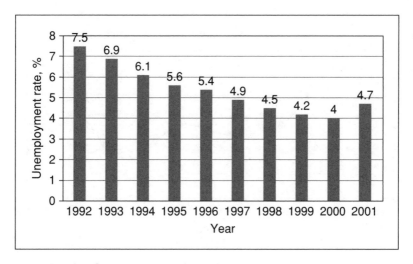

Figure 4.3 *Unemployment rate, 1992–2001*

Source: adapted from Bureau of Labor Statistics (2009), *Labor Force Statistics from the Current Population Survey*, <http://www.bls.gov>

neither too hot (inflation) nor too cold (recession). And, for both those who
talked about the 'new economy' or the 'Goldilocks economy', it would continue,
perhaps indefinitely: 'for the believers in the New Economy, we have here the
magic bullet – a way to return to the high-growth, low-inflation conditions of
the 1950s and 1960s. Forget 2 per cent real growth. We're talking 3 per cent,
or even 4 per cent. Forget double-digit inflation and the natural rate of
unemployment' (Shepard, 1997).

For its part, *Business Week* was cautious and distanced itself from the more
extravagant visions of a 'new economy'. However, it insisted at the same time
that there had been fundamental economic changes that permitted a higher
long-term 'trend' rate of growth.

> Even though we haven't ended the business cycle, outlawed recession, or banished
> inflation, the business cycle really has changed…And this may well enable us
> to grow faster than before without renewed inflation. Perhaps the 4 per cent rate
> of the past 12 months is too high…But the 2 per cent-to-2 ½ per cent speed
> limit is probably obsolete…the speed limit for the U.S. economy is probably
> 3 per cent to 3 ½ per cent a year. (Shepard, 1997)

In the early years of the new century, and despite the uncertainties of 2000–1,
some threw caution to the wind. In 2003, in his presidential address to
the American Economics Association, Robert Lucas declared that the 'central
problem of depression-prevention…has been solved, for all practical purposes'
(Krugman, 2008: 9). Similarly, Ben Bernanke, who was to become chairman

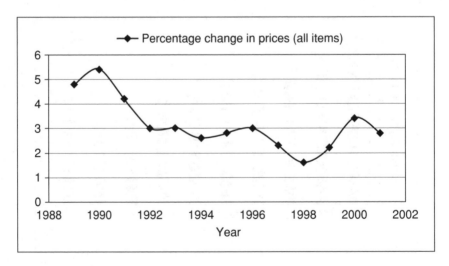

Figure 4.4 *Inflation (CPI-U), 1989–2001*

Source: adapted from Bureau of Labor Statistics (2008), *CPI-U, US City Average, All Items
(1989–2001)* <http://data.bls.gov>

of the Federal Reserve, conveyed the message that the business cycle was, as Paul Krugman was later to describe it, 'more of a nuisance than a front-rank issue' (Krugman, 2008: 10).

The optimism that underpinned pronouncements such as these also found expression on the equity markets. On January 19, 1993, the day before Bill Clinton took office, the DJIA closed at 3255.99. In early 2000, the DJIA reached 11500. AS Burns and Taylor record: 'The average annual return for both measures was just more than 26 per cent from January 1993 through January 2000. By a considerable margin, these numbers are the best annualized returns during any presidential tenure since World War II' (Burns and Taylor, 2001: 339). Average share prices rose to an even greater extent on the NASDAQ Composite Index. The index was under 1000 in 1994. At the end of the decade, in 2000, it reached 5000.

Causes

What, then, contributed to the period of economic growth during the Clinton presidency? Those who talked of a 'new economy' offering low inflation and low unemployment at the same time pointed to accelerating productivity growth and increased competition between producers.

But what explains increased productivity growth? Studies concentrate on the role of new technology and the development of the internet. Both production and distribution were, it was said, being transformed. A desktop PC could undertake the work that had formerly been the responsibility of several people. Internet retailing cut costs and extended competition. Markets were being perfected. Stephen B. Shepard spoke of all this in almost lyrical terms:

> All of this entrepreneurial energy is transforming Corporate America...there sure as hell is a new business cycle. Housing and autos used to drive the U.S. economy. Now, information technology accounts for a quarter to a third of economic growth. And remember, this is an industry that pays very good wages. And it is an industry, bless its heart, in which prices actually fall every year. How's that for noninflationary growth? Furthermore, information technology affects every other industry. It boosts productivity, reduces costs, cuts inventories, facilitates electronic commerce. It is, in short, a transcendent technology – like railroads in the 19th century and automobiles in the 20th. (Shepard, 1997)

The picture that Shepard painted seems to be supported by the productivity growth statistics for the 1990s (Figure 4.5). If output per hour (excluding agriculture) is considered, there is evidence of a marked rise during the latter half of the decade.

Technology was not the only factor. Other commentators stress the importance of changes in the character of distribution and retailing processes.

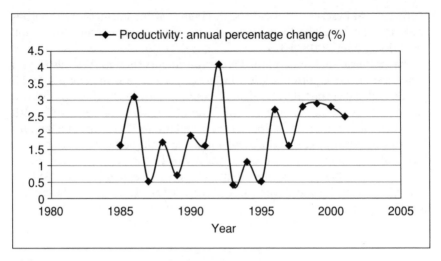

Figure 4.5 *Productivity growth (output per hour – non-farm business), 1989–2001*

Source: adapted from Bureau of Labor Statistics (2008), *Output Per Hour (Nonfarm Business)*, <http://data.bls.gov>

The relative costs of both distribution and retailing were reduced. For his part, Warren Buffett, one of America's wealthiest individuals and the chairman of Berkshire Hathaway, has argued that the economic successes of the 1990s owed much more to what is sometimes described as 'the Wal-Mart effect rather than the PC and new forms of software. Because of its size, Wal-Mart secured extensive economies of scale allowing it to keep operating costs to a minimum, sell goods at a low price, and limit price increases to an absolute minimum (Malanga, 2008).

The technological revolution and the retailing revolution should be seen within the context of another development. Intensified competition, including that resulting from foreign competition, added to the pressure for efficiency savings. Globalisation, the rise of China and India, and the enactment of trade liberalisation measures such as the North American Free Trade Agreement (NAFTA) opened up new markets, reduced and removed the barriers between existing markets, and thereby kept many price increases in check:

> As trade barriers fall, cheaper goods are available around the world. Cheaper labor, too, whether you're talking about software programmers in Russia or textile workers in China. The cheaper goods prompt people to buy more of them, and workers everywhere get the chance to share in economic growth. The result is increased global demand and a supply explosion that helps keep costs down for both labor and products. (Shepard, 1997)

Table 4.2 *Federal Funds effective rate (%)*

Year	1989	1990	1991	1992	1993	1994	1995	1996	1997	1998	1999	2000	2001
%	9.21	8.10	5.69	3.52	3.02	4.21	5.83	5.3	5.46	5.35	4.97	6.24	3.88

Source: adapted from US Census Bureau (2008), *The 2008 Statistical Abstract – Banking, Finance, & Insurance: Money Stock, Interest Rates, Bond Yields*, <http://www.census.gov>

Interest rate policy also, it was said at the time, played its part in shaping the 'new economy'. Although higher during the mid and late 1990s than in the immediate aftermath of the recession at the beginning of the decade, rates were much lower than they had been at the end of the 1980s and early 1990s when the reduction of inflation had been the principal policy goal.[5] The Federal Reserve responded quickly to the anxieties engendered by the world financial crises of 1998. Indeed, Alan Greenspan's ability to judge the nation's monetary policy needs led to him being judged 'the Maestro'. Table 4.2 shows the Federal Funds rate (governing other short-term interest rates) between 1989 and 2001.

Others pointed to the long-term impact of policy shifts during the Reagan era. The conquest of inflation, deregulation, tax reductions and the taming of the labour unions had, it was said, laid the basis for the boom years. Despite pressures from some aligned with the Democratic Party and policy uncertainties during his first two years in office, Bill Clinton had for the most part followed in Reagan's path.[6]

> Although President Bill Clinton did push through a small increase in income taxes, he reversed course by 1997, signing a major cut in the capital gains tax. In fact, President Clinton built upon and brought to completion several of Reagan's ideas, including most significantly the consummation of the North American Free Trade Agreement (NAFTA), an idea Reagan first proposed in the late 1970s. (Hayward, 2006: 62)[7]

Assessing the Clinton administration

What else can be said about President Clinton's contribution to the upturn? He and his supporters would reject claims that he simply continued the policies pursued in the Reagan era. Clinton described himself as a 'new Democrat'. In doing so, he reaffirmed his loyalty to the party but at the same time distanced himself from the traditional Democratic attachment to what Republicans derided as 'tax and spend' policies. He emphasised the dynamism and potential of the free market and criticised dependency upon welfare provision. At the same time, however, he pointed to a substantial role for governmental activism in, for example, healthcare. He often talked of 'investing in people'.

A month after he entered the White House, Clinton put before congress a set of legislative proposals, *A Vision of Change for America*. The plans, which drew upon Clinton's campaign rhetoric promising government investment in education and the infrastructure, incorporated a relatively short-term fiscal stimulus package resting upon expenditure increases and temporary investment tax credits. Brit Hume, a conservative commentator, was scathing:

> The stimulus package was a grab-bag of spending ranging from child immunization to summer youth jobs to unemployment compensation. The money was to come from deficit spending, which required the White House to declare it an 'emergency' to get around budget rules. Part of the money, about $2.5 billion, was to be distributed to states and cities for spending on projects mayors and governors had placed on their 'ready-to-go list.' It included such things as swimming pools in Midland, Texas, public housing for artists in San Francisco, and an Alpine slide in Puerto Rico. (Hume, 1993)

Although there was still a Democratic majority in both chambers of Congress at that time, the stimulus package was defeated. In response, the administration drew on other strands in Clinton's election platform and placed fiscal probity at the top of its agenda. It committed itself to the reduction and eventual elimination of the federal government budget deficit. Clinton drew upon his own convictions as a 'new Democrat' and was undoubtedly pushed by budget 'hawks' in his administration such as Leon Panetta, Alice Rivlin and Robert Rubin. Indeed, such was Rubin's influence that some commentators described White House policies as 'Rubinomics'. So as to reduce the deficit, the highest rates of personal taxation and corporate taxes were to be raised (Rosenberg, 2003: 281). In all, the package represented one of the largest tax increases in US history, about $240 billion over five years (Burns and Taylor, 2001).

Winning a Congressional majority was not straightforward. The administration faced Republican opposition and equivocation by some Democrats who feared the political consequences of tax rises. As Samuel Rosenberg records, the mood among some Democrats reflected the shift in economic and political values that the Reagan years had wrought: 'The supply-side economics rhetoric of Reaganomics had so influenced the policy debate that an income tax increase narrowly focused on the top 1.2 per cent of taxpayers had great difficulty being passed by a Democratic majority in Congress' (Rosenberg, 2003: 283). Nonetheless, the 1993 deficit-reduction law was based on a commitment to cut the deficit by $496 billion over five years.

Clinton's commitment to deficit reduction paid off, although it would have been unrealised had the economy not boomed during the second half of the 1990s.[8] Economic growth led to increases in wages and salaries and significant numbers of people thereby moved into higher tax brackets without changes in the tax code. As Table 4.3 indicates, in 1998 the federal government budget showed a surplus for the first time since 1969.

Why did the budget deficit matter? Some commentators stressed the ways in which the budget deficit boosted overall demand levels and thereby added

Table 4.3 *Federal government budget/deficit (US$bn), 1990–2001*

Year	Deficit/surplus (US$bn)
1990	−221.0
1991	−269.2
1992	−290.3
1993	−255.1
1994	−203.2
1995	−164.0
1996	−107.4
1997	−21.9
1998	69.3
1999	125.6
2000	236.2
2001	128.2

Source: adapted from US Census Bureau (2002), *The 2008 Statistical Abstract*, <http://www.census.gov>

to inflationary pressures (Morgan, 2004: 1024). Others argued that the borrowing required to fund deficits and the growing size of the national debt diverted savings and put upward pressure on the interest rate, thereby reducing or 'crowding out' private sector borrowing and the funds available for investment.[9] Deficit reduction allows interest rates to be set at a lower rate than they would otherwise be (or at the least limited rises) and thereby contributed to the boom of the late 1990s.[10] In a study published in 2009, the Congressional Budget Office has spelt out the potential economic consequences of long-term and sustained budget deficits:

> More government borrowing would drain the nation's pool of savings...If the budget continued along the path of rising debt, serious concerns about fiscal solvency would arise. Investors would require the government to pay an interest premium on its securities to compensate for the risk that they might not be repaid or that the value of their securities would be eroded by inflation. Such a premium would drive up the cost of borrowing.... As investment was displaced by government debt, GDP would grow more slowly and eventually decline. In the longer run, as the debt continued to grow and unless the interest premium was very large, capital would probably flee the United States, further reducing investment. (Congressional Budget Office, 2009: 18)

The priority assigned to deficit reduction angered more radical and progressive Democrats who would have rather seen more funding given to social provision. They were also at odds with other policies pursued by the Clinton administration. Although there were tax rises for those in the highest brackets at the beginning of his first term, Clinton's commitment to governing as a 'new Democrat' ensured that if the overall taxation structure is assessed in terms of 'who pays what' it remained broadly unchanged. As Burns and Taylor record:

> We would have expected a Democratic president to alter policy to force the rich to pay more, but under Clinton the rich are contributing as much to total revenues from the individual income tax as they did in the 1980s. Indeed, it has been argued that the pattern under Clinton closely resembles that under Reagan and Bush – that is, the highest-income quintile of the population has carried more of the tax burden only because its share of national income has increased. (Burns and Taylor, 2001)

Difficulties

Others, both during the 1990s and subsequently, have questioned the extent which there was a fundamental shift in the character of the US economy. Terms such as 'new economy' or 'Goldilocks economy' are, they suggest, journalistic hyperbole.

First, from this perspective, the upturn of the late 1990s was caused by temporary and short-lived developments. Increases in the cost of healthcare slowed down. The labour market was swelled by mass immigration and the Personal Responsibility and Work Opportunity Act of 1996, which reformed welfare provision and brought new entrants into the workforce. The sluggishness of the labour market in terms of recovery from the recession at the beginning of the decade created nervousness among many workers and led to moderate wage demands. There was a widespread awareness that excessive pay awards would fuel inflation and trigger interest rate rises and other deflationary measures. Larry Elliott and Dan Atkinson put this in graphic terms: 'Central banks use technical phrases such as "managing inflation expectations" but what they really mean is that the huddled masses are petrified that a recessionary thunderbolt will come thudding down from mount Olympus if they get too uppity' (Elliott and Atkinson, 2008: 118).

The appreciation of the dollar against other currencies reduced import prices (affecting consumer goods, components and raw materials) (*Business Week*, 1997). At the same time, oil prices, relative to the prices of other goods and services, were at a lower level than before the oil crises of the early 1970s. This was, in part, because demand fell in the East Asian 'tiger economies' after they crashed in summer 1997. Furthermore, the federal government budget was, after all the angst of the late 1980s and early 1990s, balanced. Indeed, during the late 1990s there was a surplus, thereby reducing upward pressures on the interest rate which could otherwise have had deflationary effects. This was partly because of the economic upturn (which bolstered federal revenue), policy decisions by the Clinton administration, and the end of the Cold War, which allowed reductions in military spending.

Secondly, the evidence for a productivity 'revolution' upon which much of the 'new economy' was constructed is limited. Insofar as there was an increase in productivity growth it was a one-off spurt (Elliott and Atkinson, 2008: 233). Furthermore, it was confined to only a few sectors of the economy. Researchers assert that multifactor productivity growth (measuring the growth in output not accounted for by a growth in inputs) was very unimpressive between 1995 and 2001 outside of computer and semiconductor-producing and communications equipment. There were, it has been argued, very few spillovers into other sectors (Marxsen, 2007: 7).

> During the postwar decades, when the economy really was a productivity powerhouse, technological advances affected every aspect of life…Has recent experience offered a comparable transformation? We have made some spectacular advances. But these have taken place on a very narrow front, tied directly or indirectly to the magic of silicon, which allows us to manipulate and transmit vast amounts of information at blinding speed. How much difference does this really make to people's lives? Information is a means, not an end: people can't eat information, wear it, live in it. (Krugman, 1996)

Paul Krugman also suggests that productivity growth in the second half of the 1990s bore little comparison to technological advances in earlier decades. This seems to be supported by some, at least, of the statistics. Indeed, if the figures from 1995 to 2001 are considered within the context of trends over about forty years (see Figure 4.6) the late 1990s hardly seem impressive.[11]

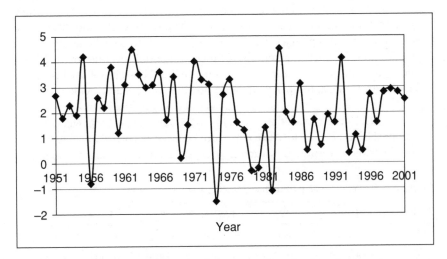

Figure 4.6 *Productivity (output per hour – non-farm business), annual percentage change, 1959–2001*

Source: adapted from Bureau of Labor Statistics (2008), *Output Per Hour (Nonfarm Business)*, <http://data.bls.gov>

Thirdly, although there was much talk of increased profits margins as a consequence of growth, profitability was limited. Profit growth between 1995 and 2000 averaged only 5.8 per cent. Indeed, profit levels were below those secured during the Bush years. As Carl Steidtmann of Deloitte Research noted in 2006:

> Profit per employee is probably the single best measure of business health. A rise in profit per employee has preceded every economic recovery, just as a decline in this metric has been an indicator of a coming recession. During the last Goldilocks era, profits per employee peaked in inflation adjusted dollars at just under $8,800 in the third quarter of 1997. Today, profit per employee stands just above $10,000 per employee, its highest level in more than 55 years. (Steidtmann, 2006)

Fourthly, the boom led to an increasing balance of payments deficit (see Table 4.4). Whereas Japan had been a major source of concern during the late 1980s and early 1990s, and there were deep-seated fears that Japan threatened American economic interests, it was displaced by China as the decade progressed (see Chapter 6).

In an era of globalisation, some suggest that balance of payments deficits have few consequences. Nonetheless, they may be a 'symptom' suggesting structural difficulties. The cause may be a lack of competitiveness or a shift in the terms of trade between different countries. A US trade deficit will also create an excess supply of dollars in the foreign markets, thereby placing downward pressure on the exchange rate. A weak dollar will increase import prices and may at some point prompt the Fed to raise interest rates, which will have a deflationary impact on demand, output and employment. The US has relied on large-scale inflows of financial capital as foreign buyers have acquired US Treasury bonds. Some see this as having given the Chinese potential leverage over the US economy and the political process. According to Robert Blecker of the Economic Policy Institute, speaking before the end of the boom became evident:

> If present trends continue, the growth in the U.S. international debt will not be sustainable in the long run. No country can continue to borrow so much from abroad without eventually triggering a depreciation of its currency and a

Table 4.4 *US balance of payments, 1989–2006 (US$mn)*

1989	1990	1991	1992	1993	1994	1995
−99,486	−78,968	2,897	−50,078	−84,805	−121,612	−113,567

1996	1997	1998	1999	2000	2001	
−124,764	−140,726	−215,062	−301,630	−417,426	−384,699	

Source: adapted from Bureau of Economic Analysis (2008), *U.S. International Transactions, 1960– Present*, <http://www.bea.gov>

contraction of its economy. The rising trade deficit and mushrooming foreign debt are thus warning signals of underlying problems that – if not corrected – could bring the U.S. economic boom crashing to a halt in the not-too-distant future. (quoted in Sandronsky, 2001)

Fifthly, the US economy was unbalanced. The financial sector, in particular the derivatives market, expanded dramatically (see below). The inflow of funds from the east, confidence in the structures on which those derivatives were based, and a faith in new technology and the overall capacity of the US economy all contributed to a rise in the prices of financial assets.[12] Manufacturing developed at a much slower speed and exporters were hit by the appreciation of the dollar: 'Strictly speaking, it was not a Goldilocks economy at all, since half the bowel of porridge was too hot and the other half was too cold' (Elliott and Atkinson, 2008: 129).

Sixthly, the upturn was, according to sceptical observers, much more of a bubble than a boom. It was, they said, sustained by a loose monetary policy (in other words, excessively low interest rates) and lax forms of regulation. While interest rates were raised from their 1992 and 1993 levels they were still, according to the Federal Reserve's critics, too low throughout the mid and late 1990s (see Table 4.2). In part, this happened because the Federal Reserve was shaken by the financial crises in Asia, Brazil and Russia as well as the collapse of Long-Term Capital Management (LTCM), and fears (which were often little more than urban myths) of a crisis as the world marked the millennium (Niskanen, 2006: 67). Against this background, there were anxieties that increased interest rates could be excessively deflationary.

Misjudged interest rates, it has been said, inflicted damage on the US economy by allowing funds to be borrowed relatively cheaply. This bloated consumer demand, unbalanced the economy by encouraging growth in the most interest-sensitive sectors, allowed the extension of the mortgage market to 'sub-prime' borrowers who had until then been regarded as too risky, and permitted inefficient companies to survive and perhaps even prosper.[13]

The stock market bubble

The excited optimism generated by new technology and the Federal Reserve's commitment to relatively low interest rates set the stage for the stock market bubble at the end of the 1990s. In 1999, there were 457 initial public offerings (IPOs) as companies, many of which were based in the new technology sector, began to offer shares on the market. Of these IPOs, 117 doubled in price on the first day of trading. Against this background, NASDAQ average share prices kept rising. As in the 1920s, however, the bubble burst. In 2001 the number of IPOs fell to 76. Average share prices crashed from 5,000 to 2,000 (see Figure 4.7) and trillions of dollars were lost. The dot.com boom

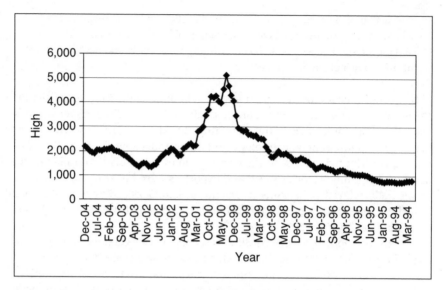

Figure 4.7 *NASDAQ average share prices, 1994–2004*
Source: adapted from Yahoo Finance (2009), *NASDAQ Composite – Historical Prices*,
<http://finance.yahoo.com>

came to an abrupt end. According to William A. Fleckenstein, Federal Reserve chairman Alan Greenspan was personally culpable:

> Whether providing fuel for the fire in the form of easy money, or rationalizations that people could use as their reason to speculate, Greenspan was the poster boy for the developing bubble. He wasn't the *only* reason there was a bubble, but without his sponsorship it could never have grown anywhere near as large or as dangerous as it did. (Fleckenstein, 2008: 31)

Apart from low interest rates, there were, as Fleckenstein acknowledges, other reasons for the bubble.

• There was a profound, almost unshakeable, optimism about the earnings potential of dot.com companies sustained by the new forms of technology that seemed to become available on a daily basis. Share prices often bore no relationship to the market opportunities of particular businesses.
• Baby boomers were becoming aware of their impending old age and increasingly sough to invest for their retirement.
• The PC and the World Wide Web offered a simple and straightforward vehicle allowing millions to buy and trade shares:

> The role of Microsoft Windows 95 in the process of seducing the crowd cannot be overemphasized. Windows 95 made personal computers far friendlier while

Table 4.5 *Median usual weekly earnings of full-time wage and salary workers (25 years and older), annual averages, 1979–2001 (2004 dollars)*

Year	Median earnings
1979	639
1980	621
1985	633
1990	629
1995	628
1996	623
1997	634
1998	662
1999	671
2000	668
2001	672

Source: adapted from Economic Policy Institute (2008), *Datazone*, <http://www.epi.org>

> making communication between PCs far easier...the Internet helped to supply the imagination component necessary to get folks really excited about how rich they might become, which served to further intensify speculation. (Fleckenstein 2008: 32)

• Some companies, it has been said, used particular accounting methods that inflated their profit margins and future earnings potential. The Enron crisis exposed these practices.

Furthermore, the 'new economy' of the 1990s did little to address the long-term difficulties faced by many wage-earners. Although the average annual growth rate of median real family income was 2.3 per cent between 1995 and 2000, this was, in reality, only a limited form of 'catch-up' for many people. For the median earner, real incomes had fallen from the 1970s onwards (Table 4.5). They then increased but only at a marginal rate during the 1980s and in the first half of the 1990s. It was only in 1998 that real median earnings exceeded those paid in 1979.

Conclusion

Few would now subscribe to terms such as the 'new' or 'Goldilocks' economy. With hindsight, the late 1990s are regarded in less effusive terms. In particular, talk of the business cycle having been in some way 'overcome' is now derided. Indeed, there have been frequent claims that the beginnings of the recession that began in late 2007 are to be found in the ways in which the financial markets developed during the 1990s. Nonetheless, particularly when compared with the downturn at the beginning of the decade and the uncertainties and sluggishness that marked the early years of the new century, the latter half of the 1990s seem to offer a picture of sustained progress. However, although Senator Hillary Clinton's 2008 primary campaign sought to capitalise on this, benign memories of her husband's administration were not sufficient to bring her victory.

Notes

1   Unemployment almost always lags behind the business cycle. Employers tend not to make large-scale layoffs at the first sign of downturn but postpone decisions. Correspondingly, they are generally slow to hire new workers once economic conditions begin improving after a downturn.
2   S & Ls (sometimes also called 'thrifts') offer opportunities for savers and provide mortgages for those buying homes.
3   Those who talked in terms of a 'new economy' also challenged the legitimacy and relevance of the statistics customarily used to measure economic progress. The 'new economy', they asserted, could not be understood by simply adding up production totals. The value of a cellphone or fax machine could not be estimated in this way (and, indeed, a drop in price for items such as these would appear – all other things being equal – as a fall in GDP).
4   In each country, NAIRU is set by a range of economic and cultural variables and can change over time. The US NAIRU is usually put at between 5.5 and 6 per cent (Roubini, 1998).
5   The Federal Reserve raised rates at times when it feared that unemployment had fallen to a point at which inflationary pressures would grow. There was also a belief that economic growth rates of more than 2.5 per cent were 'unsustainable' (Meeropol, 1998: 255). The reasons why interest rates fell are considered on p. 109.
6   Clinton was, after January 1995, faced by Republican majorities in both the House of Representatives and the Senate.
7   In 1993, there were several tax rises. For example, the highest marginal rate of tax was increased from 31 per cent to 39 per cent. However, there were only minor rises after this and large-scale spending plans (most notably proposals for universal health coverage) were abandoned. Indeed, during the Clinton years, the rate of growth of real per capita federal government spending was the lowest of any administration from 1945 onwards (Niskanen, 2006: 64–5).
8   Deficit reduction was also helped by the end of the Cold War and the US's reduced military commitments.
9   Although influential among policymakers, notions of 'crowding out' may already have become an anachronism by the time the Clinton administration sought to prioritise deficit-reduction. Japan and other nations (China was of increasing importance) were buying the Treasury securities used to fund deficits. Increased demand for securities reduced the necessity for interest rate rises (Judis, 2008). The relationship between deficits and interest rates may therefore be much weaker than some have suggested. Charles Morris concludes that 'big deficit reductions

move long-term interest rates by a few tenths of a percent, if at all' (Morris, 2008: 33).

10　Having said that, interest rates did not fall during the Clinton years. Indeed, they were at their lowest during Clinton's first year in office in 1993 (see Table 4.2). His backers would nonetheless assert that interest rates would have been significantly higher had the budget deficit not been addressed.

11　There has been some controversy about the productivity growth figures for the second half of the 1990s. There are problems in measuring productivity growth, particularly when multifactor productivity is considered (Marxsen, 2007: 7).

12　A 'derivative' is a financial instrument based upon another asset.

13　The expansion of credit, together with market activities based around securities and derivatives such as the development of collateralised debt obligations (CDOs), hedging and the use of credit default swaps, laid the basis, it has been said, for the financial collapse in 2007–8.

References and further reading

Burns, John W. and Andrew J. Taylor (2001), 'A New Democrat? The economic performance of the Clinton presidency', *Independent Review*, 5:3, January, 387–408.

Business Week (1997), 'The case against the New Economy', November 6, <http://www.businessweek.com>

Congressional Budget Office (2009), *Testimony Statement of Douglas W. Elmendorf (Director): The Long-Term Budget Outlook, before the Committee on the Budget United States Senate, July 16, 2009*, http://www.cbo.gov/ftpdocs/104xx/doc10455/07-16-Long-TermOutlook_Testimony.pdf

Elliott, Larry and Dan Atkinson (2008), *The Gods that Failed: How Blind Faith in Markets Has Cost Us our Future*, London: The Bodley Head.

Fleckenstein, William A. with Frederick Sheehan (2008), *Greenspan's Bubbles: The Age of Ignorance at the Federal Reserve*, New York: McGraw Hill.

Hall, Robert E. (1993), 'Macro theory and the recession of 1990–1991', *American Economic Review*, May, 83:2, 275–9.

Hayward, Steven F. (2006), 'The evolution of US economic policy in the 1980s', in Wojciech Bienkowski, Josef C. Brada and Mariusz-Jan Radlo (2006), *Reaganomics Goes Global: What Can the EU, Russia and Transition Countries Learn from the USA?*, Basingstoke: Palgrave Macmillan, 53–63.

Hume, Brit (1993), 'Taken for a swim – how Bill Clinton's failure to compromise cost him passage of his stimulus package in Congress', *National Review*, May 24, <http://findarticles.com>

Johnson, Julie (1989), 'Washington talk: the presidency; tough words to translate: "kinder and gentler" ', *New York Times*, January 25, <http://query.nytimes.com>

Judis, John B. (2008), 'Debt man walking', *New Republic*, December 3, <http://www.tnr.com>

Kamery, Rob H. (2004), 'A brief review of the recession of 1990–1991', *Proceedings of the Academy of Legal, Ethical and Regulatory Issues*, 8:2, <http://www.sbaer.uca.edu/research/allied/2004_maui/legal_ethical_regulatory_issues/14.pdf>

Krugman, Paul (1996), 'Stay on their backs', *New York Times Magazine*, February 4, <http://pages.stern.nyu.edu>

Krugman, Paul (2008), *The Return of Depression Economics and the Crisis of 2008*, Harmondsworth: Penguin.

Labonte, Marc and Gail Makinen (2002), *The Current Economic Recession: How Long, How Deep, and How Different From the Past?*, Congressional Research Service Report for Congress, <http://www.fpc.state.gov/documents/organization/7962.pdf>

Malanga, Steven (2008), *The Wal-Mart Effect Updated*, Real Clear Markets, November 26, <http://www.realclearmarkets.com>

Marxsen, Craig S. (2007), *Environmental Regulation Versus Productivity Growth: United States Studies and a European Comparison*, <http://www.westga.edu/~bquest/2007/productivity7.pdf>

Meeropol, Michael (1998), *Surrender: How the Clinton Administration Completed the Reagan Revolution*, Ann Arbor, MI: University of Michigan Press.

Morgan, Iwan W. (2004), 'Jimmy Carter, Bill Clinton and the New Democratic economics', *Historical Journal*, 47, December, 1015–39.

Morris, Charles R. (2008), *The Two Trillion Dollar Meltdown: Easy Money, High Rollers, and the Great Credit Crash*, New York: Public Affairs.

Niskanen, William A. (2006), 'Economic policy during the Clinton administration', in Wojciech Bienkowski, Josef C. Brada and Mariusz-Jan Radlo (2006), *Reaganomics Goes Global: What Can the EU, Russia and Transition Countries Learn from the USA?*, Basingstoke: Palgrave Macmillan, 64–8.

On the Issues (2008), *Bill Clinton on Budget & Economy*, <http://www.ontheissues.org>

Rosenberg, Samuel (2003), *American Economic Development since 1945*, Basingstoke: Palgrave Macmillan.

Roubini, Nouriel (1998), *The NAIRU Debate: Can the US Economy Grow Above 2.5 per cent and Unemployment Fall Below 5 per cent Without Causing an Increase in Inflation?*, New York University – Stern School of Business, <http://pages.stern.nyu.edu>

Sandronsky, Seth (2001), 'America's "Goldilocks" economy', *Common Dreams*, March 5, <http://www.commondreams.org>

Shepard, Stephen B. (1997), 'The New Economy: what it really means', *Business Week*, November 6, <http://www.businessweek.com>

Steidtmann, Carl (2006), *Economist's Corner: Will Goldilocks Make a Comeback?*, DeLoitte, <http://www.deloitte.com>

US Department of Labor (1999), *Futurework: trends and challenges for work in the 21st century: 7 – implications of workplace change*, <http://www.dol.gov>

5

The Bush years and the credit crunch

This chapter surveys US economic performance during the Bush years (2001–9). There had already been a significant slowdown before Bush took office. The administration responded by pursuing radical tax-cutting policies and, after initially imposing tariffs to protect the steel industry, emphasised the importance of bilateral free trade agreements. There have, however, been far-reaching criticisms of the administration's record from both left and right. These have included stagnating real wages, growing inequality and the budget deficit. Commentators have also argued that the 'Fed' adopted a lax monetary policy which contributed to a bloated housing market that would inevitably crash, as it did it in 2007–8.

As Chapter 4 noted, the dot.com boom came to an end at the close of the twentieth century. The almost unbounded optimism about the US's economic future that seemed to characterise the late 1990s gave way to some uncertainty and a degree of pessimism. The NASDAQ Composite Index, which is based upon the value of shares in the new technology sector, peaked on March 10 2000. By December 2000, it had fallen by over 50 per cent.

The effects of these stock market falls spread outwards.[1] They were compounded by rising energy prices, overcapacity in the telecom and computer industries and a tightening monetary policy as the Federal Reserve, fearing inflation, steadily raised interest rates up until the end of 2000 (Judis, 2008). Order books were shrinking. Investment was being reduced. Consumer confidence was falling.

Overall economic growth inevitably suffered. After nine years of uninterrupted expansion, the US economy shrank in the third quarter of 2000 (−0.5 per cent at an annualised rate). There was another phase of negative growth during the first three months of 2001 (again at a rate of −0.5 per cent). Then, in the summer of 2001, there was further shrinkage (GDP fell by 1.4 per cent). The National Bureau of Economic Research's Business Cycle Dating Committee,

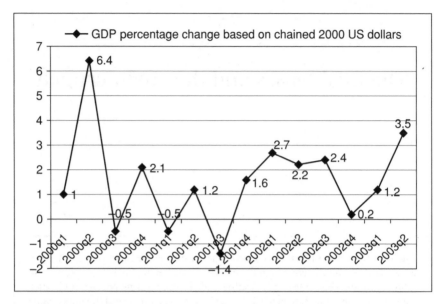

Figure 5.1 *US economy – quarterly growth rates, January 2000–June 2003*

Source: adapted from Bureau of Economic Analysis (2008), *Percent Change from Preceding Period*, <http://www.bea.gov>

whose pronouncements on the state of the economy have quasi-official weight, talked of an eight month trough between March and November 2001 (*USA Today*, 2003).

The country's economic difficulties grew in magnitude during the first year of the Bush presidency. The September 11th attacks shook confidence, shut down air transportation, disrupted production, particularly in those sectors dependent upon just-in-time deliveries from Canada or Mexico, and cost the country an estimated $100 billion in economic losses. There were also corporate scandals, most notably the collapse of Enron at the end of 2001. The demise of the energy company represented the largest bankruptcy in US history.

Against this background, unemployment inevitably rose (see Figure 5.2). It was 4.2 per cent in January 2001 when Bush took office but hit 6.3 per cent in June 2003 (Bureau of Labor Statistics, 2008).

The Bush record

Nonetheless, although European commentators and many Democrats have lambasted Bush's economic record, the effects of the downturn at the beginning of the new century could have been more severe. It was relatively shallow

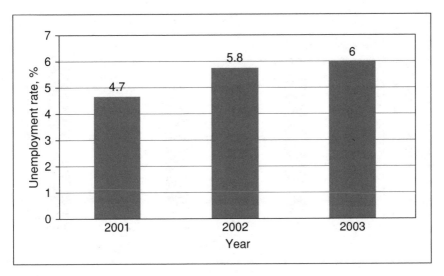

Figure 5.2 *Unemployment rate, 2001–3 (%)*

Source: adapted from Bureau of Labor Statistics (2009), *Labor Force Statistics from the Current Population Survey*, <http://www.bls.gov>

Table 5.1 *Real growth (rate of change of GDP) (%)*

Year	Real growth (rate of change of GDP) (%)
2001	0.8
2002	1.6
2003	2.5
2004	3.6
2005	2.9
2006	2.9
2007	2.0
2008	1.1

Source: adapted from Bureau of Economic Analysis (2008), *National Economic Accounts – Gross Domestic Product (GDP), Percent Change from Preceding Period*, <http://www.bea.gov>

and there was a recovery in the years that followed 2001.[2] President Bush's supporters point to fairly solid economic growth rates during many of the years after 2002. Indeed, according to Sheryl Gay Stolberg of the *New York Times*: 'Mr. Bush has spent years presiding over an economic climate of growth that would be the envy of most presidents' (Stolberg, 2008).

Furthermore, although unemployment rose during the first two-and-a-half years of the Bush presidency, and Democrats pointed in 2004 to the net job losses that there had been during the president's first term of office, the unemployment rate then fell steadily until 2007 (Figure 5.3).

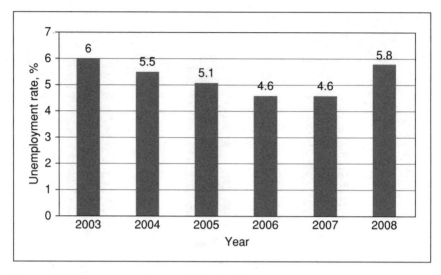

Figure 5.3 *Unemployment rate, 2003–8 (%)*

Source: Bureau of Labor Statistics (2009), *Labor Force Statistics from the Current Population Survey*, <http://www.bls.gov>

It was only in the final year of President Bush's two terms of office, they assert, that the US (and the world) economy began to falter in a serious way. By then, the country was in the grip of economic forces beyond the control of the administration and federal government agencies.

When he addressed an audience at the American Enterprise Institute (AEI) in May 2006, Karl Rove, who served as the president's chief strategist and deputy chief of staff until his resignation in August 2007, described the Bush years as a period of 'economic recovery'. He attributed this to policies pursued by the White House, which, he asserted, had 'helped strengthen the economy's foundation' by reforming the tax system, promoting trade liberalisation and imposing 'budget discipline' (Rove, 2006).

Taxation

Tax cuts were pursued as one of the administration's principal policy goals from the moment that Bush took office. With the backing of nearly all Republicans and some Democrats in Congress, the Economic Growth and Tax Relief Reconciliation Act of 2001 provided a $1.35 trillion tax cut phased in over ten years. Tax rates of 15, 28, 31, 36 and 39.6 per cent were replaced with a more simplified rate structure of 10, 15, 25 and 33 per cent. At the same time, over the years after the Act was passed, the child tax credit was to be doubled, the inheritance tax (or the 'death tax' as conservatives dubbed it) was to be phased out, and the 'marriage tax penalty' substantially reduced.[3] The Act was retrospective so that taxpayers received rebates through the post shortly after it was signed by the president.

According to a Senate Finance Committee staff estimate, once all cuts had been fully phased in, the average family of four (on $50,000 a year) would save $1,825 (Wallace, 2001). All these included 'sunset' provisions and the cuts were therefore set to expire at the end of 2010 unless further legislation was passed so as to extend them. However, few could envisage that there would be a Congressional majority for efforts to reinstate the higher tax brackets and reimpose the 'marriage tax penalty' or the 'death tax'. The cuts were widely seen as a permanent shift in the character of the tax regime.

The 2001 Act was followed up by further legislation in subsequent years. The Job Creation and Worker Assistance Act of 2002, which was passed in the wake of the September 11th attacks and amidst fears of a prolonged downturn, offered additional tax credits for individuals and added to capital depreciation credits for businesses. The Jobs and Growth Tax Relief Reconciliation Act of 2003 accelerated the implementation of provisions in the 2001 Act.

The White House and the Act's Congressional backers justified the tax cuts on both supply-side and demand-side grounds. They argued that the cuts would free up and encourage entrepreneurial initiative and thereby spur economic growth while, at the same time, adding to consumer demand. As Bush declared: 'immediate tax relief will provide an important boost at an important time for our economy' (quoted in Altman, 2004: 73).

Towards the end of Bush's second term, conservative commentators argued that the tax cuts had indeed worked in this way. According to Brian Riedl of the Heritage Foundation:

> The tax cuts are working exactly as intended...Lower tax rates have increased the incentives to work, save, and invest, and as a result, the economy has grown faster than expected. Concerns that the Bush tax cuts would lead to a long-term shortfall of government revenues have proven false...Tax revenues in 2007 are now estimated to be $70 billion above the level projected even *before* the 2003 tax cuts. In other words, tax revenues are now *above* their pre-tax cut baseline. (quoted in Murdock, 2007)

The cuts also gave rise to hopes among many on the right that government expenditure and the scope of federal provision would have, as a consequence of the tax reductions, to be curbed. Some rallied around the cry of 'starve the beast'.

The tax cuts were also tied to the visions of those Daniel Altman has dubbed 'neoeconomists' (Altman, 2004: 31–49). They were committed to a long-term and radical restructuring of the US economy so as to encourage economic growth by bolstering the position of capital and open up much more of the economy to free market forces. The tax cuts were the first step and would be followed by other measures that would reduce or abolish taxes on savings and business activity (such as taxes on interest, corporate income tax and capital gains tax) and the privatisation of Social Security so that individuals would, in readiness for retirement, hold portfolios of investment funds. George W. Bush spoke of constructing 'the ownership society' (Bienkowski, 2006: 70).

Trade liberalisation

In March 2002, the Bush administration imposed tariffs on imported steel claiming that foreign companies were dumping in US markets.[4] In late 2003, the World Trade Organisation ruled against the US, and in the context of a threatened trade war with the European Union the Bush administration withdrew the tariffs ahead of the expiration date (2005) that had been set.

There were suggestions that the imposition of the tariff owed much to electoral considerations. Steel-producing states such as West Virginia and Pennsylvania were expected to be closely contested in the 2004 presidential election. In many ways, the tariff was out of step with the Bush administration's overall trade policy. For the most part, the White House talked in expansive terms about trade liberalisation. It built upon and extended the Clinton administration's trade policy by pursuing bilateral trade agreements and at times exploring the concept of a Free Trade Agreement of the Americas (FTAA). There were discussions between the nations of north, central and south America in Quebec in 2001, Miami in 2003 and Mar del Plata (Argentina) in 2005. Talks foundered amidst demands for an end to US agricultural subsidies, US insistence upon intellectual property rights, and hopes of a radical alternative trade agreement between some of the central and south American countries.

In the absence of agreement about the construction of the FTAA, efforts were concentrated instead on bilateral trade treaties (see Chapter 6). Despite opposition by the labour movement and environmental organisations and the anxieties of Congressmen from rustbelt states, Congress agreed to renew 'fast-track' (or Trade Promotion Authority, as it was renamed), enabling the president to negotiate trade agreements with foreign governments in the knowledge that Congress would simply take an 'up or down' vote and not seek to 'renegotiate' a treaty by considering amendments. Although many of the countries with which free trade agreements were concluded were relatively small, Karl Rove stressed their collective importance: 'Our free trade partners represent 14 per cent of the world's GDP, excluding the United States from the world total, and yet they represent 52 per cent of all U.S. goods exports in 2005 – 14 per cent of the world but 52 per cent of our economic exports' (Rove, 2006).

At the same time, the Bush administration resisted pressures to curb trade with China. During the Bush years, Chinese imports into the US continued to grow at a rapid rate. Indeed, by 2005, the US trade deficit with China was nearly equal to the combined trade deficits with Japan, China and Mexico (Morrison, 2006: 2).

There were widely shared fears that imports from China were leading to the displacement of American workers. It was alleged that the Chinese *yuan* was deliberately undervalued by being pegged to the US dollar at an artificially low rate so that the country's goods and services were sold cheaply overseas. There were parallel claims that China had only partially met the obligations imposed by World Trade Organization (WTO) membership and was still failing to provide full protection for US intellectual property (Morrison, 2006: 5). In July 2005, however, the administration was able to claim a limited victory when the Chinese government decoupled the *yuan* from the dollar although critics continued to assert that that it remained undervalued.[5]

'Budget discipline'

Much has been made of the way in which the budget deficit grew during Bush's tenure at the White House. Indeed, there were bitter criticisms from within the conservative movement (see p. 129). For his part, however, Karl Rove has stressed the difficulties facing the administration and its efforts in restraining spending. The 'war on terror' required increased national security expenditure. Much government spending, such as Social Security, Medicare and Medicaid, is 'non-discretionary' and cannot be reduced. Although President Bush only vetoed one bill during the six years before the Democrats secured a majority in both chambers (from January 2007) Rove emphasises the impact of threatened vetoes. He asserts that 39 veto threats were issued by the White House when just six spending bills in total were under consideration (Rove, 2006).[6]

Furthermore, Rove records in an effort to reassure those within the conservative movement who were concerned by what they saw as fiscal recklessness, federal government expenditure was lower as a percentage of GDP than it had been under four of the five preceding presidents. At the same time, the Bush administration cut the growth of non-security discretionary spending every year it was in office. In contrast, during the final year of the Clinton administration, non-security discretionary spending increased by 15 per cent.

Seen as a proportion of GDP, the budget deficit began to fall after 2004 (Table 5.2). According to White House projections issued in readiness for the FY 2009 budget, but drawn up before the scale of the financial crisis was fully evident, the deficit would continue to shrink and government finances would be in surplus again by 2012 (GPO Access, 2008).[7]

Table 5.2 *US federal budget surplus/deficit (as a proportion of GDP), 2000–8*

Year	Surplus/deficit as a percentage of GDP
2001	1.3
2002	−1.5
2003	−3.5
2004	−3.6
2005	−2.6
2006	−1.9
2007	−1.2
2008	−3.2

Source: adapted from GPO Access (2009), *Budget of the United States Government: Historical Tables Fiscal Year 2010*, <http://www.gpoaccess.gov>

Table 5.3 *Presidential tenures and average annual economic growth rates, 1960 + (%)*

President(s)	Years	Average annual growth rate (%)
Kennedy – Johnson	1961–9	5.2
Clinton	1993–2001	3.6
Reagan	1981–9	3.4
Carter	1977–81	3.4
Nixon-Ford	1969–77	2.7
Bush II	2001–9	2.6 (* until 2007)
Bush I	1989–93	1.9

Source: Dean Baker (2008), Why Would Presidents Envy Bad Growth?, *The American Prospect – Beat the Press*, January 27, <http://www.prospect.org>

Criticisms

Despite these assertions, and some of the claims that have been made for economic growth rates during the Bush years, the administration has been subject to far-reaching criticism. Writing in *The American Prospect*, Dean Baker ranked US presidents since 1960 on the basis of annual growth during their tenures. George W. Bush and his father were in bottom place (see Table 5.3).

There are other criticisms.[8]

- The tax cuts were opposed by most Democrats and a handful of Republicans.[9] For the most part, those who voted against the measure emphasised the disproportionate gains secured by higher-income taxpayers. As Joseph Stiglitz observed, those with incomes over of a million dollars secured a tax reduction of $18,000. This was over thirty times larger than the cut extended to the average American. The 2003 cuts were skewed even more heavily toward those on the highest incomes (Stiglitz, 2007). Democratic Senator Kent Conrad spoke in similar terms to Stiglitz while the 2001 Act was under consideration:

> This bill doesn't pass any fairness test, no fiscal responsibility test. It does not pass the fundamental test we ought to apply to any tax bill. This final tax bill is clearly unfair. The top 20 per cent get 71 per cent of the benefits. The bottom 20 per cent get 1 per cent. 71 per cent of the benefits to the top 20 per cent; 1 per cent to the bottom 20 per cent. (PBS, 2001)

By giving much more to higher income groupings, it was said, the tax cuts along with large corporate profits contributed to growing levels of inequality in the US and extended the widening gap between rich and poor:

> Far from distributing money back to average American families, the Bush tax cuts overall have profited the super rich, leaving the vast majority of Americans with comparatively little or nothing to show for it. This has only made the distribution of income and wealth across America more skewed. (OMB Watch, 2006)

- Median family income barely grew during the Bush years. It was (if inflation-adjusted 2007 dollars are used) $61,083 in 2000 and $61,355 in 2007. Put another way, the average annual real growth rate of median family income was 0.1 per cent (Mishel, Bernstein and Shierholz, 2009: 46). Those on the bottom rungs of the socioeconomic ladder were hardest hit. Indeed, between 2000 and 2007, family income for those in the lowest and second lowest quintiles fell by 5.5 per cent and 1.5 per cent respectively (Mishel, Bernstein and Shierholz, 2009: 59). The difficulties facing those on the lowest rungs of the ladder were compounded by the falling value, in real terms, of the federal minimum wage. Before the Democrats secured majorities in the November 2006 Congressional elections and increased the federal minimum wage, its real value was at the lowest level in twenty years (Andrews, 2006).[10] According to Joseph Stiglitz:

> A young male in his 30s today has an income, adjusted for inflation, that is 12 per cent less than what his father was making 30 years ago. Some 5.3 million more Americans are living in poverty now than were living in poverty when Bush became president. America's class structure may not have arrived there yet, but it's heading in the direction of Brazil's and Mexico's. (Stiglitz, 2007)

This laid the basis for a widespread increase in consumer borrowing and debt. By 2007, total household debt was the highest it had ever been and constituted 141 per cent of disposable income (Mishel, Bernstein and Shierholz, 2009: 286). As Mishel, Bernstein, and Shierholz record: 'debt is a more important feature of the household economy than at any time in modern history. Over the last decade, especially, many American households have become dangerously overleveraged' (Mishel, Bernstein and Shierholz, 2009: 286).

- Because the highest income earners gained so much from the 2001 and 2003 tax cuts, the measures did little to stimulate the economy. As Joseph Stiglitz argued: 'The bang for the buck – the amount of stimulus per dollar of deficit – was astonishingly low' (Stiglitz, 2007). Those on high incomes who already lead comfortable lives are only likely to spend a proportion, perhaps quite a small proportion, of a tax rebate. They have, in the language of economics textbooks, a high marginal propensity to save. If, on the other hand, more of the cuts had been directed towards those on lower incomes, much more would have been spent, thereby adding to demand for goods and services and stimulating increased output and employment.
- Those who opposed the tax cuts pointed to their fiscal consequences. As the 2001 Act was under consideration, the budget surplus that had accumulated during the latter half of the 1990s seemed to be in jeopardy. Their fears were more than confirmed as the budget deficit returned and burgeoned (Table 5.4).

By mid-2008, as the economic slowdown became evident, the fiscal outlook appeared to have worsened. The White House's prediction for FY2009 (beginning in October 2008) was that the budget deficit would rise to nearly $490 billion, creating significant dilemmas for President Bush's successor. The increase was attributed to both the slowdown and the cost of stimulus measures intended to alleviate the impact of the 'credit crunch'. Some suggested that the deficit might be even higher than this. The federal government has major spending commitments including transportation, farm subsidies, education, Social Security and veterans' education benefits. Indeed, Bush secured passage of a new entitlement programme providing prescription drugs for those on Medicare (Wilson, 2009: 152). It also had to fund the wars in Iraq and

Table 5.4 *US federal government budget, 2000–8, (US$mn)*

Year	Budget surplus/deficit ($m)
2000	236,241
2001	128,236
2002	−157,758
2003	−377,585
2004	−412,727
2005	−318,346
2006	−248,181
2007	−160,701
2008	−458,555

Source: adapted from GPO Access (2009), *Budget of the United States Government: Historical Tables Fiscal Year 2010*, <http://www.gpoaccess.gov>

Afghanistan. Furthermore, they have asserted, the slowdown could be more severe than initial forecasts suggested (Wolf, 2008).

- Some within conservative and Republican ranks hoped that this might create political pressures that would lead to reductions in government expenditure and the reining in of social provision. Nonetheless, the deficit also provoked anxiety among those on the right. According to Bruce Bartlett, author of *Impostor: How George W. Bush Bankrupted America and Betrayed the Reagan Legacy*, a bitter indictment of the Bush administration's fiscal record, the deficit would not lead to calls for a reduction in government spending (as some conservatives hope) but to an increase:

    unless spending is checked or revenue raised, we are facing deficits of historic proportions. It is simply unrealistic to think we can finance a 50 per cent increase in spending as a share of gross domestic product – which is what is in the pipeline – just by running ever-larger deficits. Sooner or later, that bubble is going to burst and there will be overwhelming political support for deficit reduction, as there was in the 1980's and early 1990's. When that day comes, huge tax increases are inevitable because no one has the guts to seriously cut health spending. (Bartlett, 2005)

- The Bush administration failed to secure some its major policy goals. In particular, despite the hopes of both the 'neoeconomists' and the Bush administration, efforts to reform Social Security provision for senior citizens so that it was less a government entitlement and more a semi-privatised investment portfolio had to be abandoned. The White House also threw its weight behind immigration reform so as to meet US economic needs and establish a legal framework to accommodate the twelve million or so illegal immigrants living in the country. However, although there were Republican majorities in Congress for much of the time that Bush held the presidency, there was insufficient backing on Capitol Hill for these initiatives.
- 'Outsourcing' and 'offshoring' by US companies became an increasingly visible economic and political issue. With the backing of Republicans, corporate interests were, it was said, reallocating particular stages of the production process to foreign countries so as to reduce labour costs. This had long affected the manufacturing and assembly sectors but increasingly threatened those in services and the 'knowledge economy'. Lee T. Todd Jr spelt this out:

    My native state, Kentucky, has traditionally lured good-paying manufacturing jobs through a combination of cheap land, cheap labor, and tax incentives. But as soon as cheaper land and even cheaper labor comes along, many of those companies – from Appalachian call centers to 'cut and sew' manufacturing jobs – make the bottom-line economic decision to move. Now, many high-tech, professional jobs are joining the overseas exodus…more than

Table 5.5 *Current account, 2000–7 (US$mn)*

2000	2001	2002	2003	2004	2005	2006	2007	2008
−417,426	−398,270	−459,151	−521,519	−631,130	−748,683	−803,547	−726,573	−706,068

Source: adapted from Bureau of Economic Analysis (2009), *International Economic Accounts: Balance of Payments (International Transactions)*, <http://www.bea.gov>

> 150,000 technology jobs have been lost to offshoring since 2000. Software and programming jobs, research and clinical positions, and even financial services jobs are being shipped outside the U.S. borders. (Todd, 2006)

As a consequence, American workers were losing their jobs. During the 2004 election campaign, Senator John Kerry, the Democratic presidential candidate, invoked memories of Benedict Arnold who betrayed the American cause during the War of Independence. 'Benedict Arnold CEOs', said Kerry, were similarly betraying the American people by seeking to bolster their fortunes through outsourcing (*Business Week*, 2004). The Bush administration's pursuit of free trade agreements with other countries would, it was said, extend outsourcing by lowering remaining trade barriers. US jobs would be 'exported' to low-wage countries at an increasing rate. There was particular opposition to the Central American Free Trade Agreement (CAFTA) in 2005 which attracted the backing of just fifteen Democrats in the House of Representatives and the White House's proposed trade deal with Colombia in 2008. Indeed, the Democratic leadership in Congress refused to allow legislative consideration of the Colombia Free Trade Agreement.

- 'Outsourcing', a lack of competitiveness, the under-valuation of China's currency, and the failure of the US to pursue 'fair trade' rather than free trade policies contributed (at least in the eyes of the White House's critics) to an increasing balance of payments deficit. Although the deficit fell during the 2001 downturn, as consumer demand (and the country's thirst for imported goods) slumped, it then rose fairly steadily in subsequent years (see Table 5.5).
- The value of the dollar, against other major currencies, tumbled. It fell from just under 0.9 euro to 0.64 between 2003 and July 2008 (see Figure 5.4). This was caused, in part, by the balance of payments deficit which led to an outflow of dollars. However, this was compounded by other difficulties. There was uncertainty about the US's economic future and potential investors delayed or cancelled plans. Low US interest rates encouraged speculators to seek out assets denominated in other currencies. The relative strength of 'Euroland' countries such as France and Germany and increased demand for their products increased the attractiveness of the euro.
- The Bush administration has also been accused of offering lavish 'corporate welfare'. Those who make the charge not only cite the cuts on corporate

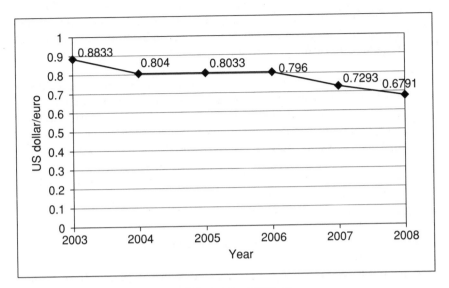

Figure 5.4 *US dollar to euro exchange rate, 2003–8*

Source: Measuringworth (2009), *Exchange Rates Between the United States Dollar and Forty-one Currencies*, <http://www.measuringworth.org>

taxes but also point to the White House's backing for agricultural subsidies. These, it is said, primarily favour corporate farming interests.[11]

• The US also faces entrenched, long-term difficulties that the Bush administration, according to its critics, has failed to acknowledge or address. Although the No Child Left Behind Act (2001) established standardised educational targets and testing in schools and while US school students are, on average, above the international average in terms of attainment in some studies, the largest ethnic and racial minorities lag behind whites. Furthermore, a 2003 survey put US school students behind the OECD average in terms of science literacy (National Center for Educational Statistics, 2008a). The survey also put American fifteen-year-olds behind their peers in twenty-three other OECD countries including France and Denmark, in combined mathematics literacy (involving an understanding of space and shape as well as change and relationships) (National Center for Educational Statistics, 2008b). Little has been done to reduce the country's dependency upon non-sustainable resources, most particularly oil and coal. Indeed, the vocal calls which were made in the wake of world crude oil price rises in 2008 to allow drilling in the Alaska wildlife refuge and along the Atlantic coast suggest that the commitment to oil has, if anything, become stronger. The events that followed Hurricane Katrina in New Orleans highlighted the unpreparedness of the federal government, its seeming indifference to the country's poorest citizens, and the extent to which the nation's infrastructure had decayed. *In These Times* writer, David Sirota, drew a connection between the administration's commitment to tax cuts and events in Louisiana:

> Year after year, the Bush administration insisted on massive tax cuts for the wealthy. And year after year, the White House refused to provide the funding government experts said was needed to strengthen levees, beef up hurricane preparedness and get federal emergency response ready for an onslaught from Mother Nature. America's budget surplus, built in the '90s to serve as a rainy day fund, was robbed to provide more and more giveaways to the rich. When the rainiest day of them all came, our country was left totally – and unnecessarily – vulnerable. (Sirota, 2005)

The mortgage market

The Bush years will probably be remembered, above all else, for the explosion of borrowing, growing indebtedness, and the economic consequences of this that became only too evident during his final year in office.

The background to these developments lay, at least in part, in the decline of manufacturing and the process of financialisation. Between 1980 and 2005, the contribution of manufacturing to GDP fell from just over 20 per cent to 12 per cent. At the same time, financial services increased from 15 per cent to over 20 per cent (Phillips, 2009: 31). As the financial sector expanded, all sorts of financial products proliferated, in particular *derivatives*, and levels of indebtedness grew.[12]

Alongside this, developments in Asia also played a part. A savings surplus in China (derived from household, corporate and government savings) as well as other Asian countries and the oil-producing states in the Gulf, made funds available for loan in the west and, in particular, the US. Alan Greenspan, chairman of the Federal Reserve, talked of a 'global savings glut' (Altman, 2009: 4). As the *Economist* reported in January 2009, between 2000 and 2008 the US attracted $5.7 trillion from abroad, which was equivalent to more than 40 per cent of its 2007 GDP (*Economist* 2009: 4).[13]

Foreign borrowing not only provided a basis for consumer loans.[14] It had also funded federal government budget deficits for several decades (through purchases of US Treasury bonds). This allowed the US to hold down interest rates despite high levels of borrowing which, in turn, spurred further lending and borrowing and fuelled consumer demand. The process of 'crowding out' that the economics textbooks had predicted as large-scale borrowing squeezed up interest rates and thereby constrained private sector investment, was averted. Thus, for much of the 1990s the Federal Reserve maintained low interest rates and did so again in the wake of the dot.com stock market crash and downturn at the beginning of the new century when the Federal Funds target rate was cut to 1 per cent.[15] Writing in the *New Republic* John Judis has spelt out the terms of the informal 'pact' between the US and the nations whose savings it absorbed:

> For decades, the United States has relied on a tortuous financial arrangement that knits together its economy with those of China and Japan. This informal system has allowed Asian countries to run huge export surpluses with the United States, while allowing the United States to run huge budget deficits without having to raise interest rates or taxes, and to run huge trade deficits without abruptly depreciating its currency. (Judis, 2008)

Against this background, funds (from both domestic and foreign sources) became available for loan in the US housing market and, because the cost of borrowing seemed relatively low, individuals who would not, in the past, have been considered for mortgages, were now regarded as potential customers.[16] Many loans were therefore directed towards the sub-prime and 'Alt-A' markets. In other words, mortgages and other types of credit were being offered to those whom loan companies had avoided in earlier years either because their incomes were too low and unpredictable or because they had a poor credit score.[17] Indeed, particular efforts were made to lure these individuals and families into the credit market. Low 'teaser rates' were charged for an initial period but customers then had to make much higher payments (and some commentators assert that this was hidden in the contractual small print). In an effort to extend the market still further and because sellers often worked on a commission basis, some of the mortgages – sometimes dubbed NINJA (No Income, No Job, (and) no Assets) loans – were offered to those whose applications were patently fraudulent. Through all of this, although some sub-prime mortgages had long been available, the number being offered expanded dramatically.

Other developments also contributed to the housing boom. Large-scale immigration, increases in household income amongst higher-income groupings as well as cheap and easy credit added to demand. In the wake of the dot.com boom, which had come to an end at the close of the 1990s, there was a feeling that property (and perhaps speculation on property) was a more secure prospect than share ownership. There was also a drive by both left and right to increase home ownership levels. Those on the left were conscious that racial and ethnic minorities were under-represented in the ranks of homeowners. The right sought to extend home ownership within lower-income groupings, arguing that this would bring them into the market order. Indeed, Grover Norquist, a highly influential conservative organiser, 'predicted that the ownership society would be Bush's greatest legacy, remembered "long after people can no longer pronounce or spell Fallujah"' (Klein, 2008).

Mortgage debt rose by $2.3 trillion between 2000 and 2003. New homes were constructed at a record rate. The buying of existing homes hit 6.1 million in 2003. This was more than half a million above the earlier record which had been set in 2002 (Baker, 2004). Against this background, house prices rose dramatically. As Roger C. Altman records: 'Whereas the average US home had appreciated at 1.4 per cent annually over the 30 years before 2000, the appreciation rate roared forward at 7.6 per cent annually from 2000 through mid-2006. From mid-2005 to mid-2006, amid rampant speculation in the housing market, it was 11 per cent' (Altman, 2009: 4).

Alongside the mortgage market, the growth of other forms of credit provision accelerated. As Dean Baker notes in a 2004 commentary published in *The Nation*: 'This borrowing has sustained consumption growth in an environment in which firms have been shedding jobs and cutting back hours, and real wage growth has fallen to zero' (Baker, 2004). Consumption exceeded income. Against this background, credit continued to expand and indebtedness grew. As the *New York Times* recorded:

> Through the years of the housing boom, many Americans came to treat their homes like automated teller machines that never required a deposit. They harvested cash through sales, second mortgages and home equity lines of credit – an artery of finance that reached $840 billion a year from 2004 to 2006...That allowed Americans to live far in excess of what they brought home from work. (Goodman, 2008)

'Shadow' banking

Within the shadow banking sector that provided much of the finance for the housing boom, many of the mortgages were, once sold, packaged together with other forms of loan and resold as securities (some of which known as collateralised loan obligations (CLOs) and collateralised debt obligations (CDOs)) that were then traded on the financial markets. Although divided into different tranches, portfolio-based financial instruments such as CDOs seemed largely risk-free. Those who purchased them were, furthermore, 'insured' for losses through derivatives such as credit default swaps.[18] As Charles Morris has recorded: 'Lulled by the presence of credit insurance, investors who might have been wary of the lowest rated CLOs and CDOs snapped them up for their extra yields. And why not? The mathematicians had banished risk' (Morris, 2008: 60–1).

The Securities and Exchange Commission (SEC), the federal government agency charged with regulating the financial industry, played only a limited role in monitoring developments. Risks were repeatedly underestimated. The Commission allowed the banks to use their own highly complex models in evaluating the degree of risk attached to their assets and permitted them to adopt looser capital requirements. As Helen Thomas and Miles Saltiel have concluded: 'This is why banks ended up operating at 20–30 times leverage, undoubtedly contributing to the boom in borrowing' (Thomas and Saltiel, 2009). In a celebrated phrase, Alan Greenspan attributed the crisis to the worldwide 'underpricing of risk' (Andrews, 2008).

Crisis

Developments gathered pace during the latter half of President Bush's second term.[19] Real wage growth continued to be very sluggish indeed. Indeed, real wages fell by 0.8 per cent in 2005 (Foster and Magdoff, 2009: 28). However, despite this, household spending increased still further. As John Bellamy Foster and Fred Magdoff noted in May 2006: 'Yet, rather than declining as a result, overall consumption has continued to climb. Indeed, US economic growth is ever more dependent on what appears at first glance to be unstoppable increases in consumption' (Foster and Magdoff, 2009: 28).

The gap between earnings and consumption continued to be filled by rising debt. By the end of 2005, $838 billion was owed in credit card debts (Foster and Magdoff, 2009: 34). Home-secured loans expanded still further and the sub-prime market was being extended to those who were, in credit terms, even riskier. Indeed, a sub-prime loan obtained in 2005 was twice as likely not to be repaid as one taken out in 2002: 'Subprime loans originated in 2002 have a one-in-ten lifetime chance of foreclosing. For loans originated in 2005 and 2006, the probability shoots up to one in five' (quoted in Elliott and Atkinson, 2008: 226). At the same time, lending to other sectors of the housing market also expanded. Indeed, there was a higher percentage increase in adjustable rate *prime* mortgages than in the sub-prime market. Significant numbers of people, amounting perhaps to a quarter of all purchases, engaged in speculative home buying (Woods, 2009: 23).

Many borrowers began to encounter difficulties. From late 2006, house prices fell. Whereas average housing values rose 53 per cent to 86 per cent between the mid-1990s and 2006 (depending on the index that is employed), they dropped by about 25 per cent during 2006–7. This made it more difficult for them to extend their mortgages or secure refinancing deals. A growing number of households found themselves in negative equity.

> Falling prices landed like a bomb. Homeowners fell behind on their loans and could not qualify for new ones: There was no value left in their house to borrow against. As millions of people defaulted, the banks confronted enormous losses in a bloody period of reckoning. (Goodman, 2008)

Some borrowers also faced problems when the initial 'teaser' interest rate expired. Many were vulnerable when the Federal Reserve increased the Federal Funds target rate. Others, apart from sub-prime borrowers, were hit. In April 2008, the proportion of 'Alt-A' mortgages in arrears quadrupled to 12 per cent from a year earlier. Furthermore, the problems were not confined to the sub-prime and 'Alt-A' markets. 'Delinquencies' among prime borrowers doubled to 2.7 per cent over the same period (Bajaj, 2008). At the same time, personal bankruptcies rose.[20]

Against this background, the number of people who defaulted increased and there were more foreclosures. In 2007, 405,000 households lost their home, a 51 per cent rise on the 2006 figure (Christie, 2008). In 2008, there was a further 81 per cent increase as foreclosures exceeded 3 million. One in 54 homes was repossessed (Armour, 2009). Many of the non-white families who had moved to the emerging suburbs in states such as Virginia earlier in the Bush era were disproportionately hit (Davis, 2009: 21–2).

By July 2008 house prices continued to fall and had lost about 17 per cent of their peak value, representing about 25 per cent in inflation-adjusted terms (Goodman, 2008). Roger C. Altman has described the process and the impact of the recession on other assets:

> Total home equity in the United States, which was valued at $13 trillion at its peak in 2006, had dropped to $8.8 trillion by mid-2008…Total retirement assets, Americans' second-largest household asset, dropped by 22 per cent, from $10.3 trillion in 2006 to $8 trillion in mid-2008. During the same period, savings and investment plans (apart from retirement savings) lost $1.2 trillion and pension assets lost $1.3 trillion. Taken together, these losses total a staggering $8.3 trillion. (Altman, 2009: 5)

Against this background, the financial sector began to feel the consequences. As Elliott and Atkinson note: 'insolvent borrowers meant insolvent lenders' (Elliott and Atkinson, 2008: 243). First, mortgage companies collapsed. One of the biggest of these, New Century Financial, filed for bankruptcy in April 2007. In 2008, Countrywide, which had sold a large number of sub-prime mortgages, hit difficulties and was bought by Bank of America. Washington Mutual was taken over.

In March 2008, the US Federal Reserve had to organise an emergency bailout for Bear Stearns, the US's fifth biggest investment bank. It was taken over by the Federal Deposit Insurance Corporation and eventually sold to J.P. Morgan Chase. Four months later, IndyMac Bank, the largest mortgage provider in the Los Angeles region and the seventh largest in the US, collapsed. It also became clear that Fannie Mae (the Federal National Mortgage Association) and Freddie Mac (the Federal Home Loan Mortgage Corporation), which were created on the basis of federal government sponsorship in 1938 and 1978 respectively to encourage home ownership, and which owned or guaranteed nearly half of the US's $12 trillion home loan market, were in trouble (Benner, 2008). Despite unease among many free market conservatives, Treasury Secretary Henry Paulson and President Bush moved to organise a prop-up. This placed $5 trillion worth of mortgages ($1 trillion of which were sub-prime) on the federal government's books and required $200 billion to guarantee Fannie Mae and Freddie Mac's debts (Flynn, 2009). Merrill Lynch and Wachovia were bought by Bank of America and Wells Fargo respectively. In September, Lehman Brothers collapsed. No buyer could be found and there was no bailout. The collapse added to a sense of panic. There was a feeling that everybody and everything was vulnerable. As Alistair Darling, Britain's chancellor of the exchequer, said later in an interview: 'What I don't think they realised was that when Lehman went down, people looked round the world and thought: well if Lehman can go down, and it's one of the world's biggest investment banks, then what else can go down' (Alistair Darling, quoted in Oakeshott, 2009). The American International Group (AIG), which had sold credit default swaps, faced difficulties because the securities from which they were derived had lost much of their earlier value. The AIG therefore had to be given an $85 billion credit facility by the Federal Reserve.[21] By late 2008, as the presidential election approached, there were fears for the future of the entire financial sector.

Against this background, the Emergency Economic Stabilization Act of 2008 was passed by Congress at the prompting of the Bush administration and the Troubled Asset Relief Program (TARP) was established. This allowed the US Treasury to buy up or guarantee collateralised debt obligations (CDOs) which had, by then, been dubbed 'toxic assets' because they had lost so much of their former value. TARP also permitted capital injections into banks.[22] In total, $700 billion was made available.[23] Some expressed surprise that a Republican administration was ready to follow such an interventionist course. However, President Bush is said to have put the matter in stark terms: 'If we don't loosen up some money into the system this sucker could go down' (quoted in Mason, 2009: 28).

Wider consequences

The wider consequences of developments in the housing market and the financial sector had been felt well before TARP was enacted. Anxieties among banks triggered the 'credit crunch'. Banks were increasingly unwilling to lend to each other or would only do so if they could secure a relatively high rate of interest. The risks had become too great. As Roger C. Altman records:

> Starting in late 2007, institutions became so concerned about the creditworthiness of borrowers, including one another, that they would no longer lend. This was evidenced by the spread between three-month US Treasury bills and the three-month LIBOR borrowing rate, the benchmark for interbank lending, which quadrupled within a month of the collapse of the investment bank Lehman Brothers in September 2008. (Altman, 2009: 7)

Against this background, both personal consumption and corporate investment plans were inevitably placed in jeopardy. The construction industry contracted as the demand for new homes fell. Because of this and developments in the financial sector, the crisis spread outwards to affect other sectors of the economy.

In mid-2008, the growth figures for the last three months of 2007 (which had been recorded as 0.6 per cent) were revised downwards to minus 0.2 per cent (Stelzer, 2008). There was growing talk of a recession both in the US and across the globe. The crisis intensified as 2008 progressed. Share prices fell steadily as investors lost confidence. During 2008, the Standard and Poor's 500 index lost over 38 per cent of its value. The Dow Jones Industrial Average (DJIA), which had reached an all-time high in October 2007, lost about 30 per cent. There was, as Figure 5.5 shows, a particularly significant slide in the DJIA during September and October.

This directly affected many households. Mutual funds, 401(k) savings plans and pension funds lost much of their former value. As a consequence, and because some began to save again, spending levels dropped.

The contraction of economic activity inevitably had consequences for the labour market. Unemployment began to rise from early 2007 and the rate of increase accelerated at the beginning of 2008 (see Table 5.6).

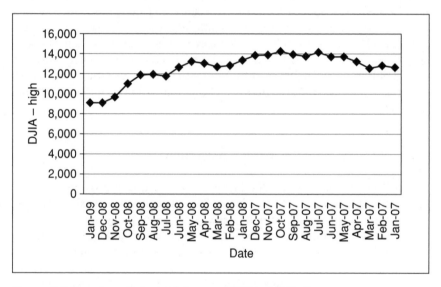

Figure 5.5 *Dow Jones Industrial Average (DJIA), 2007–9*
Source: Yahoo Finance (2009), *Dow Jones Industrial Average*, <http://finance.yahoo.com/>

Table 5.6 *Unemployment rate, 2007–8 (%)*

Year	Jan	Feb	Mar	Apr	May	Jun	Jul	Aug	Sep	Oct	Nov	Dec
2007	4.6	4.5	4.4	4.5	4.5	4.6	4.7	4.7	4.7	4.8	4.7	4.9
2008	4.9	4.8	5.1	5.0	5.5	5.6	5.8	6.2	6.2	6.6	6.8	7.2

Source: Bureau of Labor Statistics (2009), *Labor Force Statistics from the Current Population Survey – Unemployment Rate*, <http://data.bls.gov>

Alongside these developments, there was a growing awareness that the restabilisation of the financial sector through TARP and subsequent initiatives were not, in themselves, enough to lay the basis for economic recovery. And, as the depth of the crisis became evident, it was becoming clear that monetary policy was a necessary but not sufficient condition for the restoration of economic confidence. As Table 5.7 shows, the Federal Reserve repeatedly reduced the Federal Funds target rate as 2008 progressed. Indeed, by December 2008, the Federal Reserve had reduced the rate to almost zero.

Against this background, commentators recalled Keynes's claim that if business confidence was at rock bottom, minimal interest rates were likely to be an insufficient economic stimulant. The assertion that a loose monetary policy would, in such circumstances, be like 'pushing on a piece of string' was often heard. Increasingly, therefore, policymakers including many conservatives who would in other circumstances have eschewed increases in government spending turned to fiscal policy.

Despite partisan tensions between the White House and Congress and between Democrats and Republicans within Congress, they agreed upon a fiscal stimulus package at the beginning of 2008. It offered tax rebates to individuals and tax concessions for businesses. Most individual taxpayers gained $600 and married taxpayers filing joint returns were given $1,200. The rebates were limited to those earning under $75,000 (individuals) and $150,000 (couples). There was also a $300 per child tax credit (CNNPolitics.com, 2008). The total cost of the package was estimated at $152 billion for 2008. For his part, President Bush spoke of his belief that the stimulus would ensure recovery:

> In the past seven years, the system has absorbed shocks: recession, corporate scandals, terror attacks, global war; yet the genius of our system is that it can absorb such shocks and emerge even stronger…In a dynamic market economy, our economy will prosper and it will continue to be the marvel of the world. (CNNPolitics.com, 2008)

Table 5.7 *Federal Funds target rate, 2008 (%)*

Date (2008)	Federal Funds rate (%)
December 16	0.00–0.25
October 29	1
October 08	1.5
April 30	2
March 18	2.25
January 30	3
January 22	3.5

Source: Federal Reserve Bank of New York (2009), *Historical Changes of the Target Federal Funds and Discount Rates*, <http://www.newyorkfed.org/>

This was over-optimistic. By the end of the year, the scale of the crisis, both within the US and worldwide, had become only too evident.[24] However, the relatively long two-and-a-half month transition period between the election of a new president and his inauguration (during which the incumbent president continues to serve but is widely regarded as a 'lame duck') delayed further federal government initiatives.[25]

Conclusion

President Bush ended his presidency with rock-bottom approval ratings. Although perceptions of events in Iraq and the difficulties that are almost always a feature of presidential second terms played a part, economic uncertainties were also pivotal. Nonetheless, the Bush presidency has shaped the agenda for his successors. The 2008 Republican candidate, Senator John McCain, had originally opposed the tax cuts of 2001 and 2003 but subsequently accepted them. The Democratic contender, Senator Barack Obama, spoke out against trade liberalisation and the North American Free Trade Agreement (NAFTA) during the primary season but the evidence suggested that this would not last. Few expect President Bush's tax cuts to be entirely reversed by Congress when they expire. Furthermore, although the 2009 fiscal stimulus did not attract a single Republican vote in the House of Representatives, the Bush administration had already set the stage for extensive government interventionism through its own rescue packages. George W. Bush may therefore have made much more of a mark on economic policymaking than his many critics would wish to concede.

Notes

1   The Dow Jones Industrial Average, which records the value of stocks in some of the largest older companies, began to dip from the middle of January 2000, a year before George W. Bush took office.
2   For those who are critical of the Bush record, the relative shallowness of the recession and the subsequent recovery can in large part be attributed to the buying of US Treasury bonds by overseas sources. These funded the federal government budget deficit, permitted tax cuts in 2001 and 2003, and allowed the Federal Reserve to lower interest rates (see pp. 00–00). John Judis has pointed to the way in which the seeds of the later crisis were sown during Bush's first term of office: 'The economy barely recovered over the next four years. Businesses, still worried about overcapacity, remained reluctant to invest. Instead, they paid down debt, purchased their own stock, and held cash. Banks and other financial institutions, wary of the stock market since the dot-com bubble burst, invested in mortgage-backed securities and other derivatives' (Judis, 2008).

3   The 'marriage tax penalty' was imposed when married couples paid more in taxation than an unmarried couple or singles. Because the tax system is progressive, couples were more likely to reach the higher tax thresholds that required the payment of higher taxation rates.

4   'Dumping' is the selling of a product at below cost-price. NAFTA's provisions ensured that Canada and Mexico were exempted from the tariff. Some developing countries were also excluded.

5   All of this was underpinned by a further concern. Because of the trade deficit, China holds many of the US Treasury bonds that fund the federal government budget deficit, other dollar denominated assets, together with dollars in their foreign exchange reserves (see Chapter 7).

6   Under Article I of the US Constitution, the president has the power to veto legislation. A veto can only be overridden if there is a two-thirds majority so to do in both chambers of Congress. Before May 2007 the only legislation that President Bush vetoed concerned federal funding for embryonic stem cell research.

7   According to Paul O'Neill, who served as President Bush's Treasury secretary between the beginning of 2001 and the end of 2002, he was told by Vice-President Dick Cheney that 'deficits don't matter (Stelzer, 2005).

8   Joseph Stiglitz, chairman of President Clinton's Council of Economic Advisors and winner of the Nobel Prize for Economics in 2001, put forward a sweeping indictment of the Bush administration's record at the end of 2007. His comments are representative of opinion on much of the left. The Bush administration had bequeathed: 'a tax code that has become hideously biased in favor of the rich; a national debt that will probably have grown 70 per cent by the time this president leaves Washington; a swelling cascade of mortgage defaults; a record near-$850 billion trade deficit; oil prices that are higher than they have ever been; and a dollar so weak that for an American to buy a cup of coffee in London or Paris – or even the Yukon – becomes a venture in high finance' (Stiglitz, 2007).

9   Twenty-eight House and twelve Senate Democrats joined Republicans in supporting the tax cuts (Stevenson, 2001). Senator John McCain, the Republicans' 2008 presidential nominee, was one of those opposing the 2001 and 2003 tax cuts on their final passage.

10 However, many states have legal minimum wages that are set at a higher level. At the beginning of 2009, the minimum wage in both California and Massachusetts was $8.00 an hour (US Department of Labor – Wage and Hour Division (WHD), 2009).

11 It should be noted that Congressional Democrats as well as Republicans have also backed the system of extensive agricultural subsidies. (See, for example, Herszenhorn, 2008.)

12 Derivatives are financial instruments or products that are based on, or *derived* from, some other asset (the underlying).

13 As a corollary to the increase in borrowing, Americans more or less stopped saving. The US savings rate fell from about 10 per cent of disposable income in the 1970s to 1 per cent after 2005 (*Economist*, 2009: 4).

14 The inflow of funds from overseas sources also prevented further slides in the dollar's exchange rate as a consequence of the US's balance of payments deficit.

15 The Federal Funds target rate is set by the Federal Open Market Committee. It is
    the interest rate at which banks can borrow on an overnight basis and is the
    foundation for other interest rates. Changes affect the money supply.
16 Conservative commentators stress the extent to which financial institutions were
    placed under political pressures to lend to minorities and low-income earners so
    that home ownership was extended.
17 The 'Alt-A' market lies between the 'prime' and 'sub-prime' markets.
18 'Credit default swaps' cover the buyer against the possibility that an asset-based
    security or other derivative, including a CDO, might default.
19 There are very different narratives of the crisis. There are competing accounts of
    its severity and causes as well as the policies that should be adopted.
20 In April 2005, a bill was passed making the process of clearing debts by filing for
    bankruptcy more difficult (Sahadi, 2005).
21 Credit default swaps (CDS) are another type of security that is traded. They offer
    a form of 'insurance' if there is a default on a bond. When the crisis took hold,
    and mortgage defaults became commonplace, AIG was faced by CDS payment
    claims. AIG's credit rating was therefore downgraded and the company could not
    raise sufficient capital to cover its anticipated losses.
22 The Troubled Asset Relief Program (or 'bailout' as it was commonly dubbed) was
    initially rejected by the House of Representatives. It was passed, albeit in a revised
    form with about $100bn in new tax breaks added, some days later.
23 Some of funds from the bailout were repaid by the banks. The *New York Times*
    reported in August 2009 that the US taxpayer had made about $4 billion in profit
    from eight of the biggest banks that had repaid the obligations in full (Kouwe,
    2009).
24 In December 2008, President Bush announced that he had approved a bailout plan
    for General Motors (GM) and Chrysler to prevent the companies going bankrupt.
    The Obama administration took further steps during 2009. See pp. 00–00.
25 There is also a two-month period between the election of a new Congress and
    the beginning of a new legislative session. The 111th Congress only began on
    January 3, 2009.

References and further reading

Altman, Daniel (2004), *Neoeconomy: George W. Bush's Revolutionary Gamble with
    America's Future*, New York: Public Affairs.
Altman, Roger C. (2009), 'The Great Crash, 2008', *Foreign Affairs*, 88: 1, January/
    February, 2–14.
Andrews, Edmund L. (2006), 'Democrats link fortunes to rise in minimum wage', *New
    York Times*, July 13, <http://www.nytimes.com>
Andrews, Edmund L. (2008), 'Greenspan concedes error on regulation', *New York Times*,
    October 23, <http://www.nytimes.com>
Armour, Stephanie (2009), '2008 foreclosure filings set record', *USA Today*, March 2,
    <http://www.usatoday.com>
Bajaj, Vikas (2008), 'Housing lenders fear bigger wave of loan defaults', *New York Times*,
    August 4, <http://www.nytimes.com>

Baker, Dean (2004), 'Bush's house of cards', *The Nation*, August 9, <http://www.thenation.com/>

Baker, Dean (2008), 'Why would presidents envy bad growth?', *The American Prospect – Beat the Press*, January 27, <http://www.prospect.org>

Bartlett, Bruce (2005), 'Feed the beast', *New York Times*, April 6, <http://www.nytimes.com>

Benner, Katie (2008), *The $5 Trillion Mess*, CNNMoney.com, July 14, <http://money.cnn.com>

Bienkowski, Wojciech (2006), 'The economic policy of George W. Bush: a continuation of Reaganomics?', in Wojciech Bienkowski, Josef C. Brada and Mariusz-Jan Radlo (2006), *Reaganomics Goes Global: What Can the EU, Russia and Transition Countries Learn from the USA?*, Basingstoke: Palgrave Macmillan, 69–79.

Bureau of Labor Statistics (2008), *Labor Force Statistics from the Current Population Survey – Unemployment Rate*, <http://www.bls-gov/data/>

Business Week (2004), 'Kerry's "Benedict Arnold" Investments', *Business Week*, April 22, <http://www.businessweek.com>

Christie, Les (2008), *Foreclosures Up 75 per cent in 2007*, CNNMoney.com, January 29, <http://money.cnn.com>

CNNPolitics.com (2008), *Bush Signs Stimulus Bill; Rebate Checks Expected in May*, <http://edition.cnn.com>

Davis, Mike (2009), 'Obama at Manassas', *New Left Review*, 56, March/April, 5–40.

Economist (2009), 'A special report on the future of finance', January 25, 1–21.

Elliott, Larry and Dan Atkinson (2008), *The Gods that Failed: How Blind Faith in Markets Has Cost Us our Future*, London: The Bodley Head.

Federal Reserve Bank of New York (2008), *Historical Changes of the Target Federal Funds and Discount Rates*, <http://www.newyorkfed.org>

Flynn, Michael (2008), 'The roots of the crisis: how did Wall Street get into this mess?', *Reason*, October 1, <http://www.reason.com>

Flynn, Michael (2009), 'Anatomy of a breakdown', *Reason*, January, <http://www.reason.com>

Foster, John Bellamy and Fred Magdoff (2009), *The Great Financial Crisis: Causes and Consequences*, New York: Monthly Review Press.

Goodman, Peter (2008), 'Uncomfortable answers to questions on the economy', *New York Times*, July 19, <http://www.nytimes.com>

Gordon, Robert (2008), 'Did liberals cause the sub-prime crisis?', *The American Prospect*, April 7, <http://www.prospect.org>

GPO Access (2008), *Budget of the United States Government: Historical Tables Fiscal Year 2009*, <http://www.gpoaccess.gov>

Herszenhorn, David M. (2008), 'Farm income up, but subsidies stay', *New York Times*, April 24, <http://www.nytimes.com>

Judis, John B. (2008), 'Debt man walking', *New Republic*, December 3, <http://www.tnr.com>

Klein, Naomi (2008), 'Disowned by the ownership society', *The Nation*, January 31, <http://www.thenation.com>

Kouwe, Zachery (2009), 'As banks repay bailout money, US sees profit', *New York Times*, August 31, A1 and A11.

Mason, Paul (2009), *Meltdown: The End of the Age of Greed*, London: Verso.

Mishel, Lawrence, Jared Bernstein and Heidi Shierholz (2009), *The State of Working America 2008 – 2009*, Economic Policy Institute, Ithaca, NY: Cornell University Press.

Morris, Charles R. (2008), *The Two Trillion Dollar Meltdown: Easy Money, High Rollers, and the Great Credit Crash*, New York: Public Affairs.

Morrison, Wayne M. (2006), *China-U.S. Trade Issues*, CRS Issue Brief for Congress, http://fpc.state.gov/documents/organization/67147.pdf

Murdock, Deroy (2007), 'Tax-happy Dems jeopardize U.S. economy', *National Review Online*, September 21, <http://www.nationalreview.com>

National Center for Educational Statistics (2008a), *Program for International Student Assessment, 2003: Figure 9: Average Reading Literacy and Science Literacy Scores of 15 Year-Old Students in the OECD Countries and the United States*, <http://nces.ed.gov>

National Center for Educational Statistics (2008b), *International Comparisons in Science and Math*, <http://nces.ed.gov>

Oakeshott, Isabel (2009), 'Admit it: I was right', *Sunday Times* (News Review), August 16, 5.

OMB Watch (2006), *Income Inequality Has Intensified Under Bush*, OMB Watch, March 21, <http://www.ombwatch.org>

PBS (2001), *Feeling the Tax Cut*, PBS Online NewsHour, May 28, <http://www.pbs.org>

Phillips, Kevin (2009), *Bad Money: Reckless Finance, Failed Politics and the Global Crisis of American Capitalism*, Harmondsworth: Penguin.

Rove, Karl (2006), 'The Bush economy', *Real Clear Politics*, May 16, <http://www.realclearpolitics.com>

Sahadi, Jeanne (2005), *President Signs Bankruptcy Bill: What You Should Know About a New Law that Will Make It Tougher for Consumers to Clear their Debts*, CNNMoney.com, April 20, <http://money.cnn.com>

Sirota, David (2005), 'Hurricanes rain on Bush's tax cut parade', *In These Times*, September 27, <http://www.inthesetimes.com>

Stelzer, Irwin M. (2005), 'Do deficits matter? It depends on where you sit – and on which type of deficit you're talking about', *Weekly Standard*, February 15, <http://www.weeklystandard.com>

Stelzer, Irwin M. (2008), 'Don't make a recession out of a downturn', *Sunday Times*, Business, August 3, 4.

Stevenson, Richard W. (2001), 'Congress passes tax cut, with rebates this summer', *New York Times*, May 27, <http://www.nytimes.com>

Stiglitz, Joseph (2007), 'The economic consequences of Mr. Bush', *Vanity Fair*, December, <http://www.vanityfair.com>

Stolberg, Sheryl Gay (2008), 'Echo of first Bush: good economy turns sour', *New York Times*, January 28, <http://www.nytimes.com>

Tamny, John (2008), *Economic Policy and the Bush Era*, Forbes.com, December 15, <http://www.forbes.com>

Thomas, Helen and Miles Saltiel (2009), *What Really Happened? Understanding the Credit Crunch*, February, Policy Exchange research note, http://www.policyexchange.org.uk/images/publications/pdfs/What_Really_Happened.pdf

Todd, Lee T. Jr (2006), 'Domestic Inshoring: Creating the New American Economy', *EDUCAUSE Review*, 41: 1, January/February, 10–11, <http://connect.educause.edu>

USA Today (2003), 'It's official: 2001 recession only lasted eight months', July 17, <http://www.usatoday.com>

US Department of Labor – Wage and Hour Division (WHD) (2009), *Minimum Wage Laws in the States – January 1, 2009*, <http://www.dol.gov>

Wallace, Kelly (2001), '$1.35 trillion tax cut becomes law', *CNN Inside Politics*, June 7, <http://edition.cnn.com>

Wilson, Graham (2009), 'President Bush and the economy', in Andrew Wroe and Jon Herbert (2009), *Assessing the Bush Presidency: A Tale of Two Terms*, Edinburgh: Edinburgh University Press, 149–65.

Wolf, Richard (2008), 'Record deficit expected in 2009', *USA Today*, July 28, <http://www.usatoday.com>

Woods, Thomas E. (2009), *Meltdown: A Free-Market Look at Why the Stock Market Collapsed, the Economy Tanked, and Government Bailouts Will Make Things Worse*, Washington, DC: Regnery Publishing.

6

Foreign trade

This chapter considers trade policy. It looks at the imposition of trade barriers, such as the Smoot-Hawley Tariff Act of 1930 and post-war efforts to promote trade liberalisation, most notably the North American Free Trade Agreement (NAFTA). Within this context, the chapter surveys and assesses the arguments that have been put forward both for and against unrestricted trade.

For much of the twentieth century, foreign trade contributed relatively little to US GDP. Indeed, the country was largely self-sufficient. From the 1970s onwards, exports and imports began to increase in economic importance. As a consequence, trade issues played much more of a part in shaping political discourse. Figures such as Patrick J. Buchanan and Ross Perot sought votes on the basis of calls to protect American jobs by restricting the flow of imports.

Why did foreign trade make more of a contribution to GDP? Studies suggest that (at least in the years between 1980 and 2006) much of the growth in trade was because of the opportunities offered by the overall expansion of the world economy and the demand that this created for goods, products or components from other countries. The process of liberalisation (the lowering of trade barriers) was also important and falling transportation costs made a small contribution (Adler and Hufbauer, 2009).

Nonetheless, although foreign trade grew as a proportion of GDP after 1970, there is still a striking contrast between the US trade record and that of many European countries. Even in 2005, despite all the talk of 'globalisation', foreign trade constituted just 13.4 per cent of US GDP. In contrast, almost half (46.2 per cent) of Denmark's output was traded. The figure for the United Kingdom was well over a quarter. When considering the role of foreign trade in the different OECD countries, only Japan matches the US in terms of self-sufficiency (see Table 6.1).[1]

Table 6.1 *Selected countries – share of trade in GDP, 1970–2000*

Year	Denmark	Germany	United Kingdom	United States	EU15 average	Japan
1970	29.9	17.2	21.9	5.6		10.2
1975	31	19.4	26.2	8	32.3	12.8
1980	34	22.7	26	10.4	36.3	14.2
1985	37.6	25.9	28.3	8.6	40.2	12.7
1990	34.9	24.8	25.3	10.3	37.4	10
1995	35.6	23.7	28.6	11.7	39.9	8.5
2000	43.6	33.2	29.1	13.2	50.8	10.3
2001	44	33.8	28.7	12.1	50.2	10.3
2002	44.4	33.4	27.8	11.7	47.9	10.7
2003	42	33.7	27	11.8	46.2	11.2
2004	42.8	35.7	26.9	12.7	48.4	12.4
2005	46.2	38.1	28.3	13.4	50.7	13.6

Notes: These figures show the average of both exports and imports as a percentage share of GDP.
EU15 refers to the fifteen countries that constituted the European Union until expansion in 2004.
Source: adapted from Swivel.com (2007), *Share of Trade in GDP* (from OECD),
<http://www.swivel.com>

Why has foreign trade been so much less important for the US than the countries of Europe? In part, the answer lies in the relative size of the different national economies. The US and Japan are large, developed nations and therefore produce many of the goods themselves that are required for their domestic markets. Smaller countries (defined in terms of either geographic size or population), particularly if adjoined by neighbours that are open to commerce, have always been much more engaged in trading relationships. The high transportation costs of importing and exporting to the countries of Europe and Asia also deterred trade. Furthermore, both the US and Japan are advanced economies and, as such, have significant service sectors. Services are much less 'tradeable' than goods.

Government policies have also played a role. The Japanese government has done much to encourage exports (although it accepted restraints imposed upon it by other nations) while at the same time reputedly doing little to address the formal and informal barriers facing foreign companies seeking to secure a foothold within Japanese markets. For its part, the US federal government traditionally pursued a policy of imposing tariffs on imports so as to shelter US commerce and production.[2] Alexander Hamilton, one of the 'founding fathers' of the US and the first secretary of the Treasury, wrote a *Report on Manufactures* in 1791 advocating the imposition of moderate tariffs so as to protect, and subsidies to bolster, domestic producers – although he tied tariffs to notions of reciprocity with other nations. Some taxes on imports would, Hamilton asserted, encourage the growth of industry and thereby strengthen national security. Tariffs would 'tend to render the United States, independent on foreign nations for military and other essential supplies' (Hamilton, orig. 1791).

Over the coming half-century, such a policy added to the tensions between the northern states, some of which were becoming industrialised and therefore sought continuing protection, and the south, which was much more dependent upon agricultural exports and believed that its interests were more fully served by free trade. These sectional differences culminated in the Civil War (or 'war between the states' as it is still sometimes called by southerners) in the years between 1861 and 1865.

The emergence of the Republican Party and its dominance within the federal political process until just before the First World War strengthened the hand of those committed to tariffs. President Abraham Lincoln vigorously opposed free trade and a 44 per cent tariff was adopted during the Civil War. It was only after the Democrats captured both the White House and Congress that the 1913 Underwood-Simmons Tariff Act, which lowered trade barriers, was passed.

The post-war return of the Republicans led to a reversal of policy. The 1921 Emergency Tariff Act and the 1922 Fordney-McCumber Tariff Act imposed ad valorem (or proportionate) tariffs of between 60 and 100 per cent. In 1930, in the wake of the Wall Street Crash, the Smoot-Hawley Tariff Act was passed. This raised tariffs to 60 per cent on more than 3,200 products and materials imported into the US. Some earlier tariff rates were quadrupled.

In the years that followed, few historians have been generous to Smoot-Hawley. In their eyes, the measure invited retaliation by other countries, contributed to a contraction in world trade, and intensified the economic depression of the 1930s. As Douglas Irwin has noted:

> The U.S. imposed the protectionist Smoot-Hawley tariff in 1930. Two years later, Britain abandoned its traditional free trade policy by imposing a General Tariff and signing the Ottawa agreements with its former colonies, creating a preferential trading bloc that discriminated against nonmembers. Germany strong-armed countries in southeastern Europe into special bilateral trading arrangements with the Reich. Japan created the Greater East Asian Co-Prosperity Sphere to siphon off Asian trade for its own benefit. Although the world economy recovered slowly from the depression, the spread of high tariffs, import quotas, discriminatory practices and foreign exchange restrictions meant that world trade remained stagnant and compartmentalized throughout the 1930s. (Irwin, 2007)[3]

At the end of the Second World War, politicians or economists sought to ensure that there would be no return to the conditions of the 1930s and therefore committed themselves to the mutual lowering of tariffs and the provision of a stable exchange rate regime that would facilitate international trade. These sentiments laid the basis for Bretton Woods (1944) and the General Agreement on Tariffs and Trade (GATT).

The Bretton Woods conference in July 1944 established the International Monetary Fund (IMF) and created a fixed exchange rate system within which the US dollar was pegged to gold (at $35 an ounce). Other currencies were, in turn, pegged to the dollar. Although the western European currencies did not become entirely convertible for some years, the system established at Bretton Woods lasted until the economic and currency upheavals of the early 1970s.

GATT sought to reduce tariffs, quotas and subsidies. There were eight 'rounds' of talks held under the auspices of GATT between its founding in 1947–8 and the creation of the World Trade Organisation (WTO) during the Uruguay Round (1986–94), each of which slowly weakened the many barriers to trade. The average tariff imposed by the US was reduced by almost 92 per cent between GATT's founding and the Tokyo Round of 1973–9. Irwin records the cumulative impact of the GATT rounds:

> Initially, the tariff reductions...had a limited impact on international trade because wartime exchange controls and quantitative restrictions remained in place. However, as these controls were phased out during the 1950s, the lower tariffs allowed world trade to grow rapidly. The expansion of world trade promoted the rapid economic recovery of Europe and Japan. In turn, the spread of economic growth allowed democracy to become firmly established in a way that had failed dismally during the interwar period. (Irwin, 2007)

Non-tariff barriers (NTBs)

The expansion of world trade was tied to a shift in the character of trade away from raw materials and towards finished goods and then towards the provision of services. Against this background, trade policy debates were increasingly structured around non-tariff barriers to trade (NTBs) rather than tariffs. These include subsidies to domestic producers (those in farming are often cited) to provide them with a competitive advantage over foreign suppliers. Trading relationships can also be held back if a country fails to offer the full protection of intellectual property rights. Licensing requirements can often discriminate against imports. An artificially high exchange rate can raise the price of imported goods to uncompetitive levels.

The labour unions, anti-poverty organisations and the environmental lobby have also had an impact on trade negotiations. Negotiators have, at least to some extent, acknowledged the social consequences of the trading process. They consider the conditions under which people work, the environmental implications of the production process, and the impact of trade on world poverty and developing countries.

The case for free trade

> the case for free trade is as compelling as ever. Protectionism cheats consumers out of money that they could save by purchasing inexpensive imports. (A Nixon

Administration task force once estimated that quotas on oil imports alone cost the U.S. consumer $5 billion a year.) Limiting imports also restricts the consumer's freedom of choice...By shielding inefficient industries from the kind of competition that forces them to improve, protectionism works against the best use of a nation's resources. Beyond all that, protectionism, modern as it may seem in its new guise, is incompatible with the deeper reality of a world in which nations have an increasing need to get along with each other economically as well as politically. (*Time*, 1971)

From about 1970 onwards, the major parties shifted their positions. Increasingly, most Democrats emphasised what they regarded as the threat posed by free trade to the interests of workers and 'Main Street' America. Unrestricted imports, they argued, jeopardised American jobs and threatened smaller companies. For their part, nearly all Republicans talked of the export opportunities and the prospects for economic growth offered by free trade.

Nonetheless, although each of the parties is to some extent defined by its position on trade, there have been some who have broken with party positions. The 'new' Democrats around the Democratic Leadership Council, which was formed in 1985 and served as an ideological springboard for Bill Clinton's presidential bid in 1992, distanced themselves from established party positions and embraced calls for free trade. Within the Republican Party, those with ties to the US textile industry and some 'paleoconservatives' who talked in terms of 'America First', most notably the hardline commentator Patrick Buchanan, sought limits and restraints on trade.

Those in either of the parties who called themselves 'pro-trade' pointed to the opportunities offered by trading relationships.[4] In a free trade regime, they said, consumers would be offered a greater choice of products. Businesses operating across countries or continents would gain economies of scale so that their unit costs would be reduced.[5] There would be greater competition as producers would have to face foreign as well as domestic rivals. Competition, they insisted, invariably led to lower prices and increased quality. This, in turn, laid a basis for productivity gains as companies would seek to outstrip their competitors through greater efficiency. Faced by competitive pressures, free trade advocates noted, businesses quickly 'learn' from the experience of others. Both US and European automobile manufacturers sought to emulate Japanese business practices during the 1980s. For example, *Kaizen* groups based around the principle of small-scale continuous improvement through collective participation were established within companies. Although jobs in some, less competitive, sectors will inevitably be lost and there may be transitional unemployment (perhaps on a large scale), the gains from trade more than compensate for this. This, it is said, is particularly evident in some of the Latin American countries: 'Argentina lost much of its automobile industry while seeing an expansion in more sophisticated chemicals and capital- and labor-intensive manufactures' (World Bank, 2005: 149).

The arguments for free trade go, however beyond this. According to the canons of economic theory, trade allows countries to make gains by specialising in delivering the goods and services that different factor endowments (the availability of land, labour, capital and entrepreneurship) allow them to produce most efficiently. Nearly all those who advocate trade liberalisation cite the principles of *absolute* and *comparative advantage*. The principle of *absolute advantage*, which is associated with the work of Adam Smith, rests upon the factor endowments in different countries. Nations, he argued, have an interest in producing the goods or delivering the services that they can produce or deliver more efficiently than other nations. In other words, absolute advantage is:

> An advantage that a country has in producing certain goods or services relative to all or many other countries due to specific factors of production at its disposal – such as rich farmland and a favorable climate for agricultural production or a highly educated labor force for high-tech manufacturing. A country's absolute advantage means that it can produce certain goods or services at a lower cost than would be possible for other countries. Thus it is clearly beneficial for this country to specialize in producing and exporting these goods and services. (World Bank Group, 2004)

The concept of *comparative advantage* is associated with the name of David Ricardo. Writing in 1817 (*On the Principles of Political Economy and Taxation*), he built on the claim, embodied in the notion of absolute advantage, that countries gain by trading the products that they produce more efficiently than another country. Ricardo argued that, subject to certain assumptions, even countries which produce all goods and services less efficiently than other nations can gain from specialisation and trade. In the short term, the advocates of free trade concede that workers in less efficient industries may well lose their jobs. However:

> they also believe that the economy will change structurally in the long term to provide new jobs, because, after all, the economic pie has gotten larger as a result of specialization. Predicting what these may be, however, is difficult, and it may still be the case that those who have lost their jobs will have to upgrade or change their skills to work in these new jobs. (Global Trade Negotiations Home Page, 2004)

From this perspective, protectionism prevents the logic and dynamic of comparative advantage from working itself out. It 'cushions' inefficient industries and impedes a process of specialisation in those sectors that a country can produce or deliver most efficiently: 'The economic case *against* protectionism is that it distorts incentives: each country produces goods in which it has a comparative disadvantage, and consumes too little of imported goods' (Krugman, 2009).

Theoretical propositions such as these are backed by empirical claims. The office of the United States Trade Representative (USTR), the trade negotiating arm of the administration, points to what it regards as the overall gains from trade. It has claimed that annual incomes in the US are $1 trillion higher (representing $9,000 per household) because of increased trade liberalisation since 1945 (Bivens, 2007). Globalisation, global competition and the reduction of trade barriers across the world (as well as parallel developments) allow US consumers to purchase consumer durables and other products at prices that are cheaper, often in absolute terms, than those charged just a few years earlier:

> It's hard to think of much that didn't go down in price over the past few decades
> – cars, electronics, consumer goods of all kinds, services like banking and tele-
> communications – as the global movement of goods, labor and capital played
> out around the world, enriching developed countries and emerging markets
> alike. In fact, between 2003 and 2007, world GDP grew 5 per cent per year –
> faster than it ever has – even as inflation remained under 4 per cent. Freer trade,
> cheaper emerging-market labor, better technology and more plentiful capital all
> collided to make this early part of the century the most prosperous in the history
> of the planet. (Foroohar, 2008: 18)

Fears

Despite the vigour with which free trade arguments were put forward by business interests and many Republicans, anxieties about the impact of foreign trade became increasingly visible. The uncertainties of the 1970s and the recession of the early 1980s triggered a sense of national vulnerability. There were growing questions about US national competitiveness.[6] The arguments for protectionism were increasingly heard. The conclusion of free trade agreements, it was said, simply led to *trade diversion*. If an agreement is reached with a nation that supplies a product or service less efficiently (and therefore at a higher cost) than another nation, the removal of tariffs will encourage buyers to switch to the less efficient supplier. In such circumstances, free trade encourages inefficiency, threatens economic welfare and jeopardises the interests of the consumer.

Against the background of economic uncertainty in the 1970s, Japan began to be increasingly seen as a threat to US interests. The country had risen from the destruction of 1945 to become the third largest economy (in terms of GDP) in the world after the US and the Soviet Union.[7] In March 1970, *Time* magazine spoke of the coming 'Japanese century': 'No country has a stronger franchise on the future than Japan. No developed nation is growing faster. Its economy quadrupled in the past decade, and will triple again in the next ... Says Economist Peter Drucker: "It is the most extraordinary success story in all economic history"' (*Time*, 1970).

American companies and the lobbyists who represented them complained of 'unfair' competition and pointed to hidden subsidies. Japanese law, for example, was said to offer tax concessions to companies that directed their efforts towards the export markets (*Time*, 1971). Successive administrations persuaded Japan to accept 'voluntary' limits on the volume of their exports to the US. Nonetheless, anxieties about the Japanese 'threat' continued and came to be reflected in the popular culture of the period. Michael Crighton's 1992 novel, *Rising Sun*, (which was made into a film with Sean Connery and Wesley Snipes) conveyed some of these fears. Citing the Japanese motto that 'business is war', it depicted what it saw as the hidden face of Japanese business operations in the US. Nonetheless, the novel and the film appeared just as the Japanese economy hit the doldrums and stagnated for much of the decade that followed. Talk of a 'Japanese century' evaporated. By the end of the 1990s, American fears about Japan had been almost entirely displaced by concerns about China.

NAFTA

Despite these sentiments, the US signed a free trade agreement with Canada in January 1988. Although there had long been anxieties in Canada that trade liberalisation might place some industries in jeopardy, undermine the country's sovereignty and weaken its distinct cultural identity, the measure was relatively uncontroversial in the US. Wage costs were broadly similar in the two countries and there few fears that American jobs would be lost as a result of competition from workers north of the border.

The North American Free Trade Agreement (NAFTA), which was signed in December 1992 and included Mexico as well as Canada, provoked a much more hostile response in the US.[8] In a celebrated comment, Ross Perot, the Texan billionaire who contested the 1992 and 1996 presidential elections, spoke of a 'giant sucking sound' in warning that if Mexico was included in a free trade agreement with the US and Canada yet more jobs would be lost, because of much lower labour costs, to the *maquiladoras* and other enterprises south of the Rio Grande. Patrick J. Buchanan, a committed 'paleoconservative' and former White House speechwriter who contested the Republican Party primaries in 1992 and 1996 and stood as the Reform Party's presidential candidate in 2000, spoke in similar terms:

> Two years after NAFTA, the predictions of its opponents had all come true. The U.S. trade surplus with Mexico had vanished; a trade deficit of $15 billion had opened up. Trucks heading north out of Mexico were hauling more and more manufactured goods, while those going south carried machinery and equipment for the new factories going up, pointing to endless and deepening U.S. trade deficits. By 1997, 3,300 maquiladora factories were operating, employing 800,000 Mexican workers in jobs that not long ago would have gone to Americans. (quoted in Cato Institute Center for Trade Policy Studies, 2008)[9]

Claims such as those made by Perot and Buchanan have been countered by NAFTA's backers. Although some perhaps exaggerate the overall significance of the pact for the US (in the 1990s Mexico was comparable with Los Angeles in terms of economic size), NAFTA's supporters have subsequently pointed to the economic track record since its passage.[10]

- As Dan Griswold of the free market Cato Institute has recorded, trade between the US, Canada and Mexico has dramatically increased since NAFTA was signed. Between 1993, the year before the agreement was implemented, and 2004, trade between the US and Mexico more or less tripled from $81 billion to $232 billion (Griswold, 2004). Mexico became the US's second largest market for exports (after Canada), only fractionally ahead of Japan.[11] Nonetheless, the overall impact of NAFTA should not be exaggerated. Its importance lies in the way it guaranteed – or codified – the economic ties between the two nations. As Bradford De Long, Christopher De Long and Sherman Robinson have argued:

   The trade agreement did not greatly expand Mexico's access to the U.S. market; the market was already largely open to Mexican imports. Rather, NAFTA made Mexican businesses and investors a solemn promise that they would not be bankrupted by a sudden wave of U.S. protectionism. (De Long, De Long and Robinson, 1996: 9)

- Despite Perot's predictions of a 'giant sucking sound' as jobs were lost to Mexico, the trading process has created employment in net terms. The Department of Commerce estimated that the five years after the implementation of the pact, US exports to Canada and Mexico supported over 600,000 more jobs than in 1993:

   U.S. exports to Canada support an estimated 1.7 million jobs, over 300,000 more jobs than in 1993. Exports to Mexico in 1998 supported almost a million jobs, up over 350,000 jobs from 1993. Jobs supported by exports pay 13 to 16 percent more than other U.S. jobs. (Fitzgerald, 2001)

- Those who support NAFTA emphasise the impact of the agreement and the opening up of Mexican markets on particular sectors of the US economy. Total employment in the US motor industry grew five times faster following NAFTA than in the years prior to the pact (Fitzgerald, 2001).[12] There have also been export opportunities for US companies in information technology, transportation equipment (for example, diesel-electric locomotives) and oil and gas field equipment. Alongside this, US agriculture also made significant gains from increased trade. In 1993, Mexico purchased $3.6 billion worth of US agricultural products. A decade later, it bought $7.9 billion (2003) and $8.5 billion in 2004 (FASonline, 2005). NAFTA's backers argue that although the devaluation of the *peso* in 1995 made US exports to Mexico much more expensive the reduction of tariffs under the provisions of NAFTA ensured that the long-term growth of agricultural exports continued. Both countries, it is said, have increasingly structured agricultural production around the principles of absolute and comparative advantage. Because of unrestricted trade, both the US and Mexico are increasingly concentrating on the forms of production that because of the countries' different endowments they can undertake most efficiently. The US can produce animals and animal products, grains and oilseeds more efficiently than Mexico. At the same time, Mexico can produce vegetables, fruits and fresh flowers.

- NAFTA has, furthermore, added to wages in some sectors. Earnings in export-based firms are on average about 10 to 15 per cent higher than those paid by non-exporting firms. Insofar as NAFTA has increased overall US exports, it has therefore added to US wage levels (Bergsten and Schott, 1997).
- Despite the claims made by figures such as Pat Buchanan, most job losses over the past two decades can be attributed to the process of technological change and changing patterns of demand rather than foreign competition. The NAFTA labour adjustment programme was established to address the difficulties of those who might be displaced by the expansion of trade that had been brought about by the agreement. However, only about 40,000 workers annually were certified under the terms of the programme in the years that followed NAFTA's passage (Bergsten and Schott, 1997). As Griswold noted ten years after the agreement was implemented:

> Since NAFTA, about 400,000 Americans have qualified for trade adjustment assistance under a special program for workers displaced by imports from Mexico, but that is a small number when spread over a decade and when compared to the millions of jobs being eliminated and created every quarter in the U.S. economy. (Griswold, 2004)

- A World Bank study found no significant evidence of *trade diversion* (see p. 152). There had been no switch away from more efficient producers of, for example, textiles in neighbouring central American countries and the Caribbean (Hornbeck, 2004: 3).
- NAFTA includes provisions to ensure the full protection of intellectual property rights so as to prevent the importation of 'pirated' products into the US across an often porous border. NAFTA's Chapter 17 refers to '[C]opyright and related rights, trademark rights, patent rights, rights in layout and design of semiconductor integrated circuits, trade secret rights, plant breeders' rights, rights in geographical indications and industrial design rights' (Terry, Ederer and Orange, n.d.).
- NAFTA was the first international trade agreement in US history to include agreement on environmental policies. This was negotiated by the Clinton administration (together with another side agreement addressing labour issues) and signed in September 1993. The White House hoped to use these to win over Congressional Democrats who were deeply sceptical about NAFTA and free trade principles more generally. The side agreements were

Table 6.2 *Mexican investment in the US, 1990–2005*

Average % change from 1990 to 1992	Average % change from 1993 to 1995	Average % change from 1996 to 1998	Average % change from 1999 to 2001	Average % change from 2002 to 2005
37.1	14.8	15.9	87.8	8.0

Source: Elena Labastida-Tovar, 'The impact of NAFTA on the Mexican-US border begion', in Edward Ashbee, Helene Balslev Clausen and Carl Pedersen, *The Politics, Economics and Culture of Mexican–US Migration: Both Sides of the Border*, Basingstoke: Palgrave Macmillan (2007), 115.

also a response to broadly held fears that NAFTA would create a 'race to the bottom' in terms of both environmental regulation and labour rights between signatory countries. The Commission for Environmental Cooperation (CEC) was established to assess the environmental consequences of the agreement. Since the side agreements were signed, Mexico has passed environmental laws comparable with those in the United States and Canada.

• NAFTA encouraged cross-border foreign direct investment (FDI). Between 1994 and 2002, US FDI in Mexico increased from $16.1 billion to $58.1 billion (a rise of 259 per cent) (Hornbeck, 2004: 3). At the same time, although some of those on the left depicted NAFTA as an opportunity for US corporate interests to control Mexican markets, the picture is not so straightforward. Mexican investment in the US rose dramatically at least in proportionate year-on-year terms. Indeed, it almost doubled during the 1999–2001 period (Table 6.2).[13]

The passage of NAFTA contributed to restructuring and reform in Mexico. Indeed, even before NAFTA was signed, the promise of free trade accelerated the process of liberalisation and deregulation in Mexico. Once NAFTA's provisions had been implemented, the pact (along with the international financial rescue package) helped Mexico recover from the 1995 peso crisis. It avoided the temptation to impose restrictions on trade and the movement of capital and instead opted for policies based upon fiscal restraint and currency devaluation. This, free market commentators insist, contributed to the process of recovery from the crisis and there was 5.1 per cent real growth in 1996 (Bergsten and Schott, 1997). This had a significant impact on Mexican living standards. Estimates suggest that without NAFTA, Mexico's per capita GDP growth would have been 4–5 per cent lower by 2002 (Hornbeck, 2004: 4). All of this, the pact's backers have argued, is important for strategic reasons because of Mexico's proximity to the US and the long, shared border between the two nations. Furthermore, it was said, the strengthening of the Mexican economy through neo-liberal reforms would slow down the growing inflow of illegal immigrants into the US: 'NAFTA locks in these policy changes...successful growth and structural change in Mexico increase job creation and reduce pressure for migration to the United States' (De Long, De Long and Robinson, 1996: 10).

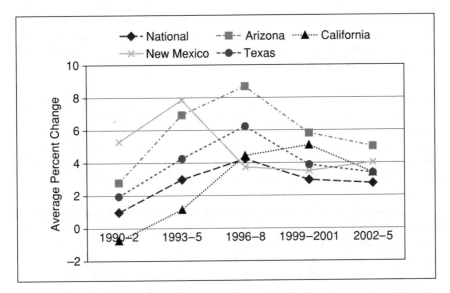

Figure 6.1 *US border states and economic growth (percentage change in real GDP), 1990–2005*

Source: adapted from Elena Labastida-Tovar, 'The impact of NAFTA on the Mexican-US border region', in Edward Ashbee, Helene Balslev Clausen and Carl Pedersen, *The Politics, Economics and Culture of Mexican–US Migration: Both Sides of the Border*, Basingstoke: Palgrave Macmillan (2007), 111.

Those who support NAFTA and the principle of free trade also point to the pace of economic development in the region around the US-Mexico border. Elena Labastida-Tovar has charted real growth rates in the US border states (Arizona, California, New Mexico and Texas) and compares these with the overall growth rate for the US. Although California faced difficulties during the first half of the 1990s, all of the border states had higher growth rates than the national average by the beginning of the new century (Figure 6.1). This, she argues, can be attributed to the dynamic gains from trade in the border region that accrued in the wake of NAFTA.

NAFTA revisited

For some free trade advocates, NAFTA fell short. There were claims that it was leading to the creation of a new trading bloc that would erect walls against non-member nations and that therefore, like the European Union, it constituted a barrier to the process of global trade liberalisation.[14] Free market organisations such as the Cato Institute were critical from NAFTA's inception:

With each passing month, the North American Free Trade Agreement (NAFTA) is acquiring more protectionist overtones...the pact contains Byzantine 'rules of origin' for products to qualify as North American products...Free trade is not complex – it is protectionism that requires endless administrative gimmicks to camouflage its true nature. NAFTA amounts to a proliferation of new definitions of fair trade. (Mass, 2009)

There were also disputes among the three signatory countries that required resolution, including a long-running battle between the US and Canada about softwood lumber. From the early 1980s onwards, the US asserted that Canadian lumber was being subsidised by the provincial governments. In 2002, the US imposed retaliatory duties on lumber imports. In turn, Canada challenged these. Although a NAFTA panel ruled in Canada's favour, an international arbitration court backed the US.

The issue of Mexican trucks on US roads provoked rather more bitter controversy and disagreement. Under NAFTA's provisions, Mexican long-haul trucking firms were to have been granted access to roads in the border states from 1995, and allowed to drive anywhere in the US by January 2000.[15] However, the Clinton administration, citing safety and environmental concerns, refused to allow Mexican trucks to operate beyond a narrow strip just north of the US-Mexico border. As a consequence, goods heading northwards had to be transferred to US trucks, adding to the time and cost of transportation. For their part, the US trucking companies and the unions representing drivers forcefully asserted that the Mexican trucks did not meet US safety standards: 'Mexico's truck inspection system is riddled with holes that allow vehicles with major safety defects to stay on the road...Mexican trucks are three times more likely to have safety deficiencies than U.S. trucks' (Public Citizen, 2008).[16]

In September 2007, a pilot programme was launched allowing a small number of Mexican long-haul trucking companies that met US requirements to operate throughout the country. However, in March 2009, in a move depicted by its critics as a form of hidden protectionism, Congress ended the programme.[17] Those directly affected pointed to the financial consequences of this:

> Because of the suspension, companies that were in the program now must pay about $120 per trailer for a transfer service that hauls cargo across the border. Delays compound those costs because shippers must drop the trailers on the Mexican side of the border, hook them up and deliver them to the U.S. side, where an American trucking company picks them up...The delays can last as long as a day as the three trucks complete their maneuvering...The system puts North America at a disadvantage to the European Union where trucks travel freely among member nations. (Black and Rodriguez, 2009)

The Mexican authorities retaliated against the US by imposing tariffs on ninety American products (including grapes and toilet paper) that were worth a total of about $2.4 billion in trade in 2007.[18]

The future of NAFTA also emerged as an issue during the 2008 Democratic presidential primaries. In October 2007, Senator Hillary Rodham Clinton, who was at the time still seen as the frontrunner for the party's nomination, distanced herself from the agreement by saying that NAFTA should be reassessed and 'adjusted' and any further free trade agreements (beyond the bilateral trade agreements that had subsequently been agreed by Congress) postponed (Page, 2007). For his part, Barack Obama spoke in similar terms. As primaries in key 'rustbelt' states approached, his campaign sought to associate Clinton with NAFTA and issued calls for renegotiation of the pact.

At the time, a key adviser to Obama sought to reassure the Canadian government by distancing the candidate from his own comments and campaign. Later in the year, the assurances that NAFTA would be renegotiated seemed to have been forgotten. In April 2009, the White House made it clear that the agreement would not be changed. The *Wall Street Journal* was elated:

> Three cheers for President Obama's decision, announced quietly on Monday, to repudiate a campaign promise and not press for new labor and environmental regulations in the North American Free Trade Agreement. The last thing the Western Hemisphere needs are more trade barriers that would snarl supply chains and damage commerce. (*Wall Street Journal*, 2009)

'Fair', 'managed', 'responsible' and 'strategic' trade

There is, however, a very different perspective. Very few of those who have reservations or concerns about free trade embrace the term 'protectionism' or wish to be described as 'protectionists' but they do talk in terms of 'managed', 'responsible' or 'fair' trade. Some justify this by portraying restrictions on trade as a way of safeguarding the nation itself. Writing at the end of the 1990s, Patrick J. Buchanan bitterly criticised what he saw as the consequences of unrestricted trade:

> At the end of sixty years of free-trade policies, America found itself as dependent on foreign imports, foreign markets, and foreign capital as it had been in the infant days of the new republic. In a few decades the globalists had reverse-engineered American history, inaugurated a new era of American dependency, and thrown away the gains of a century and a half of economic nationalism. The republic that had grown out of thirteen colonies of the British Empire to become the most self-sufficient nation in history was now a colony of the world. (Buchanan, 1998: 259)

Although there are conservative 'fair traders' such as Buchanan, most 'protectionists' have, since the early 1970s, been associated with the left. In particular, individuals and organisations associated with organised labour and the environmental movement have spoken out against the recent free trade agreements that the US has concluded.

Against this background, many Congressional Democrats opposed most of the free trade agreements agreed by the Clinton and Bush administrations as well as other, earlier trade liberalisation measures. Protectionist or 'fair trade' sentiments led to the passage of the Byrd Amendment (The Continued Dumping and Subsidy Offset Act of 2000). This required that the duties obtained from goods imported by foreign companies guilty of 'dumping' goods (selling below cost price) on the US market should be awarded to the American companies that filed an initial complaint about the practice. It thereby gave US companies a financial incentive to 'police' the distribution of products and initiate legal proceedings against importers.[19] More significantly, as in Europe, agriculture remains heavily subsidised and protected.

What arguments are put forward by those who seek trade controls and the reining in of trading relationships?

- There have been calls for the adoption of a 'strategic' or 'managed' trade. Some of those talking in these terms held up Japan as an example to be emulated. Until the Japanese economy stalled in the early 1990s, some western commentators held that the policies pursued by the Japanese Ministry of International Trade and Industry (MITI) explained the country's hitherto successful growth record. MITI guided companies and, for example, encouraged automobile manufacturers to concentrate on the production and export of a few selected models. When, in the early 1980s, the US imposed voluntary restraint arrangements (or quotas) upon Japanese cars, MITI allocated the quotas to individual Japanese companies. Others did not much look towards the Japanese model but felt that Ricardo's theory of *comparative advantage* had been overtaken by events. Writing in the early and mid-1980s, Paul Krugman questioned the traditional claim that countries could necessarily gain by specialising on the basis of their *factor endowments*. The character of world trade had, he argued, shifted:

  > a large and generally growing part of world trade has come to consist of exchanges that cannot be attributed so easily to underlying advantages of the countries that export particular goods. Instead, trade seems to reflect arbitrary or temporary advantages resulting from economies of scale or shifting leads in close technological races. (quoted in Kuttner, 1996)

Although Krugman himself came to fear that governments might simply adopt retaliatory policies against each other, the conclusion to be drawn from this proposition was that there was a case for the managed creation of comparative advantage by aiding and encouraging industries that had export market potential, spillover effects and technological dynamism. While there were to be serious rifts with Krugman in the years that followed, Laura D'Andrea Tyson, who chaired President Clinton's Council of Economic Advisers and went on to serve as a policy adviser to President Obama, was among those who followed the logic of the argument and, in very cautious terms, made the case for exceptions to the free trade principle. In particular, she argued, free trade may not produce an optimum outcome if another country is managing its trade relations:

> free trade is often a chimerical goal, doomed to be thwarted in one way if not another. And, she believes, government can do better by recognizing as much and by confronting those who would manage their markets with an equal, sophisticated, and determined strategy for getting part of the deal. Well-designed trade policies amount, in her view, to bilateral management of outcomes that would otherwise be, not free, but unilaterally managed – by the other side. (Galbraith, 1993)

- Others, more recently, have also suggested that the principle of *comparative advantage* no longer applies. In 2004, Democratic Senator Charles Schumer and Paul Craig Roberts (who served as an assistant secretary of the Treasury in the Reagan administration) argued that economic realities had changed since the time when Ricardo had been writing. Ricardo assumed that factors of production could not be easily moved between nations and a country's best interest would be served by specialisation in the production or delivery of the goods and services they could develop most efficiently. All countries, thereby, gained from trade. In today's world, however, 'some countries win and others lose'. This is because, in recent decades, there have been three developments. First, capital and technology flow far more freely around the world. Second, there are now many highly educated and committed workers in developing countries, most notably India and China, who are prepared to work at much lower wage levels than their counterparts in the west. Third, high-speed internet connections allow for large workforces to be based anywhere and managed from another country. As Schumer and Roberts put it: 'This is a very different world than Ricardo envisioned. When American companies replace domestic employees with lower-cost foreign workers in order to sell more cheaply in home markets, it seems hard to argue that this is the way free trade is supposed to work' (Schumer and Roberts, 2004).
- Those who back protectionism have gone beyond Tyson's tentative policy suggestions and have long argued that trade barriers (either tariffs or subsidies) are required so that infant industries can develop and grow. Established businesses are often large and enjoy economies of scale. In other words, the scale of production allows individual goods to be produced at a relatively low unit cost. Without protection, such infant industries will be unable to secure a foothold in a market and compete effectively. Alexander Hamilton seems to have been thinking in these terms when he wrote the *Report on Manufactures*. As John M. Rothgeb Jr records:

> Higher prices for imports are a key factor in the establishment of new enterprises, because new firms always confront substantial start-up costs that they

pass along to consumers in the form of higher prices...In Hamilton's day, unless a trading system forced the prices for foreign goods upward, America's infant industries would have little prospect of reaching adulthood. (Rothgeb, 2001: 8)

- Some industries or economic sectors are essential to the life of the nation and its overall wellbeing. Subsidies to agriculture and the imposition of tariffs on agricultural imports are often justified in both the US and Europe on this basis. If exposed to competition from across the globe, farm incomes would be unstable and lower than those in the industrial sector. As a consequence, there would be further rural depopulation and the communities that are sustained by farming would be placed in jeopardy.
- Critics of free trade assert that the gains that a country makes by trading depend upon the 'terms of trade'. This is the price at which the exchange of goods or services takes place. If supply or demand is manipulated (by, for example, placing limits on the amount of oil made available), the price can be raised so as to disproportionately benefit some countries while damaging the interests of others.
- The trading process is creating imbalances within the country's economic and occupational structure. Manufacturing jobs have been disproportionately lost to trade and there have been large trade deficits in manufactured goods. These are the jobs that traditionally offered higher wages and fringe benefits, particularly for workers who had not taken degree-level courses. Workers who have been displaced have had to turn to the service sector where wages are lower. Lester Thurow, who backs strategic trade and the adoption of *industrial policy* (whereby some selected industries are encouraged and subsidised), has argued that, as a result of this process, real wages in the US fell by 6 per cent during the Reagan-Bush years (1981–93) (Krugman, 1994: 35–6).[20]
- Free trade will probably increase socioeconomic inequalities: 'exporters – who benefit from trade reforms – need to hire skilled workers to succeed in world markets...suggesting that as countries turn to exporting, the demand for skilled workers will rise, pushing up their wages relative to those of unskilled workers' (World Bank, 2005: 151).[21] The US tends to export advanced services (for example, finance) and capital-intensive products (such as aircraft) while importing labour-intensive products. This is of direct benefit to those in the capital-intensive sectors (who gain from the export trade) while it has negative consequences for those in the labour-intensive sectors, who face competition from abroad (Bivens, 2008). This widens the gap between higher- and lower-income groupings.
- For some on the further reaches of the right, unrestricted trade represents a threat to national sovereignty. Free trade, it is said, creates a degree of dependency upon other nations for raw materials and component parts that may come to limit the US's ability to determine its own future.

- Those on the left and many of those protesting against global trade talks stress environmental concerns as well as the threat posed to employment and wage levels. The Sierra Club, the most long-established of the US environmental organisations, asserts its backing for trade but at the same time stresses the need for it to take a 'responsible' rather than an unrestrained form:

   > The Sierra Club supports trade, but we want trade agreements that promote a higher quality of life for all, not trade that simply serves as a vehicle to increase corporate profits. Communities should have the right to determine what kind of economic development they want. They should also be able to promote local and environmentally sensitive development rather than box-store retail that increases sprawl and pollution. (Sierra Club, n.d.)

- Free trade and the globalisation process have brought forth increased competition and a more developed division of labour. The world economy has become ever more interlocked and countries have become yet more interdependent. Although this has led to lower prices, it also means that economic problems are more quickly 'exported' from one country or region to another.
- There are particular concerns about the US's trading relationship with China. China, it is said, is governed by an authoritarian regime and the labour force is compelled to work for subsistence-level wages. Furthermore, there have been repeated claims that China has undervalued its currency (the *yuan*) so that its exports have been sold at an artificially low price. According to the Economic Policy Institute (EPI), a thinktank tied to the labour movement, 1.5 million jobs were lost to Chinese competition during the period between 1989 and 2003. The states which were hardest-hit, when job losses were considered as a proportion of overall employment levels, were Maine, Arkansas, North Carolina and Rhode Island. The EPI report noted that despite common perceptions China's exports to the US of advanced electronics and communications equipment were increasing much more quickly than its exports of lower-value, labour-intensive goods. Furthermore, China was also acquiring a competitive edge in advanced sectors such as autos and aerospace products (USInfo.state.gov, 2005). Since the EPI study was concluded, the trade deficit with China has continued to grow (Table 6.3).[22]
- Free trade policies have, it is said, added to the US balance of payments deficit by opening up US markets to cheap imports from countries where labour costs are significantly lower. As Table 6.4 shows, the US deficit has grown dramatically during the years since 1990 except during periods of recession (1991) or downturn (2001) when consumer demand for imports fell away and producers had to look towards the export market. NAFTA, it is said, exacerbated the trade deficit still further.

Why is a balance of payments deficit a source of concern? First, according to 'fair traders', an excess of imports means that in net terms US jobs are being

Table 6.3 *US trade with China*

Year	Trade with China (exports-imports) – balance (US$mn)
1990	−10,431.00
1995	−33,789.50
2000	−83,833.00
2005	−201,544.80
2006	−232,588.60
2007	−256,206.70
2008	−266,332.70

Source: US Census Bureau (2009), *Trade in Goods (Imports, Exports and Trade Balance) with China*, <http://www.census.gov>

Table 6.4 *Balance of payments, 1990–2006 (US$mn)*

Year	Current account balance (US$mn)
1990	−78,968
1991	2,897
1992	−50,078
1993	−84,805
1994	−121,612
1995	−113,567
1996	−124,764
1997	−140,726
1998	−215,062
1999	−301,630
2000	−417,426
2001	−384,699
2002	−459,641
2003	−522,101
2004	−640,148
2005	−754,848
2006	−811,477

Source: adapted from Bureau of Economic Analysis (2008), *U.S. International Transactions*, <http://www.bea.gov>

lost. As the Economic Policy Institute (EPI) puts it: 'Because *trade deficits* have risen over the past decade, more jobs have been displaced by imports than created by exports' (Bivens, 2008).

Secondly, a trade deficit can lead, through the laws of supply and demand (and all other things being equal), to the depreciation of the dollar. This cuts the prices of US exports and encourages tourism, but the increase in import prices that such a depreciation will cause can add to inflation.

Thirdly, the difference between a country's exports and imports may be funded through the purchase of financial assets by other countries (a process recorded in the capital account of the balance of payments). This can give significant economic and political leverage to foreign creditors. In recent years, the US's trade deficit with China has been funded by China. The People's Bank of China does not generally hold excess dollars in its reserves for fear that the dollar will lose its value. The bank has therefore bought up American financial assets, primarily US government bonds.[23]

Criticisms of NAFTA

Alongside these generalised anxieties about unrestricted trade, there are also specific criticisms of NAFTA.

- Many opponents of the pact are drawn from the left. They see NAFTA as a vehicle for big business interests and the erosion of the gains secured by workers in recent decades in both Mexico and the US:

  > It is the constitution of an emerging continental economy that recognizes one citizen – the business corporation. It gives corporations extraordinary protections from government policies that might limit future profits...Disputes are settled by secret tribunals of experts...At the same time, NAFTA excludes protections for workers, the environment and the public that are part of the social contract established through long political struggle in each of the countries. (Faux, 2004)

- Since the passage of NAFTA, the US has had an increasing trade deficit with Mexico. Whereas the US's bilateral trade balance with Mexico was in surplus in 1993, this had turned to a $16 billion deficit by 1996.[24] NAFTA's opponents argue that if the impact of the trade deficit (which they say represents the transfer of production from the US) is included in the estimates, the job losses have exceeded the gains. According to the Economic Policy Institute, 879,280 jobs, many of which were high-wage positions in manufacturing, were lost during the period between 1993 and 2002 (Scott, 2003: 1).
- The US clothing (apparel) and textile industries were particularly badly hit. During the early years of the agreement (and until China gained a market foothold) free trade between the US and Mexico accelerated the transfer of production to the *maquiladoras* in the US-Mexico border region (Bergsten and Schott, 1997). Indeed, although free trade advocates dismiss the extent to which NAFTA has caused job losses, over half a million workers (525,000), had, by the end of 2003, been certified under the NAFTA trade adjustment assistance programme that was established to aid those displaced by the trade pact (Hornbeck, 2004: 5).
- NAFTA has had damaging environmental consequences and imposed severe strains on the infrastructure, particularly in the border region. Despite the

concerns of free market conservatives at the time of the pact's implementation, and their fears about regulatory interventionism, there is little evidence that the environmental side agreements have had an impact. Indeed, according to one commentator, the agreements rest upon 'little more than vague language, including monitoring commissions with little or no power of enforcement' (Smith, 1993).

• Those opposed to unregulated trade stress its impact when countries at different levels of development are bound together by a pact. Under the provisions of NAFTA, they say, Mexican corn farmers are compelled to compete with highly subsidised American corn. By 2004, all but one of Mexico's major banks had been sold to foreign banks. Income disparities between the US and Mexico have grown. Furthermore, economic growth in Mexico was, between 1994 and 2004, only about 1 per cent at an average annual rate if measured on a per capita basis. From 1948 to 1973, it was 3.2 per cent (Stiglitz, 2004). As an EPI briefing paper has concluded:

> Mexican employment did increase, but much of it in low-wage 'maquiladora' industries, which the promoters of NAFTA promised would disappear. The agricultural sector was devastated and the share of jobs with no security, no benefits, and no future expanded. The continued willingness every year of hundreds of thousands of Mexican citizens to risk their lives crossing the border to the United States because they cannot make a living at home is in itself testimony to the failure of NAFTA to deliver on the promises of its promoters. (Scott, Salas and Campbell, 2006: 2)[25]

• Although there were assurances when NAFTA was under consideration that growing Mexican prosperity, brought about by the pact, would reduce the numbers of illegal migrants crossing the border, their numbers grew dramatically in the years that followed NAFTA's passage. In 2008, of the 11.9 million unauthorised immigrants estimated to be in the US, about 7 million were from Mexico (Passel and Cohn, 2009: 21). Furthermore, the volume of trade generated by NAFTA made it difficult to police the border effectively and as some critics assert, this has allowed increasing amounts of narcotics to enter the US from Mexico.

The Doha round and bilateral free trade agreements (FTAs)

Despite protectionist sentiments, both the Clinton and Bush administrations remained committed, albeit within defined parameters, to the pursuit of trade liberalisation on both a multilateral and a bilateral basis.[26]

At a multilateral level, from November 2001 onwards the US was engaged in the Doha Development Round of trade talks held under the auspices of the World Trade Organization (WTO). The purpose of the talks was to reduce trade barriers. So as to facilitate the passage of trade agreements through Congress, successive presidents have sought 'fast-track authority'. Congress has the constitutional authority to regulate foreign trade, although from 1934 onwards it delegated its authority to set tariffs to the White House. Under 'fast track', or 'trade promotion authority' (TPA), which was passed for a five year period in the 2002 Trade Act, Congress agreed to consider trade agreements within a specified period once they have been submitted by the White House and to take only an 'up or down vote'. In other words, amendments which could have slowed or even derailed consideration of a trade agreement were not permitted. Foreign countries could thereby negotiate trade agreements with the US knowing that they would not be delayed indefinitely or amended beyond recognition. 'Fast track' is widely regarded as essential if an administration is to pursue credible trade negotiations.

Despite the hopes pinned on the Doha Round, a significant divide opened up between the US and the European Union (EU) and the developing countries. Agriculture in both the developed and the developing nations was a particular point of contention. For the developing countries, US and EU subsidies to farming interests as well as the tariffs they imposed on outsiders constituted a major trade distortion. The issue became even more divisive when the Farm Security and Rural Investment Act, which provided $173.5 billion in agricultural subsidies to US farmers over a ten year period, was passed in 2002 shortly after the Doha Round had begun. By the time further talks were held in Cancún (Mexico) in September 2003, it was evident that progress in the Doha Round had stalled.

At the same time, hopes for a Free Trade Area of the Americas (FTAA) also receded. First proposed in 1994, FTAA would have encompassed both American continents. However, like the Doha Round, negotiations failed to make substantive progress because of diverging interests between the developed and the less developed nations. In the FTAA talks, Brazil sought increased access to the US market for some agricultural products and its steel industry. For its part, the US was only prepared to consider changes to its farm subsidies and anti-dumping laws in global trade talks.[27]

Against this background, the Bush administration placed increasing emphasis on bilateral agreements with individual countries rather than multilateral initiatives. The pursuit of free trade agreements (FTAs) was accompanied by talk of 'competitive liberalisation' (Chorev, 2009: 144), a process through which the US would conclude bilateral and regional trade agreements with some of the more pro-US countries in the hope that this might spur other nations, who would fear for the loss of market share or potential market share in the American market, to conclude agreements with the US.[28]

Bilateral agreements were concluded with Chile, Peru, Panama, Colombia, Bolivia and Ecuador as well as countries in the Middle East, Africa and Australasia. DR-CAFTA (Dominican Republic – Central America Free Trade Agreement) encompassed Costa Rica, El Salvador, Guatemala, Honduras, Nicaragua and at a later stage, the Dominican Republic.[29] However, the White

House also faced obstacles. Although Congress had renewed fast-track procedures, there was significant opposition to many of the agreements from a majority of Congressional Democrats and some Republicans. Passage of the FTAs was sometimes uncertain. Indeed, DR-CAFTA, which was considered by Congress in 2005, secured the support of just fifteen Democratic votes in the House of Representatives and ten in the Senate.[30]

The White House's free trade strategy was frustrated still further when the Democrats won control of both the Senate and the House of Representatives in the 2006 mid-term elections. In 2008, efforts by the White House to secure passage of the FTA with Colombia were rebuffed. Congressional Democrats pointed to the country's human rights record but also felt that the Bush administration had failed to consult them sufficiently. The agreements with Panama and South Korea also remained unconsidered. A compromise pact between the White House and Congress added a provision that FTA countries would adopt and observe the core labour standards of the International Labour Organization (ILO), and direct talks took place between senior Democrats in the House of Representatives and Peruvian President Alan Garcia leading to the passage of the Peru Trade Promotion Agreement in December 2007, but Congress held back trade liberalisation in another way.[31] In May 2008, Congress passed (and overrode a presidential veto on) a further farm bill providing increased subsidies. Some funds were assigned to cotton farmers in defiance of a WTO ruling (Chorev, 2009: 139).

Conclusion

Although there were claims that the 2008–9 recession would strengthen protectionist sentiments, there was some evidence of a shift towards free trade. A Pew poll conducted in March–April 2009 found that although over a third of the population felt that free trade agreements such as NAFTA and the policies of the World Trade Organization were 'bad for the country', 44 per cent said that they were 'good', an increase of 9 per cent from April 2008 (Pew Research Center for the People and the Press, 2009).

The shift in attitudes might be tied to an understanding that trade flows had been seriously damaged by the downturn. US exports fell by 30 per cent and imports by 34 per cent during the first three months of the year when compared with the last quarter of 2008. As the *New York Times* ruefully noted:

> At this rate, the World Trade Organization's dire projection in March that global trade would decline 9 per cent this year will soon start to look outright boastful. The drop in trade is spreading economic weakness across the world, as one country's drop in imports translates into a fall in exports, and production, in another. (*New York Times*, 2009)

South of the border, Mexico faced even greater problems. Its exports fell by almost 29 per cent.[32] Although, in contrast to the interwar years, countries were locked into international trade agreements, there was increasing evidence of creeping, low-level protectionism. The US's trade disputes with its NAFTA partners, Canada and Mexico, have already been noted (see pp. 157–9). The IMF expressed concern about increases in import licensing requirements, tariffs, surcharges, and aid to domestic producers that provided them with a competitive advantage against foreign suppliers. The *New York Times* highlighted the efforts of European governments, such as those in the United Kingdom, the Netherlands and Switzerland, to ensure that the provision of taxpayer funds for banks was tied to the giving of preference to domestic borrowers (*New York Times*, 2009).

Although public opinion may have shifted towards the arguments made by the advocates of free trade, protectionist attitudes within Congress have, if anything, become stronger. In the wake of the Democratic victories in the 2006 mid-term elections, Congress refused to extend TPA when it expired at the beginning of July 2007 and, at the time of writing, there seemed little prospect of renewal. The bilateral free trade agreements negotiated by the Bush administration had not been considered by Congress. The gap between Congress and public opinion can be explained by the close ties that many members of Congress have with particular constituencies, most notably organised labour. These ties, and the impact of the recession, will undoubtedly continue to place significant constraints on policymakers during the years to come.

Notes

1   The OECD (the Organization for Economic Cooperation and Development) brings together thirty of the countries most committed to the free market system.
2   Tariffs are taxes on imports. The imposition of a tax increases the selling price of a product and thereby encourages consumers to buy domestically produced goods.
3   There were some efforts, even in the 1930s, to liberalise trade relationships. The Reciprocal Trade Agreements Act of 1934 allowed the executive branch to undertake bilateral negotiations with other countries to reduce tariffs. The policy had only a limited impact.
4   Those who back trade liberalisation stress that it is a necessary but not a sufficient condition for economic growth. Other policies are also required: 'Trade is an opportunity, not a guarantee. While trade reforms can help accelerate integration in the world economy and strengthen an effective growth strategy, they cannot ensure its success. Other elements that address binding constraints to growth are needed, possibly including sound macroeconomic management, trade-related infrastructure and institutions, and economy-wide investments in human capital and infrastructure' (World Bank, 2005: 133).
5   Some point to Singapore's experience. The unemployment rate fell from over 9 per cent in the 1960s to about 2 per cent in the 1990s because trade created new sectors and jobs (World Bank, 2005: 149).

6   Paul Krugman has questioned the concept of national competiveness. Nations, he argues, should not be seen in the same way as individual firms. In contrast to firms, they cannot, for example, go bankrupt. Thinking of nations as firms can, he suggests, fuel protectionist (Krugman, 1994: 28–44).

7   Following the collapse of the Soviet Union, Japan became the second largest economy in the world, at least if measured in terms of nominal GDP.

8   The pact was negotiated by George H.W. Bush's administration and signed just before he left office. President Clinton negotiated side agreements and secured Congressional assent despite opposition from many fellow Democrats. Under the provisions of NAFTA, some duties were ended immediately while others were to be phased out in the years that followed. The pact included *rules of origin* (some of which have been subsequently liberalised) so as to ensure that tariff-free treatment covered only goods that had been manufactured in Mexico, Canada or the US and was not extended to goods exported from non-NAFTA countries which had undergone only minimal processing in North America.

9   The *maquiladoras* are assembly plants, many of which are along the border between the US and Mexico. Components and parts are shipped in and the finished product is returned to the original market.

10 According to the economic model used by the Congressional Budget Office (CBO), 85 per cent of US export growth and 91 per cent of US import growth would have occurred without NAFTA (Hornbeck, 2004: 2). In overall terms, studies suggest that NAFTA will, because of Mexico's limited economic size, be very modest and the pact will eventually add only 0.1 per cent to 0.5 per cent to US GDP (Hornbeck, 2004: 4).

11 The figures change if the nations belonging to the European Union are regarded as a single entity rather than as separate countries.

12 NAFTA ended Mexican trade and investment restrictions that had required their automobile companies to manufacture in Mexico, produce for the local market, and at the same time prohibited US vehicle exports to Mexico (US Department of State, 1993).

13 Although there were significant percentage rises, Mexican investment in the US was dwarfed by US investment in Mexico. During the four years following implementation, the latter was about $4 billion annually. In 1996, the total invested by US companies was about $785 billion (Bergsten and Schott, 1997).

14 In contrast with the European Union, which is a customs union, NAFTA does not impose a common external tariff on outsider nations. Each member country retains its own tariff system.

15 Mexican trucks had to meet US safety standards. There are no operating restrictions on Canadian trucks in the US.

16 Deroy Murdock, a conservative commentator, argues that safety concerns are, in essence, a protectionist ruse. He cites data suggesting that between 2003 and 2007, 1.2 per cent of Mexican truckers in America were non-compliant with safety rules compared with 7 per cent of US drivers. He also notes that in 2007–9, during an eighteen-month pilot programme allowing a limited number of Mexican companies to operate in the US beyond the border zone, there were no significant incidents or accidents (Murdock, 2009).

17 After signing the Act that included a provision ending the pilot programme, President Obama called for legislation to create 'a new trucking project that will

meet the legitimate concerns' of Congress as well as the country's NAFTA commitments (Bulk Transporter, 2009).

18 Supporters of free trade claimed that Mexico's retaliatory trade sanctions would lead to the loss of 40,000 American jobs (Murdock, 2009).

19 The WTO ruled against the measure and it was repealed. However, duties were collected until October 2007.

20 This claim is challenged by Krugman (1994: 36).

21 Although inequalities have increased in the US over recent decades, it is very difficult to distinguish between the effects of productivity advances (which lead to a rationalisation of the labour force) and the direct consequences of foreign trade (see Chapter 7).

22 Despite the criticisms, those who are most committed to the free market point to the gains that the US makes from growing trade with China. The US, it is argued, is importing more from China because of the country's increasing importance as the final link in the East Asian manufacturing supply chain. Furthermore, the relatively low price of imports from China has increased real American wages (particularly for low- and middle-income families) and thereby allowed them to spend more on other items. Furthermore, US companies have gained from export opportunities to China. After 2000, the rate of growth of US exports to China was more than twelve times the rate of growth of US exports to the rest of the world. At the same time, Chinese purchases of US securities have put downward pressure on American interest rates, thereby reducing borrowing costs for American households and the US government (Griswold, 2006). For its part, the US Treasury used 'quiet diplomacy' rather than sanctions to persuade China to devalue its currency (Chorev, 2009: 138).

23 These bonds have financed the large budget deficits that have been incurred in recent years as well as being used to obtain both corporate stocks and bonds and real assets. There are fears that if the Chinese restricted the flow of dollars into US assets, the dollar would lose much of its value.

24 The trade imbalance between the US and Mexico may have been exacerbated by the fall in the value of the peso and the economic boom of the late 1990s. NAFTA's backers emphasise that almost all of the increase in the US trade deficit with its NAFTA partners from 2000 onwards can be attributed to increased demand for energy from Canada and Mexico (Engler, 2008).

25 Despite NAFTA, Mexico is becoming relatively *less* important as a US trading partner. Although US exports to Mexico remain very significant, China outstripped Mexico in 2003 as the second largest supplier of imports to the US market. China has made particular inroads into electronics, machinery and parts but also textiles and apparel (Wise, 2006: 3). Furthermore, the *maquiladoras* on the US–Mexico border are now losing out because, despite the increased transportation costs, production is being transferred to China (Nevaer, 2003). Nonetheless, as Dan Griswold emphasises, Mexico continues to have advantages over China. It is much closer to the US and transportation costs are therefore lower: 'For Americans, China is the big-box retailer on the edge of town, while Mexico is our next door neighbor and business partner' (Griswold, 2006). Mexico, furthermore, has democratic structures and is therefore likely to have a more stable future than China.

26 However, there were significant exceptions. Cuba remained embargoed in an attempt to isolate the Castro regime. And, despite its talk of free trade, the Bush

administration increased tariffs (to between 8 and 30 per cent) on imported steel in March 2002. This was challenged by the European Union as well as other countries, and following a WTO ruling allowing retaliatory tariffs, the US withdrew the tariffs.

27 'Dumping' is the selling of good at below cost price. See p. 160.

28 President Bush's commitment to FTAs also built upon the agreement that the Clinton administration had negotiated with Jordan. This was passed by Congress on voice votes and signed by President Bush. Passage on a voice vote indicates that there was no significant opposition to the measure in either the House of Representatives or the Senate. Jordan, like some of the other countries with which the US negotiated an FTA, was regarded as an important ally in a troubled region.

29 It should, however, be noted that trade agreements such as NAFTA and bilateral treaties have been depicted by some as a shift towards the creation of regional trading blocs, which obstruct the process of global trade liberalisation, rather than a step towards it.

30 Arguably, Democratic opposition to CAFTA was inevitable given its provisions. The agreement included an increase in funding for the enforcement of labour and environmental laws in the countries concerned but no assurance that international labour standards would be respected. At the same time, however, the Bush administration made some significant concessions to the textile and sugar industries (Chorev, 2009: 139).

31 ILO standards prohibited forced labour, child labour and discrimination in the workplace. They also extended protection to workers seeking trade union representation. The pact between the White House and Congress applied the same enforcement mechanisms that governed other disputes to labour standards. However, ILO standards were not to apply to the US (Chorev, 2009: 141).

32 The Mexican economy shrank during the first three months of 2009 by 21.5 per cent (at an annualised rate).

References and further reading

Adler, Matthew and Gary Clyde Hufbauer (2009), 'Policy liberalisation and US merchandise trade growth, 1980–2006', *Vox*, March 10, <http://www.voxeu.eu>

Bergsten, C. Fred and Jeffrey J. Schott (1997), *Testimony before the Subcommittee on Trade Ways and Means Committee, US House of Representatives*, September 11, <http://www.iie.com>

Bivens, L. Josh (2007), *The Marketing of Economics History: Inflating the Importance of Trade Liberalization*, Economic Policy Institute Issue Brief, #238, December 17, <http://www.epi.org>

Bivens, L. Josh (2008), *Trade, jobs, and wages: Are the public's worries about globalization justified?*, Economic Policy Institute Issue Brief #244, May 6, <http://www.epi.org/content.cfm/ib244>

Black, Thomas and Carlos Manuel Rodriguez (2009), *GE, 3M Freight Costs May Rise After U.S. Bars Mexican Trucks*, Bloomberg.com, March 19, <http://www.bloomberg.com>

Brainard, Lail (2008), *America's Trade Agenda: Examining the Trade Enforcement Act of 2007*, The Brookings Institution, <http://www.brookings.edu>

Buchanan, Patrick J. (1998), *The Great Betrayal*, Boston: Little, Brown and Company.

Bulk Transporter (2009), 'President Obama blinks in NAFTA truck dispute', March 17, <http://bulktransporter.com>

Cato Institute Center for Trade Policy Studies (2008), *Buchanan on NAFTA*, <http://www.freetrade.org>

Chorev, Nitsan (2009), 'International trade policy under George W. Bush', in Andrew Wroe and Jon Herbert (2009), *Assessing the Bush Presidency: A Tale of Two Terms*, Edinburgh: Edinburgh University Press, 129–46.

De Long, Bradford, Christopher De Long and Sherman Robinson (1996), 'The case for Mexico's rescue: the peso package looks even better now', *Foreign Affairs*, 75:3, May/June, 8–14.

Engler, John (2008), 'What Nafta trade deficit?', *Wall Street Journal*, April 21, <http://online.wsj.com>

European Commission (2006), *European Union in the World*, 2, <http://trade.ec.europa.eu/doclib/docs/2006/september/tradoc_122531.pdf>

FASonline (2005), *Benefits of NAFTA*, FAS Backgrounder, May, <http://www.fas.usda.gov>

Faux, Jeff (2004), *NAFTA at 10*, Economic Policy Institute, February 9, <http://www.epi.org>

Fitzgerald, Sara J. (2001), *The Effects of NAFTA on Exports, Jobs, and the Environment: Myth vs. Reality*, The Heritage Foundation, Backgrounder #1462, August 1, <http://www.heritage.org>

Foroohar, Rana (2008), 'Up, up and away...', *Newsweek*, August 11, CLII: 6, 16–20.

Galbraith, James K. (1993), 'Who's bashing Tyson?', *American Prospect*, March 21, <http://www.prospect.org>

Global Trade Negotiations Home Page (2004), *Trade, Comparative Advantage, and Their Critics*, <http://www.cid.harvard.edu>

Griswold, Daniel T. (2004), *After 10 Years, NAFTA Continues to Pay Dividends*, Cato Institute, January 8, <http://www.freetrade.org>

Griswold, Daniel T. (2006), *The Future of NAFTA: 'Hecho en China'?*, Cato Institute, November 15–17, <http://www.freetrade.org>

Hamilton, Alexander (orig. 1791), *Report on Manufactures (excerpts)*, <http://history.sandiego.edu/gen/text/civ/1791manufactures.html>

Hayes, Christopher (2007), 'The NAFTA superhighway', *The Nation*, August 9, <http://www.thenation.com>

Hornbeck, J.F. (2004), *NAFTA at Ten: Lessons from Recent Studies*, CRS Report for Congress, <http://fpc.state.gov>

Ikenson, Daniel (2005), *Felling NAFTA*, Cato Institute, October 24, <http://www.freetrade.org>

Irwin, Douglas A. (2007), 'GATT turns 60', *Wall Street Journal*, April 9, A13.

Krugman, Paul (1994), 'Competitiveness: a dangerous obsession', *Foreign Affairs*, 73:2, March/April, 28–44.

Krugman, Paul (2009), 'Protectionism and stimulus (wonkish)', *New York Times – Conscience of a Liberal*, February 1, <http://krugman.blogs.nytimes.com>

Kuttner, Robert (1996), 'State of the debate: peddling Krugman', *American Prospect*, September 1, <http://www.prospect.org>

Mass, Warren (2009), 'Obama to strengthen NAFTA without new negotiations', *New American*, April 21, <http://www.thenewamerican.com>

Murdock, Deroy (2009), 'Democrats trigger North American trade war', *National Review Online*, June 13, <http://www.nationalreview.com/archives>

Nevaer, Louis E.V. (2003), 'China poses NAFTA challenge', *Berkeley Daily Planet*, December 19, <http://www.berkeleydailyplanet.com>

New York Times (2009), 'Trade and hard times', May 25, <http://www.nytimes.com>

Page, Susan (2007), 'Clinton seeks to re-evaluate NAFTA', *USA Today*, October 9, <http://www.usatoday.com>

Passel, Jeffrey S. and D'Vera Cohn (2009), *A Portrait of Unauthorized Immigrants in the United States*, Pew Hispanic Center, <http://pewhispanic.org>

Pew Research Center for the People and the Press (2009), *Support for Free Trade Recovers Despite Recession*, April 28, <http://people-press.org>

Public Citizen (2008), *Mexico-Domiciled Trucks and NAFTA*, <http://www.citizen.org>

Rothgeb, John M. (2001), *US Trade Policy: Balancing Economic Dreams and Political Realities*, Washington DC: CQ Press.

Schumer, Charles and Paul Craig Roberts (2004), 'Second thoughts on free trade', *New York Times*, January 6, <http://www.nytimes.com>

Scott, Robert E. (2003), *The High Price of 'Free Trade': NAFTA's Failure has Cost the United States Jobs across the Nation*, Economic Policy Institute Briefing Paper, <http://epi.org>

Scott, Robert E., Carlos Salas and Bruce Campbell (2006), *Revisiting NAFTA: Still not Working for North America's Workers*, Economic Policy Institute Briefing Paper, September 16.

Sierra Club (n.d.), *Trade and Sprawl: How Global Trade Rules Could Increase Sprawl*, <http://www.sierraclub.org>

Smith, Wesley R. (1993), *Assessing the NAFTA Side Agreements*, The Heritage Foundation, Backgrounder #960, September 30, <http://www.heritage.org>

Stiglitz, Joseph E. (2004), 'The broken promise of NAFTA', *New York Times*, January 6 (Global Policy Forum), <http://www.globalpolicy.org>

Terry, John, Lou Ederer and Jennifer A Orange (n.d.), 'NAFTA: the first trade treaty to protect IP rights', *Intellectual Asset Management*, <http://www.buildingipvalue.com>

Time (1970), 'Toward the Japanese century', *Time*, March 2, <http://www.time.com>

Time (1971), 'Peril: the new protectionism', *Time*, December 6, <http://www.time.com>

US Department of State (1993), *Fact Sheet: summary of principal provisions of NAFTA – North American Free Trade Agreement*, August 30, <http://findarticles.com>

USInfo.state.gov (2005), *Study Documents Negative Impact of U.S. Trade Deficit with China*, January 11, <http://usinfo.state.gov>

Wall Street Journal (2009), 'Austan Goolsbee's vindication', April 24, <http://online.wsj.com>

Wise, Carol (2006), *China's Trade with North America: What Does this Mean for NAFTA?*, Woodrow Wilson Center, February 14, <http://www.princeton.edu>

World Bank Group (2004), *'Beyond Economic Growth' Student Book* <http://www.worldbank.org>

World Bank (2005), *Economic Growth in the 1990s: Learning from a Decade of Reform*, Herndon, VA: World Bank Publications.

7

Inequality, mobility and
the American dream

This chapter looks at inequality in the US. It considers concepts such as the *Lorenz curve* and the *Gini coefficient* and explores the reasons why there is greater inequality in the US than in the countries of Europe. It also examines the growth in inequality over recent decades and assesses why rates of economic mobility have also declined.

News commentaries often stress the inequalities that seem to define American society. Much has been said, in particular, about the gulf between rich and poor. There are frequent stories about displays of opulence as well as the hardships faced by some of those living below the poverty line. Many of the statistics support the tone and approach adopted in these reports. In 2003, the Congressional Budget Office reported that the top 1 per cent of Americans, who earn an average of $1.3m each before tax ($862,000 after tax), have an income that is, in total, more than that received by the 110 million people in the lowest 40 per cent, whose income averages $21,350 annually (Schifferes, 2003).

While the inequality gap has widened in recent decades, attacks on earnings and wealth differentials have a long history in the US. Towards the end of the nineteenth century, *populist* agitators spoke up for western farmers and poor whites and at the same time lambasted the wealthy east coast owners of the railroads and the banks. Although it adopted more restrained tones, the Progressive movement that followed in the wake of populism also attacked the wealth and power of the bankers and businessmen (dubbed 'robber barons') who controlled many of the major industries and the distribution of farm produce.

Although some attacked the 'hobos' who wandered across states during the depression years of the 1930s, popular culture has also portrayed the poor in more sympathetic terms. The song 'Brother Can You Spare a Dime?', written in 1931 and sung by Bing Crosby, told of former soldiers and workers who were now dependent upon the charity of others. Almost forty years later, at the end of the 1960s, Elvis Presley recorded 'In the Ghetto', portraying inner-city poverty and its consequences.

More recently, first-hand commentaries and narratives have told of continuing poverty in the urban neighbourhoods and the plight of low-paid workers. Barbara Ehrenreich's book, *Nickel and Dimed*, is a representative example. Ehrenreich worked 'undercover' in jobs at the lowest end of labour market, including in restaurants, a nursing home and Wal-mart. The jobs were intense and demanding but, even without dependants, the remuneration did not cover the necessities of life (Ehrenreich, 2002). For his part, the documentary film maker Michael Moore has tracked the hardships faced by workers in Flint, Michigan, following the closure of auto plants (*Roger and Me*, 1989). Moore's film *Sicko* (2007) contrasted the profits accumulated by the insurance companies with the hardships faced by those excluded from comprehensive health provision. Jacob Hacker emphasises the extent to which US family incomes are now highly unstable insofar as they rise and fall, from year to year, much more sharply than in the past and are now much more likely to undergo significant decline:

> The chance that families will see their income plummet has risen. The chance that they will experience long-term movement up the income ladder has not. For average families, the economic roller coaster takes them up and down. It doesn't leave them any higher than when they started. (Hacker, 2006: 15)

Measuring inequality

The extent to which a society is unequal or equal is customarily measured through the *Gini coefficient*. The coefficient is, in turn, derived from the *Lorenz curve* (Figure 7.1). This shows the relationship between the proportion of individuals, families or households and their acquisition of income. The reasoning begins with the line of perfect equality. In a perfectly equal society, 50 per cent of the individuals, families or households would receive 50 per cent of national income. 75 per cent would receive 75 per cent.

No society comes close to this. In practice, even in the more egalitarian societies of Scandinavia, there are deep inequalities. The lower 50 per cent of the families or households secures far less than 50 per cent of national income. While 100 per cent of the families or households will, by definition, receive 100 per cent of a country's income, the Lorenz curve always droops well below the line of perfect equality.

The Gini coefficient captures the degree of equality or inequality in a society by measuring the area between that country's Lorenz curve and the line of perfect equality and then considering this as a proportion of the entire triangular area of the graph underneath the line of perfect equality. A Gini coefficient

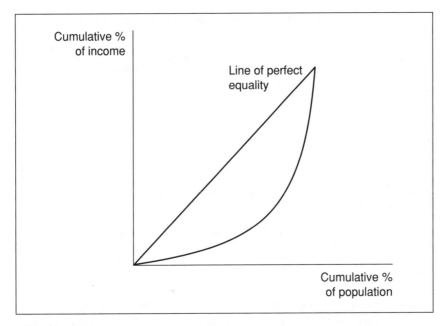

Figure 7.1 *The Lorenz curve*

Source: adapted from CyberEconomics (2008), *Measuring Income Distribution*, <http://ingrimayne.com>

of 0 (indicating that the Lorenz curve is the same as the line of perfect equality) represents a perfectly equal society.

If the Lorenz curve droops very substantially below the line of perfect equality (thereby indicating that the society is highly unequal), the area between the curve and the line of perfect equality will be relatively large as a proportion of the total area underneath the line of perfect equality. The Gini coefficient for that society will therefore be fairly high. If, on the other hand, the Lorenz curve is much closer to the line of perfect equality (and therefore droops to a much lesser extent) the Gini coefficient will be lower. In other words, if the Gini coefficient is high, a society is comparatively unequal. Table 7.1 considers some Gini coefficients for family income. Whereas Denmark has a coefficient of 0.24, the US is substantially higher and Mexico is higher still. Some African countries record very high Gini coefficients. In 1994, Botswana had a coefficient of 0.63. In 2006, the figure for Zimbabwe was 0.501 (Central Intelligence Agency – The World Factbook, 2008).

Reasons

Why is the US more unequal than most countries of Europe?

Table 7.1 *Distribution of family income (Gini coefficient), international comparisons*

Country	Gini coefficient	Year
Canada	0.32	2005
China	0.47	2007
Denmark	0.24	2005
Germany	0.28	2005
Japan	0.38	2002
Mexico	0.51	2005
United Kingdom	0.34	2005
United States	0.45	2007

Source: adapted from Central Intelligence Agency – The World Factbook (2008), *Field Listing – Distribution of family income – Gini index*, <https://www.cia.gov>
Note: Family income – like 'household income' which is another commonly used figure – may not offer a full and accurate figure. Families are of different sizes. If a family is large, its income will be spread across a greater number of individuals and each will necessarily have less.

- Some commentators suggest that the explanation lies in the tax system. They emphasise that Europeans are taxed at a higher rate and often also assert that the tax regime in many European countries, particularly the Nordic nations, is more *progressive*. (In other words, the tax authorities take a larger proportion of income as income levels rise.) Initially, there seems to be evidence to support this. According to an OECD study the US 'all-in' tax rate in 2000 for those in the higher tax bands (the OECD considered those receiving 167 per cent of average gross earnings) was 28.2 per cent.[1] In contrast, the figures for Denmark and Germany were 51.4 per cent and 49.1 per cent respectively (OECD, 2008). However, these figures are misleading.[2] Many European countries have high national sales taxes. Indeed, the Nordic nations levy a 25 per cent tax on all goods and services, which is *regressive* insofar as it takes a greater share of income from lower income groupings. Indeed, Monica Prasad and Yingying Deng conclude, if the overall tax burden is considered the US system is more progressive than others, particularly those in Scandinavia:

    the USA has a more progressive tax structure than the European welfare states. Of the six countries for which it was possible to calculate sales tax, the USA is the only country to have an overall progressive tax structure.... Of the 13 countries for which it was possible to calculate income, payroll and property tax progressivity, the USA has the most progressive tax structure; Sweden and Denmark are the most regressive. (Prasad and Deng, 2009: 443)[3]

- Some commentators stress the opportunities that the US offers to those with entrepreneurial vision. The open character of the American economy, it is said, permits the rapid expansion and growth of corporate initiatives that address gaps in the market. It also rewards those who take such initiatives. The economic rewards for those who are successful necessarily increase the gap between rich and poor.

- Supply and demand in the labour market can play a pivotal role in determining the degree of inequality. Mass immigration (including large numbers of 'illegals') and, arguably, the structural weaknesses of the public education system in poorer neighbourhoods, have added to labour supply. As a consequence, those at the bottom of the labour market are employed in insecure working conditions and are vulnerable to exploitation. A 2009 study of low-wage workers in New York, Los Angeles and Chicago found that many were paid less than the minimum wage and were not remunerated for overtime. Twelve per cent reported that their employer had stolen some of the tips that they had been given (Greenhouse, 2009).
- Although some government programmes (such as Social Security) were established during the New Deal years, traditions of self-reliance are still deeply embedded in US political culture. While charitable giving and voluntary effort should not be underestimated, and while there was some growth in government provision from the beginning of the 1990s, the US devotes fewer resources to social programmes and the alleviation of poverty than European countries (Table 7.2). As Timothy Smeeding records, in 2000 the US 'spent less than 3 per cent of GDP on cash and near cash assistance for the nonelderly (families with children and the disabled). This amount is less than half the share of GDP spent for this purpose by Canada, Ireland, or the United Kingdom; less than a third of spending in Austria, Germany, the Netherlands, or Belgium; and less than a quarter of the amount spent in Finland or Sweden' (Smeeding, 2005: 11).
- A cross-national study that considered the United States along with fifteen other countries has suggested that political-institutional variables, such as trade union density, the extent to which there is centralisation of wage bargaining, the size of the public sector, and the partisan composition of government may be more significant than economic processes. Union density is important across different countries. If there is, as in the US, relatively low union membership as a proportion of the overall workforce, there will be greater income inequality. Indeed, as Rueda and Pontusson conclude: 'Union density emerges as the single most important factor influencing wage inequality across institutional contexts; its effects are consistently egalitarian and they are greater than those of any other independent variable within the country clusters' (Rueda and Pontusson, 2000: 352). However, the impact of the other variables (such as the partisan character of the government and the extent to which it is drawn from the parties of the left or those of the right) differs between liberal market economies (such as the US or Britain) and social market economies (such as France or Germany). It only has an impact on levels of inequality in liberal market economies (Rueda and Pontusson, 2000: 379).[4]

Table 7.2 *Public social expenditure as a proportion of GDP*

Year	Denmark	Germany	United Kingdom	United States
1980	25.2	23	16.6	13.3
1981	25.4	23.7	18	13.6
1982	25.5	23.8	18.5	13.9
1983	26	23.4	19.4	14.1
1984	24.9	23.1	19.3	13.2
1985	24.2	23.6	19.6	12.9
1986	23.4	23.6	19.7	13.1
1987	24.1	23.9	18.9	13
1988	25.4	24	17.7	13
1989	25.7	23	17.1	13
1990	25.5	22.5	17.2	13.4
1991	26.3	23.7	18.6	14.4
1992	26.8	25.7	20.3	15.1
1993	28.6	26.1	21	15.3
1994	29.4	26.1	20.5	15.3
1995	28.9	26.6	20.4	15.4
1996	28.2	27.1	20.1	15.2
1997	27.2	26.4	19.2	14.9
1998	27	26.7	19.3	14.8
1999	26.8	26.7	19	14.6
2000	25.8	26.6	19.1	14.6
2001	26.4	26.7	20.1	15.2
2002	26.9	27.4	20.1	16
2003	27.6	27.6	20.1	16.2

Note: Public social expenditure comprises cash benefits, direct 'in-kind' provision of goods and services, and tax breaks with social purposes. To be considered 'social', benefits have to address one or more social goals. Benefits may be targeted at low-income households, but they may also be for the elderly, disabled, sick, unemployed, or young persons. Programmes regulating the provision of social benefits have to involve: *a*) redistribution of resources across households, or *b*) compulsory participation. Social benefits are regarded as public when general government (that is central, state, and local governments, including social security funds) controls relevant financial flows. The expenditures shown here refer only to public social benefits and exclude similar benefits provided by private charities.
Source: adapted from Swivel (2008), *Public Social Expenditure*, (OECD, April 20, 2007), <http://www.swivel.com>

Growing inequality

Although, as Thomas Piketty and Emmanuel Saez emphasise, the gap between rich and poor was still smaller at the end of the 1990s than it had been in the years before the First World War, levels of inequality have grown since the 1970s. Indeed, by the end of the twentieth century, top wage shares were much higher than during the interwar years (Piketty and Saez, 2003: 32).[5]

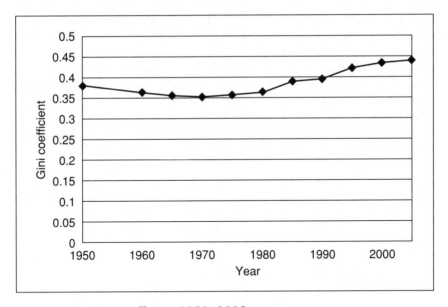

Figure 7.2 *US Gini coefficient, 1950–2005*

Source: adapted from US Census Bureau, *Historical Income Tables – Families, Table F-4. Gini Ratios for Families, by Race and Hispanic Origin of Householder: 1947 to 2006*, <http://www.census.gov>

As Figure 7.2 suggests, after falling during the long boom years of the 1950s and 1960s, the Gini coefficient for the US has risen steadily since 1968 (US Census Bureau, 2009).

As the *Economist* concluded in June 2006: 'The one truly continuous trend over the past 25 years has been toward greater concentration of income at the very top' (quoted in Reynolds, 2007: 2).[6] According to Piketty and Saez, who base their analysis on Internal Revenue Service returns, the threshold for those in the highest-earning one ten-thousandth of households in the late 1970s was about $2 million (in inflation-adjusted, pretax terms). In 2007, it was $11.5 million: 'The gains for the merely affluent were also big, if not quite huge. The cutoff to be in the top 1 per cent doubled since the late 1970s, to roughly $400,000. By contrast, pay at the median – which was about $50,000 in 2007 – rose less than 20 per cent, Census data shows. Near the bottom of the income distribution, the increase was about 12 per cent' (Leonhardt and Fabrikant, 2009).

Some have suggested that despite these claims the increase in inequality is largely illusory and reflects changes in the character of the tax regime rather than a fundamental shift in the US economic structure. According to Alan Reynolds of the Cato Institute tax changes (and in particular reductions in marginal tax rates) encouraged large numbers of businesses to change from filing tax returns as corporate taxpayers to using the individual income tax system (Reynolds, 2007: 4). Although the shift in the tax returns that were submitted was merely a technical change, it created the appearance that there were more very high earners.

Many commentators, however, challenge this. Gary Burtless of the Brookings Institution, a more left-leaning Washington thinktank, accepts that estimates of income, wealth and inequality based upon tax returns can be criticised but argues that other sources of income data, most notably the surveys of households conducted by the US Census Bureau, are valid and allow firm conclusions to be drawn that levels of inequality have increased markedly:

> Ever since the income distribution became a hot topic in the 1980s, the main source of information on which people rely comes from an annual Census Bureau survey of American households. The reason most people think inequality has risen since the late 1980s is because the household survey shows it has. (Burtless, 2007: 3)

Why, then, have levels of inequality risen?

- Structural economic change and the adoption of new forms of technology have played an important part. As Henry M. Paulson Jr, the Treasury secretary in the Bush administration, noted, 'the rapid pace of technological change has been a major driver in the decades-long widening of the income gap' (Johnston, 2007). Indeed, technological changes have magnified the effects of educational differences. Those who have the abilities and skills to use new forms of technology (who will probably have graduate qualifications) are in much greater demand and attract much higher earnings. Correspondingly, those without qualifications will have difficulty finding any form of job opening except at the lowest end of the labour market. Put another way, as Rueda and Pontusson conclude, technological changes 'have rendered more-educated workers more valuable to employers than less-educated workers' (Rueda and Pontusson, 2000: 357). Furthermore, the downsizing of companies and layoffs as a consequence of technological change disproportionately affect those in lower-income groupings.[7] It is not, Will Hutton suggests, that jobs are being sacrificed in the interest of productivity gains. Instead, he concludes that 'downsized companies have delivered the same or reduced output, but have succeeded in paying less for any given hour worked. In other words, downsizing is merely an effective way of holding down wages and transferring income from labour to capital' (Hutton, 2007: 303).
- Although the US has a more progressive taxation system than is often acknowledged, the tax code in the US and some other OECD countries has become less progressive in recent decades. This is partly because of a shift towards indirect or sales taxes (requiring all consumers to pay the same rate on purchases) and reductions in the marginal rates of income tax paid

by the highest earners. The highest rate of federal income tax was 70 per cent when President Ronald Reagan took office in January 1981. The cuts at the beginning of his first term reduced the rate to 50 per cent. Once the tax cuts proposed by President George W. Bush and passed by Congress had been implemented, the top rate had been reduced to 35 per cent (Bittle and Johnson, 2008: 59). Furthermore, inheritance tax (dubbed the 'death tax' by many conservatives) has been reduced. As of 2007, it was imposed on less than 1 per cent of American families. Up to $2 million could be inherited tax free (Bittle and Johnson, 2008: 239). As Paul Krugman has concluded, 'Americans pay low taxes by international standards. Most people's taxes haven't gone up in the past generation; the wealthy have had their taxes cut to levels not seen since before the New Deal' (Krugman, 2003). Robert Greenstein, executive director of the Center on Budget and Policy Priorities, an advocacy group campaigning on behalf of the poor, has spoken in similar terms: ' "The nation faces some very tough choices in coming years...That such a large share of the income gains are going to the very top, at a minimum, raises serious questions about continuing to provide tax cuts averaging over $150,000 a year to people making more than a million dollars a year, while saying we do not have enough money to provide health insurance to 47 million Americans and cutting education benefits' (Johnston, 2007).

- Education, particularly higher education, has always been important. It shapes the supply of labour for particular types of jobs. Arguably, there was a narrower gap between incomes during the 1950s and 1960s because there had been an expansion in the number of university places leading to an increase in the relative supply of educated labour. The rate of expansion slowed in the 1970s and 'the supply of better-educated labor subsequently failed to keep up with demand, giving rise to sharply increasing returns to education' (Rueda and Pontusson, 2000: 357). Janet L. Yellen, president and CEO, Federal Reserve Bank of San Francisco, has spelt out the ways in which the wage gap between college graduates and those with a high school education or less has widened. She noted that between 1973 and 2005, the real hourly wages of those in the top 10 per cent of earners, within which most have college or advanced degrees, rose by 30 per cent or more. Furthermore, she recorded, 'among this top 10 per cent, the growth was heavily concentrated at the very tip of the top, that is, the top 1 per cent' (Yellen, 2006). Although these differentials have encouraged increasing numbers to enrol in college, this has not been sufficient to narrow the gap.

- Alongside technological change, there have been claims that the globalisation process has widened the wage inequality gap in the OECD countries (Dreher and Gaston, 2006: 20).[8] Although the US has been less exposed to the global market than many other countries, foreign trade (exports and imports) has grown as a share of GDP. US exports, however, tend to depend upon skilled (sometimes highly skilled) labour. Imports often displace those

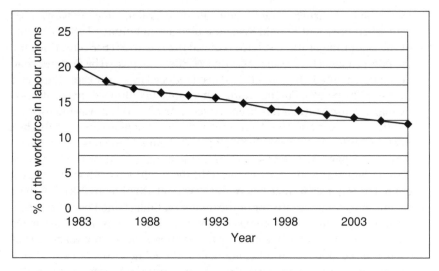

Figure 7.3 *Trade union membership, 1983–2007 (% of workforce)*

Source: adapted from Bureau of Labor Statistics (2006), *Table 38. Union Affiliation of Employed Wage and Salary Workers by Sex, Annual Averages, 1983–2006*, <http://www.bls.gov/cps/wlf-table38-2007.pdf> and United States Department of Labor (2008), *Union Members in 2007*, Bureau of Labor Statistics – News, January 25, <http://www.bls.gov/news.release/pdf/union2.pdf>

with fewer skills. Globalisation has therefore added to the demand for skilled labour and reduced the demand for those with fewer skills. Inequalities have thereby been exacerbated.

- The US labour or trades unions were always weaker than their western European counterparts but nevertheless placed upward pressure upon the wage levels of lower and middling income workers and called for overall 'wage compression'. However, they have lost much of their former leverage (see pp. 82–3). Membership has shrunk as a proportion of the labour force. In 2007, union members accounted for 12.1 per cent of wage and salary workers in employment. In 1983, the figure was 20.1 per cent. Furthermore, whereas the unions were traditionally rooted in the 'heavy' industries such as mining or steel production and could set the pace for wage increases across the labour market, they are now largely based in the public sector. Indeed, those employed in the public sector (working in white-collar occupations, such as education, training and libraries) had a union membership rate nearly five times that of private sector employees (United States Department of Labor, 2008).

- The rises in share prices in, for example, the 'dot.com boom' of the second half of the late 1990s, added enormously to the wealth of those who were share owners although, it should be noted, the 'bursting' of the stock market bubbles led to a significant fall in share prices. At the same time, some commentators point to a lack of transparency and accountability in the corporate sector that has allowed CEO salaries and the stock options offered to them to increase at a rapid rate.

- Since the 1960s there has been a significant shift towards conservative (or 'neo-liberal') ideas along with an underlying faith in an aggressive form of social Darwinism and away from more progressive notions of managed egalitarianism, 'fairness' and social justice. Oliver Stone's 1987 film, *Wall Street*, sought to capture the prevailing mood. In the film, Gordon Gekko, a savagely ruthless corporate operator played by Michael Douglas, tells stockholders in a celebrated address: 'Greed, for lack of a better word, is good. Greed is right. Greed works. Greed clarifies, cuts through, and captures the essence of the evolutionary spirit. Greed, in all of its forms, greed for life, for money, for love, knowledge has marked the upward surge of mankind.' Against this background, the payment of very high salaries, inequality and *rentier* capitalism became much more socially acceptable.

- Changes in the character of the labour force have also played a part. Some suggest that the rise in the scale of women's participation in the workforce increased the relative supply of unskilled labour, thereby depressing wage levels amongst those at the lower end of the socioeconomic scale (Rueda and Pontusson, 2000: 357). There have been suggestions that large-scale immigration, particularly from the countries of central and south America, has added to the supply of unskilled labour and thereby reduced the earnings of native-born low-income workers. As Table 7.3 shows, by 2007 there were there were an estimated 37.3 million immigrants. About a third of these (11.3 million) were in the US illegally. Economists such as George Borjas and Lawrence F. Katz suggest that immigration led to a 3.4 per cent decline in the earnings of native-born workers between 1980 and 2000. Those at the lowest end of the income distribution were most adversely affected (Borjas and Katz, 2006: 38). Others are more sceptical. They question Borjas's methodological assumptions and stress that the lowering of labour costs, as a consequence of immigration, reduces the prices of goods and services, thereby raising purchasing power (Zimmerman, 2008).

Table 7.3 *Foreign-born population in the US (millions)*

Year	Total US population	Foreign-born population
1960	178.5	9.73
1970	203.9	9.62
1980	227.2	14.07
1990	256.2	19.76
2000	281.4	31.1
2005	297.8	34.2

Source: Associated Press (2009), 'U.S. immigration boom hits record levels', *MSNBC*, December 12, <http://www.msnbc.msn.com>

The increase in inequality should, however, be put in context. The mid-century period was in some ways exceptional and should not perhaps be used as a yardstick for judging levels of inequality. There was, between the 1930s and the 1970s, a narrowing of the wage structure that some have termed the 'Great Compression'. Between 1929 and 1947, there was a 17 per cent fall in real income among the highest 1 per cent of income earners. The incomes of those in the highest socioeconomic groupings had been hit by the Great Depression of the 1930s. At the same time, the real wages of manufacturing workers increased by 67 per cent. This was because of increased demand for low-skilled labour and a growth in the relative supply of skilled workers. The highly restrictive immigration policies that had been adopted in the 1920s also limited the supply of unskilled and semi-skilled workers. The ranks of the skilled workforce swelled because much higher numbers were graduating from high school and college opportunities were beginning to expand (Lindsey, 2009: 8–19).

Wealth

Although the words are sometimes used interchangeably, there is an important distinction between income and wealth. Whereas income is a flow, wealth refers to a stock of assets (such as ownership of a house or accumulated savings). In the US, as in many other countries, including some of those regarded as relatively egalitarian, levels of inequality are very pronounced if wealth holdings are considered. As Marco Cagetti and Mariacristina De Nardi conclude in a report on the US published by the Federal Reserve Bank of Chicago: 'a large fraction of the total wealth in the economy is concentrated in the hand of the richest percentiles: the top 1% hold one third, and the richest 5% hold more than half of total wealth. At the other extreme, a significant fraction of the population holds little or no wealth at all' (Cagetti and De Nardi, 2005: 1).

Furthermore, just as the distribution of income has become more unequal in recent decades, there has also been a growing 'wealth gap'. This is partly because increasing income inequalities enable some to build up a greater stock of wealth than others. It is also because the value of assets has risen differentially. The rise in house prices in the years preceding the 'credit crunch' allowed some to gain much more than others. In particular, some saw their equity (the difference between the value of a property and the mortgage owed on it) rise rapidly:

> Higher income households grew home equity at a much faster speed than low income households. While homeowners in the top quartile of household income distribution more than doubled their home equity and nearly doubled their housing value on average, homeowners among the bottom quartile of household income distribution only saw 32 per cent gain in home equity and a 42 per cent

gain in housing values on average...A typical homeowner in the bottom income quartile only gained 12 per cent in home equity and 22 per cent in housing value. (Di, 2007: 18)

Mobility and the American dream

Some would assert that European societies are more unequal than the statistics suggest. This is partly because higher rates of tax in Europe (particularly Scandinavia) encourage tax avoidance and evasion. Income and wealth are therefore underdeclared to the authorities and the hidden economy has more of a presence. Others point to an increase in European inequalities.[9] Nonetheless, few question the claim that there is, in overall terms, greater inequality in the US.

Although inequalities are often the subject of criticism, many commentators suggest, as noted above, that inequality is acceptable because it encourages individuals to work hard and exploit opportunities.[10] This, it is said, is particularly the case in the US because America offers higher levels of mobility than the more rigid and class-based societies of Europe. With sufficient motivation, individuals can escape poverty and progress up the socioeconomic ladder. Indeed, many still talk in terms of the 'American dream'.

The 'American dream' has been defined in different ways. At times, its scope has been quite circumscribed. Although the late nineteenth-century novels of Horatio Alger Jr. are often cited when the American dream is considered, Alger's narratives do not tell of unlimited wealth but instead recount tales of young men who, mostly through their own efforts, escaped poverty and secured security, stability and respectability. In later years, the American dream referred to the economic and social integration of newcomers into the ranks of the middle class. During the years of suburbanisation after the Second World War, the 'American dream' was equated with a family's ownership of a house and an automobile.

The American dream is frequently defined in far more expansive terms, however. In these accounts, it offers the prospect of a 'rags to riches' rise from poverty to unlimited income and wealth. It is about 'long-range' economic mobility, the fulfilment of ambition and notions of boundless opportunity.

Forms of mobility

Economic or income mobility can be defined and assessed in different ways. *Intragenerational* mobility considers the position of an individual within his or her lifetime and the extent to which he or she has moved up the economic ladder.

In contrast, *intergenerational* mobility looks at an individual in relationship to his or her parents (customarily the father). There are different forms of intergenerational mobility. *Absolute* upward mobility is widespread and commonplace. Economic growth ensures that each generation has on average a higher standard of living than the preceding generation (their parents). Those born in the 1960s ('Generation X') are better off in material terms than the 'baby boomers', a generation earlier (Sawhill and Morton, 2008: 5). As the Economic Mobility Project established by the Pew Charitable Trusts has reported:

> Median family income for adults who were children in the late 1960s and are now in their 30s or 40s increased 29 per cent, from $55,600 for parents to $71,900 for their children, adjusting for inflation. Moreover, family sizes have shrunk over this same period (from 3.1 to 2.3 individuals between 1969 and 1998), so higher incomes are spread over fewer people. (Isaacs, 2008: 2)

Only major economic traumas, such as the Great Depression, prevent absolute mobility although the extent to which there is mobility depends upon long-term rates of economic growth.

Relative mobility is different. It takes place 'regardless of what is happening to the society as a whole. Individuals can change their position relative to others, moving up or down within the ranks as one would expect in a true meritocracy' (Sawhill and Morton, 2008: 4).

Mobility in comparative perspective

Despite the assertions that underpin the American dream, mobility in the contemporary US is relatively limited. Indeed, many remain within the same income quintile as their parents. As Table 7.4 shows, 42 per cent of children born to parents in the bottom income quintile remain in the bottom quintile, while 39 per cent born to parents in the highest income quintile remain there.

The American dream, as Isaacs concludes, has very limited validity if it is defined in terms of widespread long-range economic mobility: 'The "rags to riches" story is much more common in Hollywood than on Main Street. Only 6 per cent of children born to parents with family income at the very bottom move to the very top' (Isaacs, 2008: 2).

An individual's fate therefore depends, in large part, on his or her family background. Indeed, it is shaped by grandparents and preceding generations. The Economic Mobility Project concludes that for those who are on particularly high or low incomes, it may take 'five generations or more for these advantages or disadvantages to work their way out of the system' (Economic Mobility Project – The Pew Charitable Trusts, 2008). Only the life chances of those born into middle-income groupings are less predictable. They are almost equally likely to end up in any other income quintile. A third of the population are downwardly rather than upwardly mobile.

Indeed, if considered in overall terms, the US offers markedly less mobility than many other advanced nations. According to researchers, 42 per cent of

Table 7.4 *Children's prospects of relative mobility (%)*

Parents' income grouping	Children's income grouping				
	Bottom quintile	Second quintile	Middle quintile	Fourth quintile	Top quintile
Top quintile	6	10	19	26	39
Fourth quintile	11	18	17	32	23
Middle quintile	19	24	23	19	14
Fourth quintile	23	23	24	15	15
Top quintile	42	25	17	8	9

Note: The table is based upon family income averaged over several years and reported in 2006 dollars.
Source: adapted from Julia B. Isaacs (2008), *Economic Mobility of Families Across Generations*, Economic Mobility Project – The Pew Charitable Trusts, 5, <http://www.economicmobility.org/assets/pdfs/EMP_FamiliesAcrossGenerations_ChapterI.pdf>

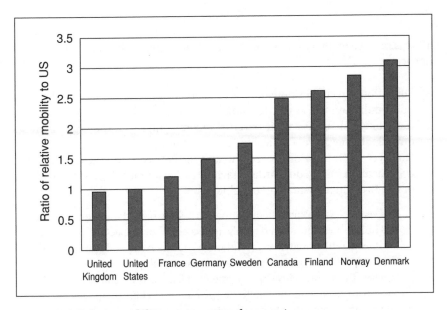

Figure 7.4 *Relative mobility – international comparisons*
Source: adapted from Isabel Sawhill and John E. Morton (2008), *Economic Mobility: Is the American Dream Alive and Well?* Economic Mobility Project – The Pew Charitable Trusts, 9, <http://www.economicmobility.org/assets/pdfs/EMP_American_Dream.pdf>[11]

US men born into the poorest quintile in terms of earnings distribution remain within that quintile as adults. The figures are between 25 and 30 per cent in some other countries (Economic Mobility Project, 2008).[12] Figure 7.4 considers the rate of relative mobility in eight countries in comparison to the US. The graph is indexed so that the US mobility rate is presented as 1. Only the United

Kingdom has a lower rate of mobility but the difference is only marginal. Rates of mobility in Germany are twice as high as those in the US and they are three times higher in Denmark.

There are, furthermore, suggestions that mobility levels may have fallen. Certainly, many Americans believe this. A 2008 Pew survey found that more than half of those asked believed that they had not moved ahead in the preceding five years (25 per cent) or felt that they had fallen behind (31 per cent). It was, according to Pew commentators, 'the most downbeat assessment of personal progress in nearly half a century' (Samuelson, 2008: 13). Pew also found evidence that the gap in terms of educational attainment (which plays a large part in determining later income levels) between Latino and black Americans on the one hand and whites and Asians on the other may be widening (Eckholm, 2008).[13]

Reasons

Why is relative mobility much more limited than talk of the 'American dream' suggests?

* Education can enable individuals from poorer backgrounds to gain the skills and qualifications needed to climb the economic ladder. Individuals are more likely to surpass their parents' income and reach the high earnings quintile if they have a college degree (Economic Mobility Project, 2008). However, such individuals are few and far between. In overall terms, the US education system does little to facilitate upward mobility. As Ron Haskins of the Brookings Institution concludes:

  > At every level from preschool, to the K-12 system, to the nation's colleges and universities, education has only modest economic impacts on the average low-income child or adolescent. Although education can and sometimes does boost the achievement and later the income of children from relatively poor families, the average effect of education at all levels is to reinforce the differences associated with the family background that children and adolescents bring with them to the classroom. (Haskins, 2008: 11)

In part this is because public schools are funded by local property taxes and poorer districts can offer only limited resources to each of their schools. However, early socialisation may also play a part insofar as it shapes attitudes towards the learning process as well as expectations and hopes. Will Hutton stresses the role played by the process of development before a young girl or boy begins school: 'Disadvantage begins at birth and continues in early childhood, now understood to be a critical period for intellectual and emotional development. It is vital for a child's development either to have an adult parent at home full time, implying forgone income, or alternatively child care, averaging

$4,500 a year, which is beyond most working families' (Hutton, 2007: 307). However, other variables, including family size and birth order, may be significant. There are suggestions, for example, that children born later have lower levels of educational achievement. This might be because of financial constraints or different relationships between parents and children as families become larger (Kronstadt and Favreault, 2008).

- Many on the left emphasise the barriers to advancement in the US that are structured around race and ethnicity. Until the passage of the 1964 Civil Rights Act, the *Jim Crow* laws in the southern states maintained a system of institutionalised discrimination that confined African-Americans to subordinate status. There were very few occupations open to those who were black and entrepreneurial opportunities were limited to the few that emerged within the black market. Although there was not *de jure* discrimination in northern states such as New York or Illinois, *de facto* discrimination (through social barriers) ensured that few within the minorities could share the 'American dream'. Arguably, despite progress over the past half-century, there are still restricted opportunities for those who are non-white. At the least, continuing racial 'segregation' (insofar as blacks and whites live in different neighbourhoods) and cultural separation may restrict the economic mobility of minorities.
- In *Race, Class and Conservatism*, Thomas D. Boston has built upon notions of institutionalised discrimination to argue that the US labour market is segmented – in other words, is divided between a primary and secondary labour market. Although there are different strata within each market, the former is structured around managerial, professional, technical, sales and craft occupations. Employment is organised around formal rules, systems of pay and institutionalised hierarchies. The secondary labour market is based around more general forms of labour, low wages and arbitrary rule-making. Blacks are largely confined to the secondary labour market 'even after having controlled for job-related attributes, age and other demographic differences' (Boston, 1988: 133). Only a very small number of individuals can pass between the two markets.
- Many commentators argue that women also face structural impediments to individual progress. Those associated with feminism and the left often insist on the existence of a 'glass ceiling'. Despite formal pronouncements of equal opportunity, the occupational structure prevents women from advancing beyond a certain level. In part, this is because many women withdraw from the labour market for a period to bring up young children. They therefore fall behind in job terms. However, many allege that corporate decision-making is dominated by male networks that look less favourably upon career women. This line of reasoning has been challenged by Diana Furchtgott-Roth and Christine Stolba of the American Enterprise Institute, a conservative thinktank in Washington DC. Women, they conclude, have

made very substantial progress and are now awarded over 50 per cent of college degrees at bachelor's and master's level. They are better represented in occupations that were traditionally male bastions. If education levels and experience are factored in, their positions and salaries are comparable with those of men. Often women have only fallen behind because of personal choices. They have chosen to stay at home with young children or work on a part-time basis (Furchtgott-Roth and Stolba, 1996: 79–80).

- Some sections of the right rallied around *The Bell Curve*, a 1994 study of intelligence (IQ), achievement and the class structure written by Richard J. Herrnstein and Charles Murray. It asserted that IQ was an important influence in determining an individual's eventual income and work performance as well as the likelihood of becoming pregnant outside of marriage or turning to criminality. The book also claimed that when IQ test results were plotted, the normal distribution curve for African-Americans was to the left (in other words, the median IQ was lower) than that for whites (Herrnstein and Murray, 1996). *The Bell Curve* was subject to criticism from the left as well as many on the right. Its authors were accused of scientific racism. They were said to imply that IQ was genetically determined by failing to acknowledge evidence suggesting that IQ was shaped in large part by cultural factors. Herrnstein and Murray were, it was said, surrendering to a crude determinism that denied the role of human agency. Glenn C. Loury, an influential black conservative, was among those criticising the 'suggestion that we accommodate ourselves to the inevitability of the difference in mental performance among the races in America' (Loury, 1994). There is, nonetheless, some research data suggesting that genetic inheritance can influence cognitive skills and antisocial behaviour. Both play a part in determining an individual's position in the labour market and their chances of upward mobility (Kronstadt, 2008).

- Many conservatives extend the critique of *The Bell Curve* and reject claims that life chances are structurally determined on the basis of race, gender or parental class position. They point to examples of black entrepreneurship and argue that obstacles can be overcome with sufficient determination and effort. They suggest that cultural variables and individual choices play a significant part in shaping an individual's economic fate. Although Robert Rector, senior research fellow in Domestic Policy Studies at the Heritage Foundation, one of the most influential of the conservative thinktanks in Washington DC, is committed to limited government, he believes that it should bolster commitment to the work ethic and strengthen traditionalist forms of morality: 'To the extent that enduring poverty continues in our society, it is largely the result of personal behavior, particularly the lack of work and marriage. Policies that require welfare recipients to work or prepare for work as a condition of receiving aid and that encourage the formation of healthy marriages are the best vehicles for further reducing poverty' (Rector, 2004). Rector's thinking underpinned the Personal Responsibility and Work Opportunity Act of 1996 that reformed welfare provision. The Act was passed by Congress in the wake of the Republican victories in the November 1994 elections and was signed by President Clinton. Assistance for single mothers was limited to two years at one time and five years in a lifetime. The Act also sought to promote two-parent families and deter out-of-wedlock births. Single parenthood and illegitimacy, it was argued, kept many in poverty and dependency. The subsequent fall in the numbers on the welfare rolls seemed to offer confirmation that the Act had been justified. For his part, Thomas Sowell emphasises human capital. He has charted what he regards as the defining cultural characteristics of particular ethnic, national and racial groupings. Some of these characteristics promoted upward economic mobility while others impeded progress. Some racial and groupings have prospered despite adversity. Sowell points to Chinese and Japanese Americans. Although they have faced enduring prejudice, they now achieve more, in terms of educational attainment and income, than whites. Richard Brookhiser, another conservative writer, emphasises the values embodied in the cultural traditions of the WASP (White Anglo-Saxon Protestant). These inspired and enabled WASPs to pursue an upward path and, through this, shape the character of the US. Although latterly corrupted by contemporary liberalism and notions of group identity, WASP values traditionally included a commitment to the work ethic, responsible individualism, civic-mindedness, diligence, sobriety and thrift (Auster, 1991).

• Some other conservatives stress economic constraints on jobseekers and those who establish their own businesses. The minimum wage, enacted under federal and different state laws, has come under fire. By setting a wage that is above the market-clearing rate for those with the lowest skills and minimal experience, 'one out of every three black teens [is] now legislatively priced out of the job market.' (*Wall Street Journal*, 2005). Conservatives also point to the barriers to entry (such as government regulation or predatory pricing by firms that are already established) that prevent the creation of new businesses in particular markets. They argue that deregulation not only offers greater consumer choice at a more competitive price but allows those at the bottom of the socioeconomic ladder to make progress. Nonetheless, although those who are self-employed achieve lower initial earnings than those in regular forms of employment, and black-owned businesses fail to match their white counterparts, once a business is established, self-employment leads to increased earnings for low-income individuals (McKernan and Salzman, 2008).

Conclusion

The evidence suggests that the US has become more unequal in recent decades and, at the same time, upward mobility has slowed.[14] Nearly all agree that inequality and immobility matter. Furthermore, few would dissent from the claim that individuals should have the opportunity to climb the socioeconomic ladder. Indeed, as noted above, the 'American dream' is generally seen as a defining feature of the US as a country. Commentators disagree, however, about the character of the consequences of inequality. For many on the right, there is a connection between inequality and economic growth. Indeed, inequality is desirable insofar as it allows the provision of material incentives to those who are successful and promotes the increased provision of goods and services. Societies that offer fewer material incentives (but are more egalitarian) are, from this perspective, more likely to have very low rates of growth or stagnate. The impoverishment of communist societies such as Cuba and North Korea is testimony to this, albeit in an extreme form.

Those who lean to the left are much more critical. It is, they assert, possible to have a more egalitarian society and for there still to be high levels of economic growth. Scandinavia is often cited in this context (see p. 219). Nolan McCarty, Keith T. Poole and Howard Rosenthal argue that rising levels of inequality are tied together with political polarisation. The US is more divided than in earlier years. Others point to the fraying of the social fabric and tie inequality together with the growth of 'gated communities' that divide the higher income groups from those left on the outside. The country, they argue, needs to rediscover the 'common good'.

Notes

1   The all-in tax rate, calculated as 'the combined central and sub-central government income tax plus employee social security contribution, as a percentage of gross wage earnings' (Organization for Economic Cooperation and Development, 2007).

2   Thomas Piketty and Emmanuel Saez take a different position and argue on the basis of tax returns that although the US had a more progressive tax structure than France and the UK until the 1970s, it has been more regressive since then. Prasad and Deng argue that this conclusion is based upon a limited range of taxes and therefore does not represent a full picture (Prasad and Deng, 2009: 435).

3   Prasad and Deng suggest that the regressive character of European taxation systems has enabled these countries to introduce extended social provision (because it faced low levels of opposition from higher-income groupings) whereas the more progressive character of US tax codes bolstered opposition to the provision of 'socialised' health and other forms of assistance (Prasad and Deng, 2009: 432). It should be added that higher-income groupings in the US contribute a very large share of total tax revenues. As Clive Crook noted in the *Financial Times*: 'The U.S. income tax collects 45 per cent of its revenues from the highest-income decile'. The average in other developed countries is 32 per cent (Yglesias, 2009).

4   Larry Bartels has drawn similar conclusions in his study of the US. He argues that although public policy is shaped by Congress as well as the presidency, the

partisan character of the White House has made a significant difference to levels of economic inequality. When there is a Republican president, those at the top of the income distribution scale experience much larger real income gains than those at the bottom. However, when a Democrat is in the White House, those in the lowest quintile make the largest gains: 'In his first four years in office, President George W. Bush presided over a 2% cumulative increase in the real incomes of families at the 95th percentile of the income distribution, but a 1% *decline* in the real incomes of middle-class families and a 3% decline in the real incomes of working poor families...had President Al Gore governed under the same economic circumstances, the real incomes of working poor families would probably have grown by about 6% (1.5% per year) over those four years, and the real incomes of middle-class families would probably have grown by about 4.5% (1.1% per year), while the real incomes of families at the 95th percentile would have remained unchanged' (Bartels, 2008: 63).

5 If the income earned by those at the top is considered, the depression years and the Second World War had, despite fluctuations, a levelling effect that, Piketty and Saez suggest, lasted until the 1970s (Piketty and Saez, 2003: 12).

6 The recession that began in late 2007 has brought a halt to this trend. Indeed, although the rise in unemployment has hit those in the lower income groupings, the rich have also been squeezed. As David Leonhardt and Geraldine Fabrikant noted in the *New York Times*: 'The rich, as a group, are no longer getting richer. Over the last two years, they have become poorer. And many may not return to their old levels of wealth and income anytime soon' (Leonhardt and Fabrikant, 2009). Leonhardt and Fabrikant pointed to the fate of John McAfee, who established the antivirus software company named after him, and was said in August 2009 to be worth only about $4 million compared with an earlier peak of more than $100 million.

7 For their part, Piketty and Saez question the extent to which technological change has led to growing income inequality. They note that much of the increase can be attributed to 'the huge increase in top wage shares since the 1970s' . Yet, 'such a large change in top wage shares has not taken place in most European countries which experienced the same technical change as the United States' (Piketty and Saez, 2003: 34).

8 Most economists believe, however, that when growing inequality is considered, 'globalization takes a backseat' and that technological change has played more of a role (Braeuninger, 2008).

9 See, for example, Wirtén, 2007.

10 Arguments such as these have been challenged by the *Kuznets curve* and the reasoning that underpins it. This suggests that while inequality plays an important role during the early stages of industrialisation, insofar as it encourages savings and investment, more developed economies depend upon human capital. Inequality tends to deny educational opportunities to those in lower income groups.

11 See also Markus Jantti et al., *American Exceptionalism in a New Light: A Comparison of Intergenerational Earnings Mobility in the Nordic Countries, the United Kingdom and the United States*, Bonn: Institute for the Study of Labor Discussion Paper 1938 (2006), <http://papers.ssrn.com> and Miles Corak, 'Do poor children become poor adults? Lessons from a cross country comparison of generational earnings mobility', *Research on Economic Inequality*, 13:1 (2006): 143–88.

12 Americans must 'travel' further if they are to climb the economic ladder. This is because there is greater inequality in the US than many comparable countries (Economic Mobility Project, 2008).

13 Robert J. Samuelson has noted that at the same time, about two-thirds of Americans assert that they have higher standards of living than their parents (Samuelson, 2008).

14 Mobility depends, to some degree, upon equality and inequality. Individuals have to 'travel' further if they are to advance in more unequal societies. Arguably, growing inequality has played a part in limiting rates of mobility.

References and further reading

Auster, Lawrence (1991), 'The way of the WASP: how it made America, and how it can save it, so to speak', *National Review*, January 28, <http://www.nationalreview.com>

Bartels, Larry (2008), *Unequal Democracy: The Political Economy of the New Gilded Age*, Princeton, NJ: Princeton University Press.

Bittle, Scott and Jean Johnson (2008), *Where Does the Money Go? Your Guided Tour to the Federal Budget Crisis*, New York: Collins.

Borjas, George J. and Lawrence F. Katz (2006), *The Evolution of the Mexican-Born Workforce in the United States*, March, <http://www.economics.harvard.edu/faculty/katz/files/mex_immig_nber_wp.pdf>

Boston, Thomas D. (1988), *Race, Class and Conservatism*, Boston: Unwin Hyman.

Braeuninger, Dieter (2008), *Has Globalization Deepened Inequality?*, YaleGlobal, February 6, <http://yaleglobal.yale.edu>

Burtless, Gary (2007), *Comments on 'Has U.S. Income Inequality Really Increased'*, <http://www3.brookings.edu/views/papers/burtless/20070111.pdf>

Cagetti, Marco and Mariacristina De Nardi (2005), *Wealth Inequality: Data and Models*, Chicago: Federal Reserve Bank of Chicago.

Central Intelligence Agency – The World Factbook (2008), *Field Listing – Distribution of family income – Gini index*, <https://www.cia.gov>

Di, Zhu Xiao (2007), *Growing Wealth, Inequality, and Housing in the United States*, February, Joint Center for Housing Studies, Harvard University, <http://www.jchs.harvard.edu/publications/markets/w07-1.pdf>

Dreher, Axel and Noel Gaston (2006), *Has Globalisation Increased Inequality?*, Konjunkturforschungsstelle Swiss Institute for Business Cycle Research, Arbeitspapiere/Working Papers, <http://www.kof.ethz.ch/publications/science/pdf/wp_140.pdf>

Eckholm, Erik (2008), 'Higher education gap may slow economic mobility', *New York Times*, February 19, <http://www.nytimes.com>

Economic Mobility Project (2008), *Summary of Key Findings: 'Getting Ahead or Losing Ground: Economic Mobility in America'*, <http://www.economicmobility.org/assets/pdfs/Economic_Mobility_in_America_Key%20Findings.pdf>

Economic Mobility Project – The Pew Charitable Trusts (2008), *Economic Mobility Factsheet*, <http://www.economicmobility.org/reports_and_research/Economic%20Mobility%20Project%20Fact%20Sheet.pdf>

Ehrenreich, Barbara (2002), *Nickel and Dimed: On Getting by in America (Spare Change?)*, New York: Saint Martin's Press.

Furchtgott-Roth, Diana and Christine Stolba (1996), *Women's Figures: The Economic Progress of Women in America*, Washington DC: AEI Press.

Greenhouse, Steven (2009), 'Low-wage workers are often cheated, study says', *New York Times*, September 2, A11.

Hacker, Jacob (2006), *The Great Risk Shift: The Assault on American Jobs, Families, Health Care, and Retirement and How You Can Fight Back*, Oxford: Oxford University Press.

Haskins, Ron (2008), 'Education and economic mobility', in Julia B. Isaacs, Isabel V. Sawhill and Ron Haskins (2008), *Getting Ahead or Losing Ground: Economic Mobility In America*, <http://www.economicmobility.org/assets/pdfs/EMP_Education_ChapterVIII.pdf>

Herrnstein, Richard J. and Charles Murray (1996), *Bell Curve: Intelligence and Class Structure in American Life*, New York: Simon & Schuster.

Hutton, Will (2007), *The Writing on the Wall: China and the West in the 21st Century*, London: Abacus.

Isaacs, Julia B. (2008), *Economic Mobility of Families Across Generations*, Economic Mobility Project – The Pew Charitable Trusts, <http://www.economicmobility.org/assets/pdfs/EMP_Across_Generations_ES.pdf>

Johnston, David Cay (2007), 'Income gap is widening, data shows', *New York Times*, March 29, <http://www.nytimes.com>

Kronstadt, Jessica (2008), *Genetics and Economic Mobility*, Economic Mobility Project – The Pew Charitable Trusts, <http://www.economicmobility.org/assets/pdfs/EMP_LitReview_Genetics.pdf>

Kronstadt, Jessica and Melissa Favreault (2008), *Families and Economic Mobility*, The Urban Institute, <http://www.urban.org>

Krugman, Paul (2003), 'The tax-cut con', *New York Times*, September 14, <http://www.nytimes.com>

Leonhardt, David and Geraldine Fabrikant (2009), 'Rise of the super-rich hits a sobering wall', *New York Times*, August 20, <http://www.nytimes.com>

Lindsey, Brink (2009), *Paul Krugman's Nostalgianomics: Economic Policies, Social Norms, and Income Inequality*, Washington DC: Cato Institute.

Loury, Glenn C. (1994), 'Dispirited – race and intelligence – "The Bell Curve": a symposium – cover story', *National Review*, December 5, repr. in R. Jacoby and N. Glauberman (eds) (1995), *The Bell Curve Debate*, New York: Times Books (Random House), 346–50.

McKernan, Signe-Mary and Hal Salzman (2008), *Self-Employment and Economic Mobility*, Economic Mobility Project – The Pew Charitable Trusts, <http://www.economicmobility.org/assets/pdfs/EMP_LitReview_SelfEmployment.pdf>

Organization for Economic Cooperation and Development (2007), *OECD Tax Database: Table I.2 Average personal income tax and social security contribution rates on gross labour income*, <http://www.oecd.org>

Piketty, Thomas and Emmanuel Saez (2003), 'Income inequality in the United States, 1913–1998', *Quarterly Journal of Economics*, 118:1, 1–39.

Prasad, Monica and Yingying Deng (2009), 'Taxation and the worlds of welfare', *Socio-Economic Review*, 7:3, 431–57.

Rector, Robert (2004), *Understanding Poverty and Economic Inequality in the United States*, The Heritage Foundation – Backgrounder #1796, September 15, <http://www.heritage.org>

Reed, Deborah (2001) 'Immigration and males' earnings inequality in the regions of the United States', *Demography*, 38:3, August, 363–73.

Reynolds, Alan (2007), 'Has U.S. income inequality *really* increased?', *Policy Analysis* (Cato Institute), January 8, no. 586, <http://www.cato.org>

Rueda, David and Jonas Pontusson (2000), 'Wage inequality and varieties of capitalism', *World Politics*, 52:3, April, 350–83.

Samuelson, Robert J. (2008), 'Progress rips entitlement hopes', *Japan Times*, May 25.

Sawhill, Isabel and John E. Morton (2008), *Economic Mobility: Is the American Dream Alive and Well?* Economic Mobility Project – The Pew Charitable Trusts, <http://www.economicmobility.org/assets/pdfs/EMP_American_Dream.pdf>

Schifferes, Steve (2003), *US Inequality Gap Widens*, BBC News, September 25, <http://news.bbc.co.uk>

Smeeding, Timothy (2005), *Poor People in Rich Nations: The United States in Comparative Perspective*, Luxembourg Income Study Working Paper Series, Working Paper No. 419, October, <http://www.lisproject.org/publications/LISwps/419.pdf>

US Census Bureau (2009), *Income – Historical Income Tables – Families*, Table F-4, <http://www.census.gov>

United States Department of Labor (2008), *Union Members in 2007*, Bureau of Labor Statistics – News, January 25, <http://www.bls.gov/news.release/pdf/union2.pdf>

Wall Street Journal (2005), 'Job slayers', August 29, <http://online.wsj.com>

Weeks, J. (2007), 'Inequality trends in some developed OECD countries', in J.K.S. and J. Baudot (eds), *Flat World, Big Gaps*, New York: ZED Books (in association with the United Nations), 159–74.

Wirtén, Per (2007), *Unacknowledged, Unseen, Unmentioned: Poverty in Europe*, <http://www.eurozine.com>

Yellen, Janet L. (2006), *President's Speech – Economic Inequality in the United States*, November 6, <http://www.frbsf.org>

Yglesias, Matthew (2009), 'The next tax revolt: progressives need to stop worrying and learn to love taxes', *American Prospect*, June 17, <http://www.prospect.org>

Zimmerman, Seth (2008), *Immigration and Economic Mobility*, Pew Charitable Trusts – Economic Mobility Project, <http://www.urban.org/UploadedPDF/1001162_Immigration.pdf>

8

Drawing comparisons: the US and Europe

American conservatives often argue that overbearing state regulation has stifled economic growth and initiative in many European countries. They point to *Eurosclerosis*. This chapter assesses the legitimacy of these claims. It considers comparative growth rates and the variables that should be factored in when comparisons are drawn. It also surveys the relative tax burden on both households and companies as well as living standards, poverty rates and leisure time.

The European countries, particularly those in western Europe, have long been subject to criticism by American conservatives. The criticisms took a particularly vigorous form as the 2008 presidential election approached. One of the leading Republican candidates, former Massachusetts governor Mitt Romney, emphasised the US's superior economic performance by pointing to comparative job creation rates in the US and Europe: 'We've added – during the time Europe added 3 million jobs, we've added about 50 million jobs in this country' (Council on Foreign Relations, 2007). Another Republican contender, former New York mayor Rudy Giuliani, criticised the concept of government-based or 'socialised' health provision by invoking the record of the National Health Service in the United Kingdom:

> I had prostate cancer five, six years ago ... My chance of surviving prostate cancer – and, thank God, I was cured of it – in the United States? Eighty-two percent. My chance of surviving prostate cancer in England? Only 44 percent under socialized medicine. (quoted in Bosman, 2007)

Claire Berlinski, author of the 2007 book, *Menace in Europe: Why the Continent's Crisis is America's, Too*, shares these sentiments but has gone far beyond the Republican candidates in terms of both the forms of rhetoric she employs and the substance of her comments. She offers a broad-ranging and abrasively worded indictment of Europe or, at least, the countries that former secretary of defense Donald Rumsfeld once dubbed 'old Europe':

Europeans are lazy, unwilling to fight for anything and willing to surrender to anyone; they are fascinated by decadence; they favor the bureaucracy over the corporation; they are unable to assimilate their immigrants; they no longer have children; they no longer produce much of cultural or scientific significance; they have lost their religious vocation and they no longer hold their lives to be meaningful. (quoted in Glazov, 2006)

Comments such as these are tied to a broader and more systematic critique of Europe that underpins many of the commentaries in conservative journals such as *National Review* and the *Weekly Standard* and reports published by Washington thinktanks, most notably the American Enterprise Institute (AEI), the Heritage Foundation and the Cato Institute.

Europe in crisis

The conservative critique of the European economies rests on several claims. The continent, it is said, faces a far-reaching demographic crisis. Total fertility rates are at sub-replacement level. Although the drop in fertility is most marked in the countries of eastern Europe, population growth will be at most only marginal in the western European nations. Net immigration levels, which could compensate for the fall in the working-age population, remain at a relatively low level in most European countries. Furthermore, immigrants often come to adopt the fertility patterns of the established population.[1] In contrast to developments in Europe (and nearly all other developed nations), the US fertility rate turned upwards at the end of the 1980s. Indeed, US fertility rates are close to long-term population-replacement levels. On the basis of this, Nicholas Elberstadt of the AEI describes the US in terms of 'demographic exceptionalism'.

The decline in the European birth rate, American commentators have stressed, will have important economic and cultural consequences for the relative character of European and American society. Europe will have an increasingly 'greyer' character than the US as the age structures of the two continents diverge. Furthermore, although about 495 million people live in the twenty-seven countries of the European Union (2007), while the US claimed a population of just over 303 million (January 2008), the balance will begin to shift as the US 'catches up' in terms of relative population size.

What explains the demographic differences between the continents? Although some have pointed to the comparatively high teenage birth rate and relatively high fertility levels within the minority communities in the US as an explanation of its higher birth rate, these are not, as Nicholas Eberstadt has noted, significant variables (Eberstadt, 2007). The teenage birth rate fell steadily from the early 1990s onwards. Indeed, the birth rate for black teenagers fell by more than 40 per cent between 1993 and 2003 (National Center for Health Statistics, 2003). There are significant differences between minority and non-Hispanic white fertility rates. Hispanic women had an average of about three children whereas white, non-Hispanic women had about 1.8, a figure below the long-term replacement level. However, there is evidence of a long-term trend towards convergence. The principal reason for the US's demographic 'exceptionalism', Eberstadt suggests, lies in 'the seemingly ephemeral realm of values, ideals, attitudes and outlook'. Polling data, he has noted, suggests that Americans are more optimistic about the future, 'proud' of their country and committed to religious faith than often secular Europeans (Eberstadt, 2007). All of this encourages the bringing of children into the world and, conversely, a 'birth dearth' in many European nations. European 'Godlessness' is thereby contributing to the death of the continent.

Although some have seen signs of a revival in the growth and spiritual dynamism of some evangelical congregations, the onward march of secularisation in Europe is readily evident. As Philip Jenkins records, the Church of England closed 1,700 of its buildings between 1970 and 2005 (Jenkins, 2007: 36). When the proposed European 'constitution' was drawn up by former French president Valéry Giscard d'Estaing it had a purely secular character. Although European secularism does not take a militantly atheistic form, it is nurtured by the exclusion of faith from the 'public square'. The contrast between the US and Europe when the character of public discourse is considered is striking. Invocations of God are commonplace in the US whereas they are absent in much of Europe.[2] As George Weigel puts it: 'Europe today is profoundly shaped, however, by... a set of ideas and political default positions according to which (and in the name of democracy, human rights, tolerance, and civility) all transcendent religious or moral reference points must be kept out of European public life' (Weigel, 2006).

Europe has, from this perspective, also failed to assimilate or integrate immigrants. They remain socially and economically isolated. This, many American conservatives suggest, can in part be attributed to over-regulation, which creates barriers to entry and denies opportunity to those on the lowest rungs of the economic ladder. More importantly, however, the weak and ill-defined character of national identity in the countries of Europe and, at the same time, the lack of a defining European ideal means that integration is an uncertain and problematic process.

There is a connection between what is seen as European 'Godlessness' and Europe's failure to assimilate newcomers. Conservatives argue that insofar as assimilation in contemporary Europe means anything, it is associated with secularism and the abandonment of religious faith. In contrast, American commentaries assert, the US has a markedly stronger sense of identity structured around its governing principles: liberty, individualism and democracy. Such principles facilitate and promote integration.

At the same time, the US offers religious pluralism, respect for faith and freedom of worship. For this reason, it is significant that, reportedly, just three regional newspapers out of more than 1,400 in the US reprinted the cartoons of the Prophet Muhammad that had originally been published in a Danish newspaper (*Jyllands-Posten*) and were seen as blasphemous by many Muslims. As the late Father Richard Neuhaus, a leading US 'theoconservative', complained in a survey of European belief:

> Europeans want Muslims to assimilate, but assimilate to what? ...In the United States, a person who advocates undemocratic or intolerant views is condemned as un-American and violating the principles of the Constitution to which all swear allegiance...Europe offers nothing comparable and shows no sign of doing so... Arguably, if a 'mainstream' set of values can be deduced from the last 150 years or so of European history, they would be authoritarian, military, and hyper-nationalistic, rather than pluralist and liberal. (Neuhaus, 2007)

All this is often tied together. The failure of the integration process in Europe, the 'birth dearth' and the anaemic character of European faith have, some assert, opened the way for 'Islamicisation' of Europe. The Muslim communities are becoming larger as a proportion of the population and their commitment to religious belief and the values that are rooted in their faith lays a basis for the cultural, spiritual and political transformation of European societies (Bawer, 2007).

US and European economic performance

More than anything else, however, the conservative critique of Europe rests upon an indictment of Europe's economic performance. Although there was sustained economic growth during the 1950s and 1960s (the years of the West German *Wirtschaftswunder*) this is generally represented as a 'catch-up' process. In the aftermath of the Second World War, much of Europe had been devastated and there are often high rates of growth when a country starts from low beginnings. Furthermore, western Europe could take advantage of US technology and investment.

The boom petered out. From the 1970s onwards, it is said, the consequences of 'Eurosclerosis' became evident. Excessive taxation, bloated government sectors and overregulation have held back increases in productivity, curbed national competitiveness and stifled economic growth.[3] From this perspective, the widening and deepening of the European Union in recent decades and the prospect of reforms such as tax harmonisation have compounded the problem. What US conservatives regard as lavish social provision deters initiative, encourages dependency and 'crowds out' private sector investment. In its 2007 *Index of Economic Freedom*, the Heritage Foundation acknowledges the economic freedoms offered by the European countries but also stresses the degree to which markets are restricted: 'Europe suffers from the second-worst regional score in labor freedom and is dead last in fiscal freedom and freedom from government – the price of welfare states that are so large as a percentage of GDP. Strong state sectors and rigid labor markets have already prompted significant social turmoil, not least in France' (quoted in McNamara, 2007).

Conservative commentators stress that those European countries that make a break with the policies underpinning 'Eurosclerosis' will prosper while neighbouring countries continue to languish. Writing before the crisis took hold, they have pointed to the experience of Ireland in recent decades. It sought out foreign capital through a policy of low corporate tax rates:

> The remarkable success Ireland has experienced in improving its economic performance over the past 15 years is due to market-based forces. Although EU subsidies have been present, they have not been the driving force and may actually be holding Ireland back from growing faster. A policy environment that promotes economic freedom, enabling private entrepreneurs to promote economic development was the key to creating the Celtic Tiger. (Powell, 2003)[4]

They also point to Estonia. Whereas many countries have long, complex and punitive tax codes, the Baltic country adopted a 26 per cent flat tax in 1994 which was subsequently reduced. According to Daniel J. Mitchell of the Cato Institute: 'Combined with other free-market reforms, the flat tax has helped Estonia become one of the world's fastest-growing economies. Tallinn is now a boom town, filled with expensive cars, elegant shops, trendy restaurants and new construction' (Mitchell, 2007a).

Ireland and Estonia are, however, exceptions to the rule. 'Eurosclerosis', it is said, is deeply embedded within much of Europe. Indeed, Stefan Theil, the economics editor of *Newsweek*, suggests that it is taught in the schools. He asserts that school students in France and Germany are taught to be critical of capitalism and free market dynamism. He cites a French textbook used for university entrance examinations (*Histoire du XXe siècle*), according which: 'Economic growth imposes a hectic form of life, producing overwork, stress, nervous depression, cardiovascular disease and, according to some, even the development of cancer' (quoted in Theil, 2008: 56).

So as to make amends for its lack of economic competitiveness, conservatives have claimed, Europe is guilty of protectionism. There have been references to 'fortress Europe'. In particular, although free market advocates acknowledge that US farm subsidies constitute a form of 'corporate welfare' that props up inefficient systems of production and distribution, the European Union's Common Agricultural Policy (CAP) is, they assert, an example of the EU's protectionist mentality. In 2004, agricultural support in the EU cost about $133 billion compared with $47 billion in the US. From a free market perspective, subsidies such as these and tariff regimes not only impede growth and modernisation but by preserving inefficiencies they add substantially to the prices paid by consumers. Marian L. Tupy of the Cato Institute cites evidence to suggest that EU consumers are compelled to pay 42 per cent more for agricultural products than they would if the CAP was ended and the system opened up to market forces. For their part, he says, Americans pay 10 per cent too much (Tupy, 2005).

Those who subscribe to the conservative critique cite comparative economic growth rates in the US and Europe. Except for a brief period during 2001, recent US growth rates have been higher, often markedly so, than those of the countries that formed and then became part of the area using the euro (Table 8.1). In particular, Germany and France, the core countries within the Eurozone, performed sluggishly throughout the 1990s. Writing well before the economic crisis that engulfed both continents from 2007 onwards, Fredrik Bergström and Robert Gidehag stress what they see as the gulf between the US and Europe: 'The gaps already existing today are so great that, even if the European countries were to suddenly being growing much faster, it would still take them a long time to catch up with the USA' (Bergström and Gidehag, 2004: 9).

For the continent's critics, Europe's entrenched difficulties made it particularly vulnerable to the global recession that began in late 2007. As Anatole Kaletsky recorded in August 2009:

> Industrial production in Germany has now fallen back to the same level as in January 1991. In America, contrary to the widespread belief in catastrophic de-industrialisation, industrial production is still 41 per cent higher than it was 18 years ago, even after the post-Lehman slump. (Kaletsky, 2009)

Although there was widespread talk by mid-2009 of economic recovery in France and Germany, some observers were sceptical and felt that a 'W' shaped (or 'double dipper') recession was more likely.[5]

Living standards

The 'growth gap' between the continents has consequences for average living standards. These can be measured in different ways. Per capita income (using purchasing power parity so that countries using different currencies can be compared in a meaningful way) offers one approach (Table 8.2). Considered in this way, the US is ahead of the European countries, with the exception of Norway.

Alternatively, per capita GDP can be used as the basis for an index that allows direct comparisons between the US (and its fifty states) and Europe. The results are similar. When compared with the US states, most of the west European countries (the fifteen countries that constituted the EU before expansion in 2004) fare relatively badly (Figure 8.1). Indeed, the EU-15 has a lower level of per capita GDP than just four US states. These are the poorest in the union: Arkansas, Montana, West Virginia and Mississippi.

Per capita income and GDP statistics only, however, tell part of the story. They are gross, pre-tax figures and mask lower net standards of living. This is particularly clear in Scandinavian nations such as Norway. If the Nordic

Table 8.1 *US and European economic growth rates, 1990–2006*

Country	1990	1991	1992	1993	1994	1995	1996	1997	1998	1999	2000	2001	2002	2003	2004	2005	2006
Canada	0.2	–2.1	0.9	2.3	4.8	2.8	1.6	4.2	4.1	5.5	5.2	1.8	3.4	2.0	2.8	2.8	3.0
France	2.6	1.0	1.3	–0.9	1.9	1.8	1.0	1.9	3.6	3.2	4.2	2.1	1.1	0.5	2.3	2.0	2.2
Germany	5.7	5.0	2.2	–1.1	2.3	1.7	0.8	1.4	2.0	2.0	2.9	0.8	0.1	–0.1	1.7	0.8	1.9
Italy	2.0	1.4	0.8	–0.9	2.2	2.9	1.1	2.0	1.8	1.7	3.0	1.8	0.4	0.3	1.2	1.2	2.0
Japan	5.3	3.3	1.0	0.2	1.1	2.0	3.6	1.7	–1.1	–0.0	2.4	0.2	–0.3	1.4	2.6	0.8	1.9
United Kingdom	0.8	–1.4	0.2	2.3	4.4	2.9	2.8	3.3	3.1	2.9	3.9	2.3	1.8	2.2	3.1	2.6	2.6
United States	1.9	–0.2	3.3	2.7	4.0	2.5	3.7	4.5	4.2	4.4	3.7	0.8	1.9	3.0	4.4	3.6	3.6

Source: adapted from International Monetary Fund (2008), *World Economic Outlook Database*. <http://www.imf.org>

Table 8.2 *Per capita income using purchasing power parity exchange rates, 2004 (2004 US$)*

Country	Per capita income ($)
United States	39,728
Germany	28,565
France	29,450
United Kingdom	30,292
Denmark	32,270
Norway	41,804

Source: adapted from Economic Policy Institute (2006), *The State of Working America, 2006–07, Chapter 8 – International comparisons: How does the United States stack up?*, 74, <http://www.stateofworkingamerica.org/swa06_ch08_international.pdf>

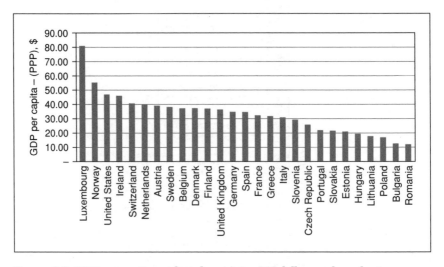

Figure 8.1 *GDP per capita – selected countries, US dollars and purchasing power parities (2008 estimates)*[6]
Source: adapted from Central Intelligence Agency (2009), *The World Factbook*, <https://www.cia.gov>

nations are considered on the basis of price levels as well as the extent to which individuals are taxed, it becomes evident that standards of living are much more modest than statistics initially suggest. Indeed, they are in some ways 'poor' when compared with other Europeans. A March 2005 study by KPMG, the accounting and consulting firm, indicated that if post-tax, disposable income was adjusted for the cost of living in different countries, 'Scandinavians were the poorest people in Western Europe. Danes had the lowest adjusted income, Norwegians the second lowest, Swedes the third. Spain and Portugal, with two of Europe's least regulated economies, led the list' (Bawer, 2005).

Writing in the *New York Times*, Bruce Bawer spells out what this means in practice for those in northern Europe by painting a critical picture of life in Norway (which, in terms of gross income, had the third highest per capita income in the world):

> One image in particular sticks in my mind. In a Norwegian language class, my teacher illustrated the meaning of the word *matpakke* – 'packed lunch' – by reaching into her backpack and pulling out a hero sandwich wrapped in wax paper. It was her lunch. She held it up for all to see. Yes, teachers are underpaid everywhere. But in Norway the *matpakke* is ubiquitous, from classroom to boardroom. In New York, an office worker might pop out at lunchtime to a deli; in Paris, she might enjoy quiche and a glass of wine at a brasserie. In Norway, she will sit at her desk with a sandwich from home. (Bawer, 2005)

Europeans lose out in other ways. In a study published in 1999, Michael Cox and Richard Alm charted the proportion of households in the US and a number of European countries owning basic household appliances. With some exceptions, US citizens used significantly more of these appliances in their homes (see Table 8.3).

Despite frequent European news reports about extreme inequalities and severe poverty in the United States, those in poverty in the US have a higher standard of living than the poor in Europe. A study published in 2004 charted the proportion of US households in poverty that had particular utilities or appliances (Figure 8.2).

Generalisations and 'shocks'

How legitimate is the conservative critique of Europe? There are certainly some significant differences in terms of economic performance if growth rates are compared (see Table 8.4).

Nonetheless, there are dangers in making the broad generalisations about a continent that are sometimes heard from those on the American right. As has already been noted, when the impact of Scandinavian tax regimes was considered, there are significant differences between particular European countries and there is a case for claiming that terms such as 'European model' should only be used with caution. There are different models within Europe. Indeed, André Sapir identifies four different and distinct European social models. The Nordic model rests upon high levels of social protection (and therefore 'big government'), much of which is offered through universal forms of provision. There are strong labour unions and 'highly compressed wage structures' (Sapir, 2005: 4). They also have active labour market policies to encourage retraining and the reallocation of labour while, at the same time, extending benefits to those who are out of work. Such 'flexicurity' contributes to fairly

Table 8.3 *Percentage of households in selected countries owning domestic appliances*

	USA	Belgium	Denmark	France	Germany	Italy	Netherlands	Spain	Sweden	Switzerland	UK
Dishwasher	53	26	36	32	34	15	11	12	32	32	11
Microwave	86	21	31	19	36	6	22	9	37	15	45
Radio	99	90	98	95	84	92	99	95	93	99	90
Television	98	97	98	93	97	98	93	98	97	93	98
Vacuum cleaner	99	92	96	89	96	36	98	29	97	93	98
VCR	83	42	63	33	42	25	90	40	48	42	69
Personal computer	40	22	30	20	20	14	25	11	29	21	25
Phones per 100 people	63	46	61	56	49	43	53	39	68	62	50
Cell phones per 1000	12.4	23.2	137.5	23.8	42.5	67.8	33.2	24.1	229.9	63.5	98
TVs per 1000	776	464	536	579	550	456	495	490	476	462	612

Source: Fredrik Bergström and Robert Gidehag (2004), *EU versus USA*, Timbro, June, 16, <http://www.timbro.se/bokhandel/pdf/917566546.pdf>

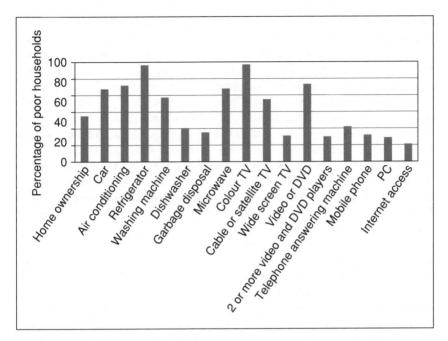

Figure 8.2 *Percentage of poor households in the US owning domestic appliances and utilities*

Source: Fredrik Bergström and Robert Gidehag (2004), *EU versus USA*, Timbro, June, 22, <http://www.timbro.se/bokhandel/pdf/9175665646.pdf>

Table 8.4 *Economic growth rates – US and selected European countries, 1990–2006*

Country	1990	1991	1992	1993	1994	1995	1996	1997	1998
France	2.6	1.0	1.3	−0.9	1.9	1.8	1.0	1.9	3.6
Germany	5.7	5.0	2.2	−1.1	2.3	1.7	0.8	1.4	2.0
United Kingdom	0.8	−1.4	0.2	2.3	4.4	2.9	2.8	3.3	3.1
United States	1.9	−0.2	3.3	2.7	4.0	2.5	3.7	4.5	4.2

Country	1999	2000	2001	2002	2003	2004	2005	2006
France	3.2	4.2	2.1	1.1	0.5	2.3	2.0	2.2
Germany	2.0	2.9	0.8	0.1	−0.1	1.7	0.8	1.9
United Kingdom	2.9	3.9	2.3	1.8	2.2	3.1	2.6	2.6
United States	4.4	3.7	0.8	1.9	3.0	4.4	3.6	3.6

Source: International Monetary Fund (2008), *World Economic Outlook Database*, <http://www.imf.org>

low levels of unemployment. According to Sapir, the Nordic model provides both equity and efficiency.[7] In the 'continental' countries (most notably France and Germany), the unemployment rate was for a long period around 10 per cent (although it gradually fell from about 2000 onwards) but the 'continental' model offers social protection to individuals and families through contributions. The unions have lost some of their former influence but continue to have a powerful voice. The 'Mediterranean' model is characterised by relatively high levels of unemployment and a high risk of poverty. Social provision is more limited and is concentrated on old-age pensions. Although unemployment benefits tend to be low, there is a higher level of employment protection legislation than is found in the Nordic countries. The Anglo-Saxon model (which through its name suggests that the United Kingdom, Ireland and the United States have much more in common than the UK and Ireland have with the other countries of Europe) is structured around weak unions and a wage structure that encompasses very high and very low levels of pay. Unemployment is lower than in the 'continental' countries but social provision is rather more of a last resort than 'continental' or Nordic regions. There are significant disincentives for those who do not take offers of employment. Those who talk in terms of an Anglo-Saxon model also suggest that from Margaret Thatcher's premiership (1979–90) onwards, successive British governments (both Conservative and Labour) have pursued a much more vigorous policy of privatisation and market liberalisation than other European countries. Some observers introduce a further model and talk of the former communist countries (such as Hungary and Poland) as a distinct economic and social system characterised, for example, by a continuing commitment, despite market liberalisation, to social provision within a market context.

Furthermore, if the size of government is used as a basis for constructing different models, there is only a loose 'fit' with empirical realities. There is a very clear contrast between the European countries and the US. The countries associated with the Nordic model have, as might be expected, the highest levels of government expenditure when measured as a percentage share of GDP. However, France, which is tied to the continental model, also has a high level of government expenditure. Spain and Italy are both 'Mediterranean' countries but have markedly different levels of government expenditure (see Table 8.5).

Even if government social expenditure is considered apart from other forms of government spending, there is a marked gap between the UK and US and the other European countries (Table 8.6). Nonetheless, there are fewer differences between the 'continental' countries such as France and Germany and those in the Nordic region.

The conservative critique is open to other criticisms. Economic difficulties such as those faced by Germany and France are not necessarily systemic. They may instead be attributable to particular exogenous (or external) 'shocks' that had damaging consequences. Some, for example, have pointed to the effects of monetary union on the countries of Europe. The introduction of the euro

Table 8.5 *General government expenditure as a share of GDP – selected countries, 2007*

Country	Government expenditure % share of GDP
United States	37.4
Denmark	50.7
France	53.0
Germany	44.3
Italy	48.4
Spain	38.8
Sweden	53.8
United Kingdom	44.6

Source: adapted from Small-M (2008), *OECD General Government Expenditure (% of GDP, 2007)*, <http://micpohling.wordpress.com>

Table 8.6 *Social expenditure as a proportion of GDP (2003)*

Country	Social expenditure as a proportion of GDP
Denmark	27.6
France	28.7
Germany	27.6
Norway	25.1
Sweden	31.3
United Kingdom	20.1
United States	16.2

Source: adapted from OECD (2008), *Selection of OECD Social Indicators: How Does Your Country Compare?*, <http://www.oecd.org>

imposed transition costs and more importantly a single interest rate across all the Eurozone countries and regions regardless of their macroeconomic circumstances. A low interest rate set by the European Central Bank (ECB) might have a reflationary impact in countries facing a recession but added to the 'overheating' process in countries nearing full capacity. Furthermore, some countries may have joined the euro at an overvalued exchange rate between the national currency and the new single currency. This was most notable in the case of Germany, with the consequence that German exports were relatively costly, thereby imposing a burden on producers. Conversely, imports were lower in price than would otherwise have been the case (Gersemann, 2004: 48). Germany faced other difficulties. The costs of reconstruction in East Germany after the two Germanies were unified in 1990 were markedly higher than expected. Industry in the former German Democratic Republic was backward, inefficient and uncompetitive. The infrastructure and basic public utilities had to be rebuilt. These costs raised taxation rates in the west. Furthermore, despite public investment in the east, economic development remained at a relatively low level. Social provision and transfers to those living there added still further to the tax burden in the west (Gersemann, 2004: 49).

Nonetheless, 'shocks' such as these cannot provide that much of an explanation. While Germany is the largest economy in the European Union, events in Germany cannot explain the economic character of the entire continent. French economic performance was also sluggish. Furthermore, the advent of the euro offered advantages as well as disadvantages to member countries insofar as the single currency facilitated trade and enabled companies to operate on a larger basis, thereby gaining economies of scale. As conservative commentators emphasise, Europe's difficulties do not stem from particular events but should instead be attributed to the policies pursued by governments. For his part, Olaf Gersemann concludes: 'sluggishness in countries like Germany and France is not the result of asymmetrical shocks but a voluntarily chosen lot' (Gersemann, 2004: 50).[8]

A 'voluntarily chosen lot'

What is this 'voluntarily chosen lot'? Conservative commentators point, first and foremost, to the tax burden that governments impose upon both individuals and companies in Europe (see Figure 8.3).

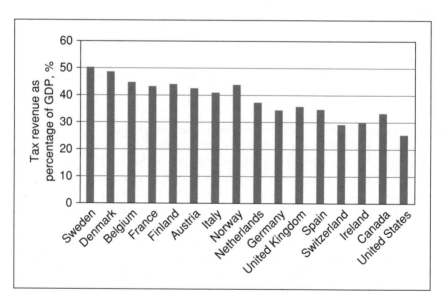

Figure 8.3 *Tax revenue as a proportion of GDP in the US, Canada and selected European countries, 2004*

Source: Organization for Economic Cooperation and Development (2006), *Tax Revenues on the Rise in Many OECD Countries, OECD Report Shows (Table A)*, <http://www.oecd.org/dataoecd/8/4/37504406.pdf>

High marginal rates of taxation, it is said, reduce individual choices and deter initiative and effort. Furthermore, as the Laffer curve suggested (see pp. 82–3), governments could reduce tax rates and, because there would be an increase in overall economic activity, would nonetheless bring in higher levels of tax revenue. Furthermore, high tax rates support a large-scale public sector that is protected from open competition or the need to secure a profit and, from a conservative perspective, is inherently inefficient and sluggish:

> the higher the tax burden and the larger the public sector become, the greater will be the power of political decision-makers and public bureaucracies. Private players, consequently, will have less scope for deploying their incomes and assets as they themselves wish to. High taxes also generate counter-incentives to work and entrepreneurial initiative. The larger the public sector is, the more dependent the population will also be on public transfers and the smaller will be the portion of the economy open to competition. This…has a negative impact on economic growth. The tax burden and the size of the public sector are indicators of the extent to which an economy is a market economy or an economy directly and indirectly subject to political decision-making. (Bergström and Gidehag, 2004: 25).

The problems posed by a high tax regime and a large public sector go further. They reduce the space open to voluntary and charitable initiatives which often, it is said, deliver aid to those who are most disadvantaged far more effectively than impersonal government services. Because incentives are reduced in the private sector (because individuals and companies are required to pay a high proportion of additional income to the tax authorities) and the public sector faces little or no competition, there are relatively few pressures to adopt new forms of technology. In contrast, in a more dynamic and competitive economy companies will be under much more intense pressure to develop new product lines, reduce production costs and employ new technology. They will otherwise lose their market share and their profit margins will be squeezed. In other words, although governments may give subsidies to encourage innovation, productivity growth rates will be lower in countries where there are higher tax rates and larger public sectors. Table 8.7 shows the rate of productivity growth (output per hour) in selected countries. The US is ahead, sometimes far ahead, of almost all the European countries.

From this perspective, the European countries lag behind the US for other reasons. Across many, there are regulatory mechanisms that limit competition and the creation of new businesses. The relative strength of the labour unions contributes to excessive wage demands, although it should be noted that while the unions became less militant and wage demands were moderated from the early 1980s, unemployment rates did not always fall. In some countries, unemployment remained high (Blanchard, 2004). Gersemann points, in particular, to Germany, and cites the former German government's provision of federal loan guarantees to ailing companies. SPD chancellor Gerhard Schröder's

Table 8.7 *Output per hour – average annual rates of change, 1979–2006 (%)*

Country	Output per hour – average annual rates of change, 1979–2006 (%)
United States	3.9
Denmark	2.4
France	3.8
Germany	2.9
Italy	1.7
Norway	2.0
Sweden	4.5
United Kingdom	3.6

Note: the figure for Germany includes only West Germany until 1991. Source: adapted from Bureau of Labor Statistics (2008), *International Comparisons of Manufacturing Productivity and Unit Labor Cost Trends 2006, Revised*, <http://www.bls.gov>

reluctance to allow bankruptcies (the process of 'creative destruction', as Joseph Schumpeter termed it) propped up firms that were either inefficient or no longer meeting consumer needs. At the same time, centralised wage bargaining systems added to labour costs in the country's more depressed regions. German education has long been vocational in character insofar as it is directed towards specific forms of employment. However, in an era when the nature of work is changing rapidly, more conceptual approaches to education have greater transferability and would strengthen human capital, one of the building blocks of economic growth (Gersemann, 2004: 57–8). Culture also plays a part, although many conservatives would also point to the system of incentives and disincentives created by what they see as lavish welfare provision. US history is full of stories of those who have moved westwards or to the metropolises to realise their hopes and fulfil their ambitions. Contemporary Europeans are more reluctant to move in search of work. In many cases there are linguistic barriers that inhibit mobility across the different EU countries. Nonetheless, there is little taste for geographical mobility even within many individual EU countries. During the 1990s, on average, 2.65 per cent of people moved to another state each year. In 2001, just 1.44 per cent moved to another state within Germany (Gersemann, 2004: 56). The lack of mobility hinders economic growth (because it restricts the labour supply) and prevents individuals securing a higher standard of living.

Public choice theory puts forward a further explanation for sluggish growth rates. Mancur Olson argues that stable democracies permit and encourage the growth of 'distributional coalitions' or 'special interests' representing particular industries or sectors who seek concessions or advantages (such as the imposition of tariffs to protect themselves from foreign competition). Such advantages constrain competition and thereby inhibit expansion. As Olson asserted: 'the higher the rate of special-interest organization membership, the lower the rate of growth' (Olson, 1982: 97). Although there has long been relative political stability in parts of the US, the 'frontier' character of some regions and the checks against the passage of legislation held 'special interests' at bay longer than would otherwise have been the case.[9]

Strengths of the European model

The conservative critique of Europe has not gone unchallenged. Indeed, liberal and progressive commentaries on both sides of the Atlantic talk about Europe in very positive terms. Extensive social provision, through relatively high taxation, it has been said, can be used to provide individual security and social cohesion but also sustained economic growth.[10] Robert Kuttner, a co-editor of *The American Prospect*, has pointed in particular to the Danish model.

> For the half of GDP that they pay in taxes, the Danes get not just universal health insurance but also generous child-care and family-leave arrangements, unemployment compensation that typically covers around 95 percent of lost wages, free higher education, secure pensions in old age, and the world's most creative system of worker retraining. (Kuttner, 2008)

- Forms of provision that are offered in the US as very much a last resort or only through private insurance schemes are routinely available to all in many European countries. Michael Moore's 2007 film, *Sicko*, conveys this message powerfully. It points to the plight of those who cannot afford insurance or have been adversely affected by the many exemptions in coverage (see also Chapter 7). European social support is much more than minimal and does not therefore carry a stigma that might deter those in need from applying to the authorities. There are fewer gaps because individuals are not at the mercy of private insurance companies seeking to maximise their profits.
- In Europe, paid parental leave ensures that infants are given proper attention in their early months and years. As T.R. Reid, an American admirer of the European model, records in a description of Norway:

> In America, the White House and state governors routinely boast about how much their welfare rolls are being reduced. In Norway, the government takes pride in statistics showing that the number of recipients has been growing rapidly . . . Other European countries can't afford to pay as much for parenting as wealthy Norway does. Still, parental leave programs are standard, whether funded through state payments or by requiring employers to continue paying a salary while the employer is at home being a parent. Beyond that, European parents can expect a monthly benefit check from the government for the first eighteen years of each child's life. (Reid, 2005: 154)[11]

- Government educational provision in Europe, which is generally offered free or at low cost, ensures social mobility because it provides an opportunity for those from lower-income households to secure advanced qualifications and climb the socioeconomic ladder. Indeed, some evidence suggests that despite frequent talk of the 'American dream' and the ability of those who work hard to reap rewards, mobility is higher in the Nordic countries (and to a lesser extent the UK) than in the US (Jäntti et al., 2006).[12]

- Those who stress the strengths of the European model argue that extended government provision not only bolsters social capital. Government spending also acts as an 'automatic stabiliser' and provides an economic 'cushion' during periods of downturn by adding to demand levels (see pp. 00–00). In the recession that began in late 2007, countries such as Germany and France did not adopt large-scale stimulus measures comparable with those adopted in the US because, through higher overall levels of government spending, they already had stabilisers in place. Furthermore, the subsidies paid to ailing firms ensured that unemployment rose more slowly than in the UK and US. As the *Wall Street Journal* recorded: 'German government subsidies for workers whose hours have been cut prevented hundreds of thousands of job losses this year' (Walker and Gauthier-Villars, 2009).

- Claims that the US is far ahead in terms of productivity growth should be qualified. Comparative productivity growth statistics need to be adjusted for different business cycles. This is because productivity growth varies depending upon the point on the cycle that a country has reached. Furthermore, there are different accounting methods. Business spending on software is, for example, handled differently in Europe and the US. US statistics use output per man-hour in the non-farm business sector. In contrast, the productivity figures issued by the European Central Bank for the euro area are based upon GDP per worker in the whole economy. Labour market reforms in Europe have brought unskilled and inexperienced workers, whose productivity rates are lower, into the workforce (*Economist*, 2002a). Furthermore, the US productivity lead is, in large part, attributable to the character of the distributive process. In the US, goods are distributed using very large trucks and the extensive network of interstate highways. Europe, as Larry Elliott and Dan Atkinson note, cannot keep pace: 'Europe could only enjoy the same sort of productivity if it was prepared to abandon its more stringent planning laws, allow 40-ton lorries to invade the centres of medieval cities and perhaps knock down the odd Gothic cathedral or two' (Elliott and Atkinson, 2008: 232–3).

- Some of the comparisons between Europe and the US (particularly those based upon growth rates and GDP per capita) are misleading. US growth is higher in part because its population has grown more rapidly, offering more in terms of human capital and a market for goods and services. Although the US has higher GDP per capita figures, Americans have to spend more than Europeans on both heating and air conditioning. Given the distances involved in much of the US and the often limited character of public transportation, Americans have to spend more on automobiles.

Table 8.8 *Prisoners – rate per 100,000 of population (2006 or latest)*

Country	Prison population – rate per 100,000
Canada	107
Denmark	77
France	88
Germany	97
United Kingdom	143
United States	738

Source: adapted from OECD (2008), *Selection of OECD Social Indicators: How Does Your Country Compare?*, <http://www.oecd.org>

At the same time, the higher crime rate in the US and the adoption of punitive approaches to criminality mean that a greater proportion of its national output has to be spent on security and prison (Table 8.8).

- It is undeniable that American living standards (GDP per capita) are higher than those in western Europe. Estimates suggest there is a 30 per cent gap between the US and Europe (if averaged out between individual nations) that has remained broadly constant over the past thirty years. Nonetheless, Americans work longer hours and take fewer holidays.[13] This can be measured through the labour supply (LS) ratio. This is the relationship between the actual number of hours worked in the economy's regular employment sector and the number of hours which would be worked if all individuals of adult age (16–64) worked full time, apart from taking five weeks' annual holiday. A ratio of 1 indicates that the entire labour force is working all of this time. A figure approaching 0 indicates that nobody is working at all. As Table 8.9 indicates, there is a substantial gulf between the US and European countries. Indeed, according to one estimate 'the average American worker clocks up 40 per cent more hours during his life time than the average person in Germany, France or Italy' (*Economist*, 2004).
- Poverty rates are significantly lower in Europe than in the United States (Table 8.10). Poverty is generally assessed in relative terms and the poverty statistics are therefore shaped by the degree of inequality within a particular country. The US is much more unequal than the European countries. For critics, a significant 'underclass' far removed from median incomes and lifestyle not only poses a threat to individuals and their life-chances but jeopardises social cohesion. They point to violent crime rates, gang-based cultures, illegitimacy and educational underachievement.
- Arguably, a considerable proportion of US growth has in recent years been based upon artificially low interest rates and widespread consumer borrowing. In 2007, the total amount of consumer debt in the US was almost $2.5 trillion dollars. This excludes mortgages and represents about $8,200 of debt for every man, woman and child in the country (Money-Zine.com, 2007). If mortgages are included, total household debt in the US amounts

Table 8.9 *Labour supply ratio – selected European countries (2000)*

Country	LS ratio
United States	0.74
United Kingdom	0.67
Switzerland	0.67
Sweden	0.66
Finland	0.63
Denmark	0.62
Ireland	0.59
Greece	0.58
Spain	0.57
Netherlands	0.55
Germany	0.53
France	0.53
Belgium	0.51
Italy	0.48

Source: Fredrik Bergström and Robert Gidehag (2004), *EU versus USA*, Timbro, June, 29, <http://www.timbro.se/bokhandel/pdf/9175665646.pdf>

Table 8.10 *Poverty rates – selected countries, 2004*

Country	Poverty (%)	Child poverty (%)
United States	17	21.9
Australia	14.3	15.8
Italy	12.7	16.6
Sweden	6.5	4.2
Norway	6.4	3.4
Finland	5.4	2.8

Source: adapted from Economic Policy Institute (2008), *Facts & Figures – State of Working America 2004/U.S. & the World*, <http://www.epi.org/books/swa2004/news/swafacts_international.pdf>

to 84 per cent of GDP compared with only 50 per cent in the euro zone. Furthermore, US households now save less than 2 per cent of their disposable income. In contrast, the saving rate in the euro area is 12 per cent (*Economist*, 2004).
- Furthermore, many of Europe's difficulties can in part be reduced to a single country. Although Germany (West Germany) was associated with the 'economic miracle' of the 1960s, it faced problems in the 1990s, when unification with the former east imposed a larger financial burden than had been forecast. If Germany is excluded from the European statistics, key economic indicators (the growth of GDP per capita, employment and productivity) are more than a match for the US.
- From the perspective of those who back the European model, there have been significant labour market reforms in many of the European countries

that have begun to address earlier problems. Denmark pioneered the concept of 'flexicurity'. There is relatively generous provision for those who are unemployed but employment protection in a particular job is limited. Active labour market policies encourage retraining and the reallocation of workers so that they only spend a short period drawing unemployment benefits. In the Netherlands, from the early 1980s onwards, the unions agreed to hold back wage demands. As part of the overall package, companies added more jobs and the government cut social security contributions. The government also restricted the availability of benefits for those who were unemployed or on disability benefits (*Economist*, 2002b).

- Lastly, liberals and progressives suggest, conservative commentators have difficulties explaining the economic success of the Scandinavian countries. Despite, or perhaps because of 'big' forms of government and very high levels of taxation, they have impressive growth rates and low unemployment. For many liberals, both in Europe and the US, they offer a model that should be emulated. As Robert Kuttner puts it: 'Denmark has forged a social and economic model that couples the best of the free market with the best of the welfare state, transcending tradeoffs between dynamism and security, efficiency and equality' (Kuttner, 2008).

Rebuttals

Many of these claims have been countered by those who continue to see Europe in critical terms. Government social spending may, it is said, be high in many European countries, particularly those in the Nordic region, but it offers no assurance in terms of outcomes. In Denmark, spending per person was estimated in 2002 to be the fourth highest in the world (NationMaster, 2008a). Nonetheless, breast cancer rates are, at 30.4 per 100,000 females, the highest, or in some years, the second highest in the world (NationMaster, 2008b).[14] At the same time, deaths from lung cancer were the third highest in the world (*Economist*, 2005: 82).[15] Although Europeans have more leisure time than Americans, they also have to undertake many more basic household chores. Americans eat out and are more likely to use laundries. They have more dwelling space and a greater number of labour-saving appliances in the home (Fogh Rasmussen, 2007: 11–12). Insofar as life expectancy is a measure of social wellbeing, most western European countries have higher rates of life expectancy (from birth) than the US (Table 8.11).

Furthermore, the European countries are heavily dependent upon indirect forms of taxation, particularly sales taxes (or 'value-added tax'). In contrast with the US, they are set at very high levels (see Table 8.12). As T.R. Reid notes: 'For an American, even an American who lives in a "high-tax" state like California, New York, or Washington, the VAT rates in European countries seem mind-boggling' (Reid, 2005: 146). Whereas income taxes tend to be

Table 8.11 *Life expectancy at birth, 2003–4*

Country	Women	Men
Denmark	79.9	75.2
France	83.8	76.7
Germany	81.4	75.7
Italy	82.5	76.8
Japan	85.6	78.6
Norway	82.3	77.5
United Kingdom	80.7	76.2
United States	80.1	74.8

Source: adapted from OECD (2008), *Selection of OECD Social Indicators: How Does Your Country Compare?*, <http://www.oecd.org>

Table 8.12 *VAT/sales tax rates, selected European Union countries, 2007*

EU country	VAT standard rate
Denmark	25
Estonia	18
Germany	19
France	19.6
Italy	20
Luxembourg	15
Sweden	25
United Kingdom	17.5

Source: adapted from European Commission (2008), *VAT Rates Applied in the Member States of the European Community*, <http://ec.europa.eu/taxation_customs/resources/documents/taxation/vat/how_vat_works/rates/vat_rates_en.pdf>

progressive insofar as they take a higher proportion of income in taxation as income levels rise, sales taxes are flat-rate and are almost always regressive. In practice, those on low incomes pay a higher proportion of their income in sales taxes than those who have higher incomes (see p. 178).

In contrast, US state and local rates of tax are set at much lower levels (see Table 8.13) or in some cases states and local governments find revenue from other sources (such as a monopoly on liquor sales).

Conservative commentators also argue that the Nordic countries should not be portrayed as a success story for social-democratic approaches to economic policymaking. In practice, despite high levels of personal taxation, the Scandinavian countries have pursued free market policies:

They have open markets, low levels of regulation, strong property rights, stable currencies, and many other policies associated with growth and prosperity. Indeed, Nordic nations generally rank among the world's most market-oriented nations. Nordic nations also have implemented some pro-market reforms. Every

Table 8.13 *State and local sales tax rates, 2006 (%)*

State	Combined state/local average tax rate (2006 rates) (%)
Alaska	1.15
California	7.95
Florida	6.7
Illinois	7.6
Massachusetts	5.0
New Hampshire	nil
New York	8.25
Oregon	nil
Pennsylvania	6.25
South Carolina	5.8
Texas	7.95
Virginia	5.0

Source: adapted from USA-Sales-Use-Tax-E-Commerce.com (2008), *Table of Sales Tax Rates*, <http://www.usa-sales-use-tax-e-commerce.com>

Nordic nation has a lower corporate tax rate than the United States, for example, and most of them have low-rate flat tax systems for capital income. (Mitchell, 2007b: 1)

However, the large welfare states that the Nordic model rests upon were only established in the 1960s and their full impact has yet to be felt. Because of the burden that government imposes, growth rates could be higher. Although unemployment is low in overall terms, there is entrenched long-term un-employment among certain segments of the population. In 2006–7, over 18 per cent of the unemployed in Scandinavia had been out of work for more than a year. In the US, fewer than 12 per cent of the unemployed had been without work for that long (Mitchell, 2007b: 8). Large numbers, who some assert could be within the labour market, are on transfer payments because of long-term illness or early retirement (*Copenhagen Post*, 2008).

Despite claims that the Nordic model addresses poverty, figures from 2000 suggest the poorest 10 per cent of Swedes and Danes receive about the same share of median income as Americans (Mitchell, 2007b: 11). However, in the US, median income is higher. Although there are high levels of national pride in the Nordic countries, punitive tax rates do lead to high levels of tax avoidance through either the hidden economy, emigration or the moving of assets to other countries with lower tax levels. In July 2008, the OECD published figures that revealed that Denmark had fallen from seventh place in 1996 in terms of gross domestic product per capita, adjusted for purchasing power to eleventh place. It had been overtaken by Canada, Australia, Ireland and the Netherlands. Furthermore, the OECD forecast that Denmark's economic growth rate would be, between 2010 and 2014, the lowest among the organisation's thirty member countries (*Copenhagen Post*, 2008).

Conclusion

'Anti-Europeanism' has a firm hold within conservative and Republican circles in the US. Alongside other charges Europe is said to be economically stultified because of excessive taxation and overregulation. This critique has nonetheless been challenged by liberals and progressives who point to European social provision. They also challenge the claim that the US is far ahead economically and suggest that the statistics do not always provide a full picture. At the same time, they stress the greater amount of leisure time enjoyed by Europeans and the ways in which this enables them to establish more of a balance between work and family life. That having been said, many European countries are increasingly embracing forms of public policy that were once decried as 'American conditions'.

Nonetheless, the claims made by different polemicists may be a poor point at which to leave the discussion. The 'Varieties of Capitalism' school divides much of the developed world between 'liberal market economies' (of which the US is the quintessential example) and 'co-ordinated market economies' such as Germany.

Varieties of Capitalism literature focuses on the forms of coordination between and within firms and, within a liberal market economy, market relationships are paramount:

> firms coordinate their activities primarily via hierarchies and competitive market arrangements... In response to the price signals generated by such markets, the actors adjust their willingness to supply and demand goods or services, often on the basis of the marginal calculations stressed by neoclassical economics. (Hall and Soskice, 2001: 8)

Other characteristics are tied to this and provide a basis for distinguishing between liberal market economies and coordinated market economies where there are, it is argued, significant non-market modes of coordination. Within liberal market economies, shareholding is dispersed and there are sizeable equity markets. The ability of a business to raise funding from outside sources will be dependent upon its valuation (the share price) in those markets. Current profitability and short-term prospects are therefore critical. Managers can 'hire and fire' relatively easily and labour markets are fluid. There is therefore an emphasis on generalized, transferable skills rather than skills that are specific to a particular company or narrowly defined sector and, particularly because welfare or social provision covering periods between jobs is limited in LMEs, workers have an incentive to invest in these (Hall and Gingerich, 2009: 138). Such characteristics are said to constitute institutional complementaries insofar as they add to, reinforce and mutually strengthen each other and the overall production regime. In other words, they 'allow arrangements in one sphere of the political economy to enhance the results secured in others' (Hall and Thelen, 2009: 8). They form an 'interlocking ensemble' (Howell, 2003: 106).

Varieties of Capitalism practitioners suggest that it is a mistake to consider which type of economy is 'best'. Liberal market economies can innovate quickly and allow innovative firms and sectors to expand rapidly. In contrast, coordinated market economies are stronger when it comes to incremental, small-scale forms of innovation. There is more of an emphasis on consensus decision-making. In other words, both types of economy have comparative institutional advantages. Each has distinct and different strengths.

Notes

1 Despite these claims, recent reports suggest a significant increase in the UK birth rate. (See, for example, Hawkes, 2007.)
2 Tony Blair's plan to include the words 'God bless you' in a television address at the time of the 2003 Iraq war were withdrawn following an intervention by his advisers. (See Jenkins, 2007: 38.)
3 Conservative commentators concede the US is also far removed from the free market model that they seek. They acknowledge, for example, that the US has very high levels of corporate taxation that are well above the OECD average (although others would contend that there is, because of the many loopholes, a far lower effective corporate tax rate).
4 Nonetheless, both Ireland and Estonia experienced a very severe downturn in 2008 and 2009.
5 European recovery from the recession was, it was said, not only held back by uncompetitiveness. There were other difficulties. German and French companies were heavily leveraged. The claims that the Chinese market would provide a demand for European exports rested on an exaggerated picture of Chinese purchasing power. Furthermore, the rise in value of the euro threatened to increase export prices (Kaletsky, 2009).
6 See p. 20 for an explanation of purchasing power parity (PPP).
7 See, however, p. 178 for a discussion of the tax regime in the Nordic countries.
8 Olaf Gersemann is a German writer but his book, *Cowboy Capitalism*, was published by the Cato Institute in Washington DC.
9 Olson acknowledges that some European countries also have institutional mechanisms that limit the passage of regulatory or anti-competitive measures. He points to Switzerland and suggests that the country's prosperity can be tied to the constitutional barriers that hold back new legislation (Olson, 1982: 88). He also argues that where 'special interests' rest upon broad, encompassing organisations rather than narrower groups the legislation that is passed will be less likely to restrict the market. In Sweden, for example, because organised interests are broad in character, there are subsidies to assist labour mobility rather than to prop up a particular firm (Olson, 1982: 90).
10 Some would also point out that some US tax rates, in particular corporate tax rates, are also high and in some instances higher than in Europe. Many American conservatives acknowledge this and cite it as evidence of creeping 'Europeanisation'.

11   There are rather bigger differences between European countries in childcare provi-
      sion than this suggests, particularly if nursery and kindergarden availability is
      considered. In mid-2008, Germany had daycare places for just a sixth of its children.
      The figure for those in the former West was lower (*Economist*, 2008: 36–7).
12   Jäntti et al. emphasise, however, that all countries, including those in the Nordic
      region, show 'substantial earnings persistence' between the generations (Jäntti et al.,
      2006).
13   There is, however, a substantial gap among Americans, if leisure time is considered,
      between the less educated and the more educated (Aguiar and Hurst, 2009).
14   In 2000, Denmark had the highest rate of mortality from breast cancer in the
      world (*Economist*, 2005: 82).
15   Many other factors, apart from the quality of health provision, shape outcomes.
      In 1990, the proportion of daily smokers in Denmark (in other words those who
      smoked at least one cigarette a day) was, at 44.5 per cent, the highest in the
      world (NationMaster 2008c). By 2002–3, Denmark had fallen to tenth and the
      proportion of daily smokers was 28 per cent.

References and further reading

Aguiar, Mark and Erik Hurst (2009), *The Increase in Leisure Inequality 1965–2005*,
    Washington DC: AEI Press.
Bawer, Bruce (2005), 'We're rich, you're not. End of story', *New York Times*, April 17,
    <http://www.nytimes.com>
Bawer, Bruce (2007), *While Europe Slept: How Radical Islam is Destroying the West from
    Within*, New York: Broadway Books.
Bergström, Fredrik and Robert Gidehag (2004), *EU versus USA*, Timbro, June, <http://
    www.timbro.se>
Blanchard, Olivier J. (2004), *Explaining European Unemployment*, National Bureau of
    Economic Research, <http://www.nber.org>
Bosman, Julie (2007), 'Giuliani's prostate cancer figure is disputed', *New York Times*,
    October 31, <http://www.nytimes.com>.
Copenhagen Post (2008), 'Denmark slides in affluence ranking: OECD figures
    show Denmark's GDP has been overtaken by other countries', July 14, <http://
    www.cphpost.dk>
Council on Foreign Relations (2007), *Republican Debate Transcript, Iowa*, August 5,
    <http://www.cfr.org>
Eberstadt, Nicholas (2007), 'Born in the USA', *The National Interest*, Summer,
    <www.aei.org>
Economist (2002a), 'Europe's work in progress', November 14, <http://www.economist.com>
Economist (2002b), 'Neighbourly lessons', March 14, <http://www.economist.com>
Economist (2004), 'Europe v America: Mirror, mirror on the wall', June 17, <http://
    www.economist.com>
Economist (2005), *Pocket World in Figures – 2006 Edition*, London: Profile Books.
Economist (2008), 'Working mothers unite!', July 12, 36–7.
Elliott, Larry and Dan Atkinson (2008), *The Gods that Failed: How Blind Faith in Markets
    Has Cost Us our Future*, London: The Bodley Head.

Fogh Rasmussen, Henrik (2007), *Amerikanske Tilstande*, Copenhagen: Forlaget Center for Politiske Studier.

Gersemann, Olaf (2004), *Cowboy Capitalism: European Myths, American Reality*, Washington DC: Cato Institute.

Glazov, Jamie (2006), *Menace in Europe*, interview with Claire Berlinski, FrontPageMagazine.com, April 07, <www.frontpagemag.com>

Hall, Peter and Daniel W. Gingerich (2009), 'Varieties of capitalism and institutional complementarities in the political economy: an empirical analysis', in Bob Hancké (ed.), *Debating Varieties of Capitalism: A Reader*, Oxford: Oxford University Press, 135–79.

Hall, Peter and David Soskice (2001), *Varieties of Capitalism: The Institutional Foundations of Comparative Advantage*, Oxford: Oxford University Press.

Hall, Peter A. and Kathleen Thelen (2009), 'Institutional change in varieties of capitalism', *Socio-Economic Review*, 7: 7–34.

Hawkes, Nigel (2007), '5,000 midwives are needed to cope with increase in birthrate', *The Times*, August 31, <http://www.timesonline.co.uk/tol/life_and_style/health/article2358440.ece>

Howell, Chris (2003), 'Varieties of capitalism: and then there was one?', *Comparative Politics*, 34: 103–24.

Jäntti, Markus, Bernt Bratsberg, Knut Røed, Oddbjørn Raaum, Robin Naylor, Eva Österbacka, Anders Björklund and Tor Eriksson (2006), *American Exceptionalism in a New Light: A Comparison of Intergenerational Earnings Mobility in the Nordic Countries, the United Kingdom and the United States*, Discussion Paper 1938, Forschungsinstitut zur Zukunft der Arbeit/Institute for the Study of Labor, <http://papers.ssrn.com/sol3/papers.cfm?abstract_id=878675#PaperDownload>

Jenkins, Philip (2007), *God's Continent: Christianity, Islam, and Europe's Religious Crisis*, Oxford: Oxford University Press.

Kaletsky, Anatole (2009), 'No cause for celebrations across Europe just yet', *The Times*, August 24, <http://business.timesonline.co.uk>

Kuttner, Robert (2008), 'The Copenhagen consensus: reading Adam Smith in Denmark', *Foreign Affairs*, March/April 2008, <http://www.foreignaffairs.org>

McNamara, Sally (2007), *Is Europe Doomed to Continued Economic Stagnation?*, Heritage Lecture #1040 Delivered June 10, The Heritage Foundation, August 23, <http://www.heritage.org/>

Mitchell, Daniel J. (2007a), *Baltic Beacon*, Cato Institute, <http://www.cato.org>

Mitchell, Daniel J. (2007b), What *Can the United States Learn from the Nordic Model?*, Cato Institute – Policy Analysis, 603, November 5, <http://www.cato.org>

Money-Zine.com (2007), *Consumer Debt Statistics*, <http://www.money-zine.com>

National Center for Health Statistics (2003), *Teen Birth Rate Continues to Decline; African-American Teens Show Sharpest Drop*, December 17, <www.cdc.gov/nchs>

NationMaster.com (2008a), *Health Statistics > Spending > Per person (most recent) by country*, <http://www.nationmaster.com>

NationMaster.com (2008b), *Health Statistics > Breast cancer incidence (most recent) by country*, <http://www.nationmaster.com>

NationMaster (2008c), *Health Statistics > Daily smokers > 1990 (most recent) by country*, <http://www.nationmaster.com>

Neuhaus, Richard John (2007), 'The much exaggerated death of Europe', *First Things*, May, <www.firstthings.com>

Olson, Mancur (1982), *The Rise and Decline of Nations: Economic Growth, Stagflation, and Social Rigidities*, New Haven and London: Yale University Press.

Powell, Benjamin (2003), *Markets Created a Pot of Gold in Ireland*, Cato Institute, April 15, <http://www.cato.org>

Reid, T.R. (2005), *The United States of Europe*, Harmondsworth: Penguin.

Sapir, Andre (2005), *Globalisation and the Reform of European Social Models*, Bruegel Policy Brief, <http://www.bruegel.org/Public/fileDownload.php?target=/Files/media/PDF/Publications/Policy%20Briefs/PB200501_SocialModels.pdf>

Theil, Stefan (2008), 'Europe's philosophy of failure', *Foreign Policy*, January/February, <http://www.foreignpolicy.com>

Tupy, Marian L. (2005), *Who Pays for Farm Subsidies?*, Cato Institute – Center for Trade Policy Studies, November 25, <http://www.freetrade.org>

Walker, Marcus and David Gauthier-Villars (2009), 'Europe recovers as U.S. lags: Germany, France escape recession even as consumer weakness hobbles America', *Wall Street Journal*, August 13, <http://online.wsj.com>

Weigel, George (2006), *Europe and America: Yesterday, Today, and Tomorrow*, The Wriston Lecture – The Manhattan Institute, November 7, <http://eppc.org>

9

The Obama administration, recession and beyond

The Obama administration took office in the midst of recession. It introduced important policy initiatives including the fiscal stimulus package, the provision of assistance to the automobile industry, and 'stress tests' on the largest banks. Although there were some signs of recovery in mid-2009, the administration and the nation faced major difficulties. These included continuing unemployment, the scale of the federal government budget deficit, and the challenges posed by the rise of the Chinese and Indian economies.

When Barack Obama took office on January 20 2009, the most recently published economic statistics made grim reading. During the last quarter of 2008, GDP fell (using real, annualised figures) by 6.3 per cent (Bureau of Economic Analysis, 2009). In December, unemployment reached 7.2 per cent (Bureau of Labor Statistics, 2009).[1] In the same month, there were 97,841 home foreclosures (Business Wire, 2009).[2] As Paul Krugman warned a fortnight before the inauguration: 'Let's not mince words: This looks an awful lot like the beginning of a second Great Depression' (Krugman, 2009a). Such was the scale of the crisis that there were parallels with Japan, which had suffered a 'lost decade' of economic stagnation from the early 1990s onwards (Kornblut and Fletcher, 2009).

Against this background, free market economics came under fire. The crisis had, it was said, illustrated the need to abandon the neo-liberalism that had governed economic thinking for three decades. The criticisms were not confined to the far left. Even moderates called for greater regulation. Robert J. Barbera spoke of the need for a form of economic thinking resting on 'an enlightened synthesis'. The Federal Reserve, he argued, should take a proactive role and deflate bubbles before they threatened national or international stability. In his book, *A Failure of Capitalism*, Richard A. Posner called for increases in marginal tax rates on those with the highest incomes so as to deter excessive risk-taking. In *Animal Spirits*, Robert J. Shiller questioned some of the most basic assumptions underpinning neo-liberalism and stressed that individuals were not cold utility-maximisers whose behaviour could be predicted but were instead guided by more irrational instincts (Leonhardt, 2009a). Across the board, there was more of an acceptance that there should be greater regulation, particularly of the banking sector, and that excessive displays of opulence, such as the payments of large bonuses, should be reined in.

Despite all the talk of change, the new administration's thinking built at least in some respects upon the steps taken by the Bush White House. There was, however, a greater sense of certainty and resolve. Furthermore, although there were still obstacles, Democratic gains in the Congressional elections made the passage of legislation more straightforward than it had been during the years of 'divided government'.[3]

'Team Obama' stressed the pivotal importance of fiscal policy and the stimulus package that was passed during the first weeks of the Obama presidency. They accepted the argument put forward by commentators, most notably Paul Krugman, that the use of monetary policy was a necessary but insufficient condition for economic recovery. From this perspective, as events in Japan during the 'lost decade' had illustrated, once interest rates have been reduced to almost zero, and this has not triggered economic expansion, other measures are required if there is to be any prospect of sustained growth. As Krugman concluded: 'For this is the third time in history that a major economy has found itself in a liquidity trap, a situation in which interest-rate cuts, the conventional way to perk up the economy, have reached their limit. When this happens, unconventional measures are the only way to fight recession' (Krugman, 2009b).

Furthermore, although the Obama White House committed itself to large-scale spending projects it also distanced itself from earlier generations of 'tax and spend' Democrats (or at least the ways in which they were portrayed by their opponents) by promising that taxes would be cut for 95 per cent of 'workers and their families'. Indeed, the Obama election campaign promised that 'no family making less than $250,000 will see their taxes increase. The typical middle class family will receive well over $1,000 in tax relief under the Obama plan' (Obama '08, 2008). Corporate tax loopholes would be ended and there would be limited tax rises for those in the highest income brackets:

> Families making more than $250,000 will pay either the same or lower tax rates than they paid in the 1990s. Obama will ask the wealthiest 2 per cent of families to give back a portion of the taxes they have received over the past eight years to ensure we are restoring fairness and returning to fiscal responsibility. But no family will pay higher tax rates than they would have paid in the 1990s. (Obama '08, 2008)[4]

In overall terms, the White House promised, the tax burden would be reduced as a proportion of US national output: 'Obama's plan will cut taxes overall, reducing revenues to below the levels that prevailed under Ronald Reagan (less than 18.2 per cent of GDP). The Obama tax plan is a net tax cut' (Obama '08, 2008). At the same time, the incoming administration talked in terms of fiscal 'responsibility'. Indeed, despite the increases in federal government spending necessitated by both the economic crisis itself and the White House's expenditure plans, the Obama campaign committed itself to 'bringing down the budget deficit' (Obama '08, 2008).[5]

The 2008 Obama campaign and the incoming administration stressed three other themes. First, they built upon the prevailing mood and emphasised the need for the tighter regulation of the financial sector so as to check speculation and prevent or at least limit future asset 'bubbles'. The crisis, it was said, had been caused by speculation, the pursuit of short-term rewards, detachment from underlying economic realities, and growing inequality that had allowed an entrenched economic elite to place its immediate interests ahead of the 'common good'. Using the soaring rhetoric that was his trademark, Obama condemned 'excess greed, excess compensation, excess risk-taking' (Ahrens, 2009a). The free market, he said, had to be reined in. As the new president said in his inauguration address:

> Our economy is badly weakened, a consequence of greed and irresponsibility on the part of some but also our collective failure to make hard choices and prepare the nation for a new age…without a watchful eye, the market can spin out of control. The nation cannot prosper long when it favors only the prosperous. (*New York Times*, 2009a)

A fortnight earlier, in a speech given at George Mason University in Virginia, Obama had been even more direct:

> For years, too many Wall Street executives made imprudent and dangerous decisions, seeking profits with too little regard for risk, too little regulatory scrutiny, and too little accountability. Banks made loans without concern for whether borrowers could repay them, and some borrowers took advantage of cheap credit to take on debt they couldn't afford. Politicians spent taxpayer money without wisdom or discipline and too often focused on scoring political points instead of problems they were sent here to solve. The result has been a devastating loss of trust and confidence in our economy, our financial markets and our government. (MSNBC, 2009)

Secondly, the White House tied the process of economic recovery and its spending plans to the task of increasing US national competitiveness. Stimulus efforts would not simply fuel demand (which might lay a basis for further asset bubbles) but would strengthen the physical and human capital upon which the country rested. Obama thereby tied the fiscal stimulus package that was passed by Congress in February 2009 as well as his proposals to reform healthcare provision together with the country's economic future:

But even as this plan puts Americans back to work today, it will also make those critical investments in alternative energy and safer roads, better health care and modern schools that will lay the foundation for long-term growth and prosperity. And it will invest in broadband and emerging technologies...because that is how America will retain and regain its competitive edge in the 21st century. (White House, 2009a)

Thirdly, there was a stress, which became more pronounced during the early months of the new administration, on the need for a coordinated global response to the economic crisis. Financial assets in the US were intertwined with those held overseas. Furthermore, regulation could only be effective if countries took broadly similar steps so that capital did not simply flee to the least controlled financial centres. At the same time, US export industries depended upon recovery in other continents. As Obama himself put it in comments he made following a meeting of the G-20 nations at the beginning of April 2009:

If people in other countries cannot spend, that means they cannot buy the goods we produce here in America, which means more lost jobs and more families hurting...And if we continue to let banks and other financial institutions around the world act recklessly and irresponsibly, that affects institutions here at home as credit dries up, and people can't get loans to buy a home or car, to run a small business or pay for college. Ultimately, the only way out of a recession that is global in scope is with a response that is global in coordination. (White House, 2009b)

The White House and Congress

Some commentators took note of Timothy Geithner's appointment as Treasury secretary and the selection of Lawrence Summers as White House economic adviser. Geithner had a background in the financial sector (he had formerly been the president of the Federal Reserve Bank of New York). Summers, who had served as Treasury secretary during the Clinton administration, also had close ties to Wall Street. The choice of Geithner and Summers therefore seemed to bode badly for those hoping (despite the generally fairly cautious commitments given by Obama himself) for radical changes, a frontal challenge to finance capital or a second 'New Deal'. Furthermore, although economic issues remained at the forefront, other concerns – including healthcare provision, the restructuring of energy industries and the battle for Afghanistan – jostled for attention during White House deliberations.

Nonetheless, some important measures were adopted during the Obama administration's first 100 days and beyond.

- The $787 billion fiscal stimulus package (the American Recovery and Reinvestment Act [ARRA]) was passed in February 2009. The measure, which *NBC Nightly News* termed 'the biggest spending bill in American history', provided tax relief, expanded social benefits and increased spending in, for example, education and healthcare provision. Despite hopes of winning across significant numbers of Republicans in Congress, there were stark partisan divisions. Sarah Palin, who had served as the party's vice-presidential nominee in 2008 and was at that point governor of Alaska, was among those Republican governors who refused the 'buckets of money' promised by the package because 'we don't want those fat strings attached, where centralized big government is going to tell us what is best'. At times, Republicans spoke in portentous terms. When asked on *Fox News* about the Obama administration and the economic policies it had adopted Palin warned of 'socialism': 'Our country could evolve into something that we do not even recognize, certainly that is so far from what the founders of our country had in mind for us' (*Huffington Post*, 2009).

Against this background, not a single House Republican backed the bill. Those Republican Congressmen who were not swayed by anxieties about creeping 'socialism' argued that much of the spending would be inefficient, 'crowd out' private investment and add to the national debt. There were also fears that government spending would be used as 'pork' so as to boost re-election efforts by particular Democratic members of Congress. In place of a spending package, Republicans and the wider conservative movement made the case for far more extensive tax cuts and credits than were offered in the stimulus.[6]

Some of these arguments were sufficient to win across seven Democrats who broke with their party and voted against the stimulus bill. With one exception, they were members of the Blue Dog Coalition. The Coalition was formed in 1995 among more conservative Democrats on the basis of a commitment to fiscal restraint, national security and other 'mainstream values'. Nonetheless, the House is a *majoritarian* institution and therefore, despite Republican opposition and the handful of dissenters within their own ranks, the package (which at that stage provided for $819 billion of spending) was passed.

The Senate version of the bill originally specified a total of $838 billion but because Senate rules require sixty votes for the passage of legislation if there is determined opposition, the Democrats had to make concessions. These enabled them to secure the votes of three Senate Republicans: Susan Collins and Olympia Snowe of Maine and Arlen Specter of Pennsylvania (who subsequently defected to the Democrats). The House and the Senate versions had then to be reconciled. At the end of the process, when President Obama signed the legislation, it totalled $787 billion.

Supporters of the package argued that it addressed short-term, medium-term and long-term economic needs. Some of its components, including tax credits and, for example, the $19.9 billion given to the food stamp programme, would not only meet urgent needs but would bolster overall demand levels.

There were also longer-term infrastructural projects that would add to employment in the medium term and strengthen US competitiveness in the longer term. As Lawrence Summers later recalled:

> As to composition, we quickly concluded that in a world of substantial uncertainty and one in which it was important to get stimulus started quickly, a diversified approach was appropriate. That is why we settled on a program that emphasized support for household consumption through tax cuts and expansions in unemployment insurance and food stamps; support for small businesses through lending and expanded access to capital; support for state and local governments; and investment in priority areas like health care, infrastructure, clean energy, and education. (Summers, 2009)

- The long-established US automobile companies, General Motors (GM) and Chrysler, had been given loans by the Bush administration to stave off bankruptcies. A month after President Obama took office, they still faced significant difficulties. The Obama administration responded by demanding a radical restructuring of both companies which included substantial job losses. Chrysler was required to merge with Fiat (Stolberg and Vlasic, 2009). Although this was intended as a temporary measure, the federal government took an 8 per cent share in the successor to Chrysler and a 60 per cent share in the company that, as a result of the restructuring, took over GM's assets (Whoriskey, 2009).[7] In June 2009, Congress established the Car Allowance Rebate System (CARS), which was quickly dubbed 'cash for clunkers'. This offered up to $4,500 to those trading in an older car (a 'clunker') for a new, fuel-efficient vehicle. Take-up was high and the $1 billion initially allocated to the programme was almost exhausted after just one week of full implementation and it was therefore extended. The programme finally came to a close towards the end of August 2009. It was said to have saved 39,000 jobs and generated a total of 690,114 sales (Ahrens, 2009b). Nonetheless, despite the seeming popularity of 'cash for clunkers', there were criticisms. Purchases that would have been made a few months later were simply being brought forward. Furthermore, the programme offered a subsidy, paid for by the taxpayer, to individuals and families who already had a comfortable income. A survey suggested that the average income of those purchasing new cars under the provisions of the programme was $57,700 (Gattuso and Loris, 2009).
- The second tranche of TARP funding, which had been authorised by legislation passed by Congress during the final days of the Bush administration, was released so as to provide a further $350 billion for the banking sector. In February 2009, the Treasury announced a plan to create a public-private partnership that would spend as much as $2.5 trillion in buying 'toxic assets'. However, in early June, the Federal Deposit Insurance Corporation, which would have guaranteed loans to investors, announced that it was placing one part of the plan on indefinite hold. This was because banks

would not sell the assets they held at the prices that were likely to be offered (*New York Times*, 2009b).

- There were 'stress tests' on the nineteen largest banks so as to assess their ability to withstand strains and crises in future years. The Treasury announced that the banks had to raise $74.6 billion as a financial 'cushion'. Although some contended that the tests were not sufficiently rigorous, there was relief that the sums involved were not larger.

- Two months after he took office, President Obama reaffirmed his commitment to new forms of 'macroprudential' supervision that 'he hopes will prevent the "bubble/bust mentality" and prevent larger systemic risk'. The Federal Reserve and other agencies would be given broad powers so as to anticipate predict bubbles and 'prick' them (through the use of deflationary measures) before they burst (Ahrens, 2009a). In mid-June 2009, the administration's proposals were unveiled. However, there was a lack of faith in the Federal Reserve among many members of Congress and a disappointed sense that the original plans had been trimmed down at the behest of lobbyists representing the financial sector. The insurance companies, for example, were able to fend off proposals for a national regulator. The *Washington Post* concluded: 'The plan President Obama unveiled yesterday to overhaul the government's oversight of the financial system was not the wholesale remaking of Washington that the administration had initially envisioned' (Cho and Goldfarb, 2009).

- The White House submitted the budget for FY 2010 (October 2009– September 2010) to Congress. President Obama's proposals envisaged spending levels of $3.6 trillion. Despite the restoration of a 39.6 per cent marginal tax rate on higher-income earners, this represented a $1.75 trillion deficit, nearly four times greater than any earlier deficit, and added markedly to the national debt. The size of the deficit reflected the scale of the fiscal stimulus, the impact of recession (additional expenditure burdens and shrunken tax revenues) and the rises in entitlement expenditure (Medicare, Medicaid and Social Security).

- The $275 billion housing programme (the Helping Families Save Their Homes Act) passed in May 2009 (and expanding an earlier programme) would, the White House and Congressional Democrats claimed, rescue as many as 9 million homeowners from foreclosure (by allowing them to swap a high interest rate loan for a thirty-year fixed loan backed by the Federal Housing Administration). By early July 2009, 131,030 mortgages had been modified on a three-month trial basis (Nocera, 2009). Set against this, however, 3.5 million foreclosures were forecast for 2009.

- Like other governments and central banks across much of the world, the US embarked upon a policy of 'quantitative easing'. This involves a process in which the Federal Reserve buys bills from the Treasury and bonds from banks using 'money' that it has itself created. This expands the money supply, particularly because funds that are deposited in a bank can then be used as a basis for loans. (This is sometimes termed the *credit creation multiplier*.)

Challenges

Although the Obama White House made much of its achievements, the administration and the Congressional Democrats on Capitol Hill faced significant challenges and difficulties. First, there were widely shared concerns about the efficacy of the fiscal stimulus package (ARRA). While Republicans condemned it as an extravagant overreaction, others argued that it was too small and wrongly 'loaded'. It should, it was said, have been based upon projects that would have more of an impact in 2009 rather than 2010. According to Paul Krugman, the package was 'about $1 trillion short of what's needed... Achieving sustained recovery will probably require spending $600 billion per year for three years on projects that put people to work while building a lasting infrastructure to support ongoing economic growth' (*Portland Business Journal*, 2009). Writing from a very different perspective, Irwin Stelzer also argued that there were relatively few 'shovel-ready' projects (which were ready to begin but were delayed because of a lack of funding) and that instead of taking new initiatives the states were using stimulus money to cover gaps created by their budget cuts (Stelzer, 2009b).

Many on the right raised more trenchant questions and attacked the underlying assumptions upon which the stimulus was based. Such policies, it was said, did not create purchasing power but instead simply redistributed it:

> Every dollar Congress 'injects' into the economy must first be taxed or borrowed out of the economy. No new income, and therefore no new demand, is created... Removing water from one end of a swimming pool and dumping it in the other end will not raise the overall water level. Similarly, moving dollars from one part of the economy to the other will not expand the economy. Not even in the short run. (Riedl, 2009: 36)

Nonetheless, many estimates concluded that ARRA saved the US from the prospect of an even deeper recession. According to Noam Scheiber, the stimulus package 'contributed roughly 3 per cent to annualized growth rates in the second quarter. This means that absent its effects, economic performance would have resembled that of the previous three quarters, when the economy contracted at an average annual rate of 4.9 per cent. In short, the recovery act turned this quarter's economic performance from disastrous to merely bad' (Scheiber, 2009). *Failure*

Secondly, unemployment levels rose far beyond the Obama administration's initial projections. With the stimulus package, his economic team had said, unemployment would probably peak at 8 per cent towards the end of 2009 (Leonhardt, 2009b). However, six months after Obama took office, the unemployment rate reached 9.5 per cent, and by October 2009 it reached 10.2 per cent (Table 9.1). Furthermore, the long-term unemployment rate (those out of work for at least fifteen weeks) reached 5.1 per cent in June 2009 and

Table 9.1 *Unemployment rate 2009 (%)*

January	February	March	April	May	June	July	August	September	October
7.6	8.1	8.5	8.9	9.4	9.5	9.4	9.7	9.8	10.2

Source: Bureau of Labor Statistics (2009), *Unemployment Rate*, <http://data.bls.gov>

for the first time since records began in 1948, those who were unemployed on a long-term basis constituted more than half all those who were out of work (Norris, 2009).

The rise in both short-term and long-term unemployment was larger than might have been expected from the fall in GDP. As Lawrence Summers noted:

> it appears that a given level of output is being produced with fewer people work-ing than historical relationships would have led one to predict. In economists' language, there is a significant residual in the Okun's law relationship: The unemployment rate over the recession has risen about 1 to 1.5 percentage points more than would normally be attributable to the contraction in GDP. (Summers, 2009)

Why did unemployment increase to this extent? In part, it was because although there had been talk of a prolonged depression at the beginning of the year the scale of the crisis had still been underestimated. There was also a sense, at least from late 2008 onwards, that the recession would be prolonged and this too may have encouraged employers to lay off workers more readily and on a larger scale than in earlier downturns (Summers, 2009). Furthermore, despite the financial 'bailout', the 'credit crunch' continued for many. Although some companies, chiefly the larger ones, could gain access to bank loans, others (particularly the smaller firms) were unable to borrow or faced punitive terms. According to a report published at the end of August 2009 in the *Wall Street Journal*, this 'divides America in two' (Tuna, Rappaport and Jargon, 2009). At the same time, excessive hopes were pinned on the ability of the fiscal stimulus package to bring about economic recovery. As noted above, much of the spending was committed to 2010 rather than 2009. The increased flexibility of the labour market, making redundancies more straightforward, may have played a part.

Thirdly, consumers were reluctant to spend and there were concerns that this would limit the extent of a recovery. Caution among consumers can in part be attributed to a negative wealth effect. As the value of assets (most notably that of houses) fell, consumers reduced their spending.[8] At the same time, people were fearful about the future and therefore sought to reduce personal debt levels and build up some savings as a safeguard against continuing hard times. Despite all the financial pressures, the savings rate (the proportion of income that is saved) rose in mid-2009 to about 4 per cent. In mid-2007, the savings rate had been just 2 per cent (Goodman, 2009).

Fourth, the scale of the federal government deficit provoked anxiety. In August 2009, the Office of Management and Budget (OMB), which is directly answerable to the president, revised its estimate of the ten-year total for deficits between 2009 and 2019 upwards to $9.05 trillion, constituting 5.1 per cent of GDP (Calmes, 2009).[9] If the entire national debt was considered, the figures looked even worse. Projections suggested that by 2019 the debt-to-GDP ratio would be about 100 per cent, a peacetime record (Samuelson, 2009). The deficits can be attributed to the 'bailouts' and the stimulus package, the tax cuts pursued by the Bush administration, the demands imposed by recession, overseas military commitments and increases in entitlement expenditure (particularly Medicare and Medicaid).[10] As *USA Today* noted: 'Of the $9 trillion, almost half can be attributed to growth in Medicare and Medicaid spending. This year, the health programs for the elderly and poor will cost about $687 billion. By 2019, they are forecast to run about $1.3 trillion' (*USA Today*, 2009).

Deficits, like any form of borrowing, have to be funded through the selling of Treasury securities (government-guaranteed bonds) at auctions. They are bought by individuals, banks and foreign governments, most notably China. The continued willingness of these parties to purchase Treasury securities cannot be assumed. Indeed, the *Financial Times* reported that an auction of thirty-year bonds in May 2009 'went badly' because of concerns about the scale of the budget deficit. There were fears that this would place upward pressure on interest rates well before economic recovery is assured (Mackenzie and Stacey, 2009). There might also, it was noted, be difficulties making interest payments:

> The growth of debt would lead to a vicious cycle in which the government had to issue ever-larger amounts of debt in order to pay ever-higher interest charges. Eventually, the government would need to adopt some offsetting measures – such as cutting spending or increasing taxes – to break the cycle and put the federal budget on a sustainable path. (Congressional Budget Office, 2009: 15–18)

If taxes were raised at some point so as to reduce the deficit and limit borrowing requirements, this would have economic as well as political consequences. Although the relationship between taxation and economic expansion is far from certain or precise, despite the claims sometimes made by supply-siders (see Chapter 3), high tax rates can pose a direct threat to enterprise and growth (Congressional Budget Office, 2009: 18).

Fifth, some raised the spectre of runaway inflation. Arthur Laffer, who made his name as a leading supply-side economist during the early 1980s (see Chapter 3), pointed to what he saw as the consequences of quantitative easing and the resultant growth of the money supply, in particular the 'monetary base' (the currency in circulation, the reserves held by member banks at the Federal Reserve and the cash held in their vaults):

The percentage increase in the monetary base is the largest increase in the past 50 years by a factor of 10 ... It is so far outside the realm of our prior experiential base that historical comparisons are rendered difficult if not meaningless ... It's difficult to estimate the magnitude of the inflationary and interest-rate consequences of the Fed's actions because, frankly, we haven't ever seen anything like this in the U.S. To date what's happened is potentially far more inflationary than were the monetary policies of the 1970s. (Laffer, 2009)

Others, however, pointed to different threats. Ambrose Evans-Pritchard noted that data from the St Louis Federal Reserve suggested that the money multiplier (the rate at which an increase in the money supply is multiplied because of the credit creation process) fell from an average for the preceding decade of 1.6 to just 0.893.[11] Instead of inflation, deflation remained a danger. If prices began to fall, there would be a crisis of business confidence and investment levels would plummet still further. Furthermore, he recorded, there was still considerable unused capacity which would also ensure that prices did not rise (Evans-Pritchard, 2009). From this perspective, the biggest danger was that 'victory' over the crisis would be declared prematurely. If they feared inflation, policymakers might adopt tighter forms of monetary policy and ease back on the spending of stimulus funds. This could, however, easily suppress a recovery and prolong the recession. Writing from a similar perspective, Christina Romer, chairwoman of the Council of Economic Advisers in the Obama administration, cited in warning the 1937 recession, which had, she claimed, been triggered by the Federal Reserve's pursuit of deflationary measures (Romer, 2009) (see pp. 37–8).

Sixth, there were growing fears for the future of the dollar. Although it may be that because quantitative easing has been pursued in many countries, investors will see few alternatives to the dollar, inflation (if it occurs) or the printing of money will lead to a process of currency depreciation. This may, in turn, trigger a reluctance to hold dollar-denominated assets:

But as the printing presses keep running, and the recession eases, investors will find the risk of being paid in dollars that have shrivelled in value too much to bear. Which is why the dollar hit its lowest level of the year last week and why for a while it cost less to buy insurance against a default by hamburger-seller McDonald's than against a default by the world's only superpower. (Stelzer, 2009a)

Seventh, the recession took its toll on the cities and the states as well as the federal government. Their budgets were squeezed by falling revenues and increased demands for services and other forms of provision. Inevitably, despite some stimulus funding, fees for services were raised while municipal employees faced lay-offs. Alongside this, there were demographic shifts as house prices plummeted, employment opportunities disappeared and migration flows dried

238

up. Florida, one of the linchpin sunbelt states, which had expanded dramatically in earlier years, lost 58,000 people in net terms during the year up to the beginning of April 2009 (El Nasser, 2009).

Eighth, the crisis intensified calls for protectionist measures within both Congress and at state level. Furthermore, despite affirmations of faith in free trade and a retreat from attempts to renegotiate NAFTA, the White House was in no mood to negotiate or implement further trade agreements. It also seemed to accept that state-level policymakers who administered and disbursed stimulus funding would impose 'buy American' conditions. There was growing talk of retaliation in some other nations and, in particular, an increasing number of trade skirmishes between the US and Canadian companies and public authorities (see Chapter 6).

Lastly, the administration (and the Congressional Democrats) seemed to lose much of the public backing that had been evident when Obama first took office and this may in turn curb its ability to take the steps it regards as necessary. Indeed, sixth months into the Obama presidency, there were signs that the conservative critique of the economic crisis had gained political traction. The bailouts of the automobile companies and the acquisition of a government stake in them were opposed by large majorities. By July 2009, the opinions polls were suggesting that many Americans identified Obama with 'big government' and were anxious about its consequences. Proposals for healthcare reform provoked increasingly vigorous opposition. Although there was backing (by about two-thirds of those asked) for the fiscal stimulus package that was enacted in February 2009, there was also some scepticism about its overall economic impact. According to a June 2009 poll 76 per cent said it was 'somewhat likely' or 'very likely' that a large amount of the funds offered by the fiscal stimulus would be wasted because of inadequate government oversight (Rasmussen Reports, 2009a). There were also major concerns about its consequences for the federal government deficit and the national debt. Some 49 per cent told pollsters that they were 'very concerned' about the size of the federal budget deficit. Furthermore, the polls suggested that there was a marked opposition to what was seen as excessive government spending. Given a choice, 50 per cent opted for tax reductions while 41 per cent supported increased government spending (PollingReport.com, 2009). A Bloomberg poll taken in early September 2009 found that 62 per cent of these asked want to see spending levels cut 'even at the risk of a longer-lasting recession' (PollingReport.com, 2009).

Conclusion

The second quarter figures for 2009 suggested that the crisis, or at least the rate of decline, was easing. In the third quarter of the year there was growth (3.5 per cent) for the first time since the second quarter of 2008. By the beginning of September 2009, Allan Meltzer could firmly assert in the *Wall Street Journal* that the US faced a recession, perhaps comparable to 1973–5, rather than a depression (Meltzer, 2009).

This form of commentary set the scene for debate about the prospects for recovery and whether that process would be 'V' shaped (implying a relatively speedy recovery), U-shaped (indicating that recovery will be significantly slower), 'W' shaped (suggesting that the US and perhaps much of the world faced a 'double-dipper', in other words a second period of recession after a brief and very limited recovery), or 'L' shaped. The 'L' was invoked by those who cited the Japanese experience during the 1990s and feared a prolonged period of downturn or, at best, very low and sluggish growth.[12]

Whatever the answer, questions remained about long-term American competitiveness and the country's economic future.[13] Asked about this in a newspaper interview, Lawrence Summers spoke in optimistic terms about structural changes that would reshape both economy and society:

> The new American economy, Summers hopes, will be 'more export-oriented' and 'less consumption-oriented'; 'more environmentally-oriented' and 'less energy-production-oriented'; 'more bio-and software-and civil-engineering-oriented'; and finally, 'more middle-class-oriented' and 'less oriented to income growth that is disproportionate towards a very small share of the population.' Unlike many other economists, Summers does not believe that lower growth is the inevitable price of this economic paradigm shift. (Freeland, 2009)

Others were much less sanguine. From this perspective, the recession has made an indelible mark on the US economy and the country's politics. In particular, the size and scale of the federal government grew in ways that policymakers will have to confront for decades to come.[14] Government spending and the imposition of additional costs upon industry (to pay, for example, for healthcare reform or to curb carbon emissions) may add to the other difficulties that the US faces. *Fortune* has reported that although the number of US companies among the world's top 500 (140) was twice as many as any other nation, it had fallen to the lowest level since the business magazine began the list in 1995 (Gunther, 2009: 67–9). Furthermore, although Chinese growth levels fell because of the global downturn, it still recorded 7.9 per cent in the first quarter of 2009. During the first half of the year, China overtook the US as the world's largest car producer. The Indian economy was, with a 5.8 per cent growth rate in the first three months, not very far behind (*Economist*, 2009: 89).

This book has charted the debates about America's economic future that have taken place from the early 1930s onwards. Despite the arguments and doubts, however, throughout the period the US has symbolised economic modernity. Although there were oft-repeated criticisms, the US was the world's economic leader and as such attracted confidence and trust even amongst those who criticised the character and uses of American economic might. All that is changing. For Kevin Phillips, the growth of Asian economic might, the 'financialisation' of the US economy (and as its corollary the decline of manufacturing) all represent signs that the US is 'an empire in decline' (Phillips, 2009: 208). Others speak of a 'post-American world'.[15] When, at the end of May 2009, Treasury secretary Tim Geithner told a student audience in Beijing in that Chinese assets were 'very safe' in the US his comment, as Reuters reported, drew laughter (Reuters, 2009). The laughter highlighted the challenges that the US economy will face over the coming decades.

Notes

1 During the three months ending in February 2009, the economy lost a total of 2.1 million jobs, the biggest three-month decline in employment numbers since 1945 (Summers, 2009).

2 A 'foreclosure' is the eviction of a homeowner (almost always because of default on loans) and the forced sale of a property.

3 The term 'divided government' is applied when Congress and the White House are controlled by different parties.

4 The Tax Policy Center, a joint project of the Urban Institute and the Brookings Institution, reported that for the approximately 147,000 families that constitute the top 0.1 per cent of the income scale, Obama's proposals would increase their taxes by, on average, $701,885 (*Washington Post*, 2008).

5 The deficit was to be reduced by ending the Iraq War, reducing some agricultural subsidies, 'cutting subsidies for private plans in Medicare, reforming student loans, cutting earmarks to at least the level they were in 1994, ending no-bid contracting, and phasing out unnecessary and duplicative programs' (Obama '08, 2008). There would also be 'pay-as-you-go budget rules' (so that spending did not add to the deficit) and 'a constitutionally acceptable line-item veto to cut pork-barrel spending' (Obama '08, 2008). Almost all of these proposals do, however, require the assent and cooperation of Congress.

6 Even some of those who backed the fiscal stimulus were concerned that the spending projects would not begin during 2009. Most, they noted, would only begin in 2010. This would be a case of 'too little, too late' and the economic impact of the stimulus would be largely lost.

7 Ford and the foreign-owned car plants in the US did not seek or secure government assistance. A July 2009 poll indicated that 46 per cent of Americans were, as a consequence, more likely to buy a car from Ford (Rasmussen Reports, 2009b).

8 The 'wealth effect' usually takes a positive form. As assets rise in value and individuals become more wealthy, they become more confident and therefore increase their spending in the following year, usually by about 2–3 per cent (Goodman, 2009).

9 Some asserted that the deficit would be at least a trillion dollars larger. The administration's projections assumed, for example, the passage of legislation bringing in carbon taxes (the 'cap and trade' proposals). As the Washington Times noted, 'a $10 trillion deficit comes out to more than $33,000 for every man, woman

and child in America. Not everyone pays federal income taxes; when counting only taxpayers, the federal deficit burden is $105,000 per household' (*Washington Times*, 2009).

10   According to David Leonhardt of the *New York Times*, the growth of the federal government budget deficit from January 2001 onwards and projected through to 2012 can be attributed to (a) the state of the business cycle (37 per cent), (b) new legislation (such as tax cuts) signed by President George W. Bush (33 per cent), (c) the extension of Bush-era policies by President Obama (such as the Iraq War and the Troubled Asset Relief Program [TARP]) (20 per cent), (d) the February 2009 stimulus package (7 per cent), and (e) Obama's plans for healthcare, education, energy etc. (3 per cent) (Leonhardt, 2009c).

11   The credit creation process is based upon banks' practice of only keeping a fraction of the funds deposited with them and lending out the remainder. The funds that are lent will then be deposited with other banks, providing a basis for yet further lending and expansion of the money supply. The extent to which more money is created depends upon the size of the fractional reserve (the proportion held back by the banks and not lent out).

12   Nouriel Roubini from the Stern School of Business, New York University, is one of the more prominent 'pessimists'. He suggested that although there might be rapid growth in the short term as stockpiles are built up again, recovery will be slow and weak (U-shaped) (Roubini, 2009).

13   Paul Krugman has questioned the notion that nations can be 'competitive' or 'uncompetitive'. Nations, he argues, are not individual companies and are not in competition with each other. See pp. 00–00.

14   Although Democrats are generally associated with a commitment to 'big government' and conservative Republicans are identified with the free market, the contours of particular policy debates has often been less clear-cut. During the 2009 debate on healthcare reform, many on the right opposed new government spending but opposed cuts in existing spending, particularly the Medicare budget (Chait, 2009).

15   In *The Post-American World*, Fareed Zakaria argues that the shift is not so much about the decline of the US, but rather about the rise of other powers (Zakaria, 2008).

References and further reading

Ahrens, Frank (2009a), 'Obama: we're moving toward broader regulation', *Washington Post* (Economy Watch – The Ticker), March 18, <http://voices.washingtonpost.com>

Ahrens, Frank (2009b), ' "Clunkers" generates 690,000 sales', *Washington Post*, August 27, A20.

Associated Press (2009), 'Congress passes bill to help stem foreclosures', *Los Angeles Times*, May 20, <http://www.latimes.com>

Bureau of Economic Analysis (2009), *National Economic Accounts – Gross Domestic Product (GDP)*, <http://www.bea.gov>

Bureau of Labor Statistics (2009), *Labor Force Statistics from the Current Population Survey – Unemployment Rate*, <http://data.bls.gov>

Business Wire (2009), *Foreclosures Surge in February to Reach Highest Monthly Level of the Foreclosure Crisis*, March 11, <http://www.businesswire.com>

Calmes, Jackie (2009), 'In revision, a 10-year deficit of $9 trillion is forecast', *New York Times*, August 26, A4.

Chait, Jonathan (2009), 'Thought rationing', *New Republic*, July 15, 240: 4863, 2.

Cho, David and Zachary A. Goldfarb (2009), 'Core reforms held firm as much else fell away', *Washington Post*, June 18, <http://www.washingtonpost.com>

Congressional Budget Office (2009), *Testimony Statement of Douglas W. Elmendorf (Director): The Long-Term Budget Outlook, before the Committee on the Budget United States Senate, July 16, 2009*, <http://www.cbo.gov>

Economist (2009), 'Output, prices and jobs', 392: 8641, July 25, 89.

El Nasser, Haya (2009), 'For Florida, "the end of an era" of growth', *USA Today*, September 1, 1A and 2A.

Evans-Pritchard, Ambrose (2009), 'Don't believe the hyperinflation hype – dare to make cuts', *Sunday Telegraph*, June 21, <http://www.telegraph.co.uk>

Freeland, Chrystia (2009), 'Crisis manager', *Financial Times*, July 11–12, Life & Arts 3.

Frum, David (2008), 'No to the auto bailout', David Frum's Diary, *National Review Online*, November 12, <http://frum.nationalreview.com>

Gattuso, James L. and Nicolas Loris (2009), *Cash for Clunkers: Just Spinning Wheels*, The Heritage Foundation, WebMemo #2579, August 5, <http://www.heritage.org>

Goodman, Peter S. (2009), 'Consumer thrift in US may last after recession', *New York Times*, August 29, A1 and A13.

Gunther, Marc (2009), 'China Inc. takes off', *Fortune* (European edn), July 20, 67–9.

Huffington Post (2009), 'Palin: Obama is leading America towards socialism (VIDEO)', *Huffington Post*, June 9, <http://www.huffingtonpost.com>

Kornblut, Anne E. and Michael A. Fletcher (2009), 'Obama says economic crisis comes first: president tells nation stimulus plan must pass, with or without GOP support', *Washington Post*, February 10, A0, <http://www.washingtonpost.com>

Krugman, Paul (2008), 'The conscience of a liberal – the Keynesian moment', *New York Times*, November 29, <http://krugman.blogs.nytimes.com>

Krugman, Paul (2009a), 'Fighting off depression', *New York Times*, January 4, <http://www.nytimes.com>

Krugman, Paul (2009b), 'Stay the course', *New York Times*, June 14, <http://www.nytimes.com>

Laffer, Arthur B. (2009), 'Get ready for inflation and higher interest rates', *Wall Street Journal*, June 11, <http://online.wsj.com>

Leonhardt, David (2009a), 'Theory and morality in the new economy', *New York Times Book Review*, August 23, 23.

Leonhardt, David (2009b), 'A forecast with hope built in', *New York Times*, June 30, <http://www.nytimes.com>

Leonhardt, David (2009c), 'America's sea of red ink was years in the making', *New York Times*, June 9, <http://www.nytimes.com>

Mackenzie, Michael and Kiran Stacey (2009), *US Bond Yields Spark Concern*, FT.com, June 10, <http://www.ft.com>

Meeropol, Michael (1998), *Surrender: How the Clinton Administration Completed the Reagan Revolution*, Ann Arbor, MI: University of Michigan Press.

Meltzer, Allan H. (2009), 'What happened to the "depression"?', *Wall Street Journal*, September 1, A17.

MSNBC (2009), *Full text of President-elect Obama's speech*, <http://www.msnbc.msn.com>

New York Times (2009a), Barack Obama's inaugural address, <http://www.nytimes.com>

New York Times (2009b), 'Credit crisis – bailout plan – overview', June 17, <http://topics.nytimes.com>

Nocera, Joe (2009), 'A big stick but no carrot on housing', *International Herald Tribune*, July 11–12, 7.

Norris, Floyd (2009), 'Joblessness is becoming a way of life', *International Herald Tribune*, July 11–12, 8.

Obama '08 (2008), *Barack Obama's Comprehensive Tax Plan*, Obama for America, <http://www.barackobama.com>

Phillips, Kevin (2009), *Bad Money: Reckless Finance, Failed Politics and the Global Crisis of American Capitalism*, Harmondsworth: Penguin.

PollingReport.com (2009), *Federal Budget, Taxes, Economic Policy*, <http://www.pollingreport.com/budget.htm>

Portland Business Journal (2009), 'Krugman: stimulus needs to be twice as big', January 30, <http://www.bizjournals.com>

Rasmussen Reports (2009a), *76% Say Government Likely to Waste Stimulus Money*, June 24, <http://www.rasmussenreports.com>

Rasmussen Reports (2009b), *46% More Likely to Buy Ford 'Cause it Didn't Get a Bailout*, July 27, <http://www.rasmussenreports.com>

Reuters (2009), *Geithner Backs Strong Dlr, Says China's Assets Safe*, June 1, <http://www.reuters.com>

Riedl, Brian (2009), 'Why the stimulus failed', *National Review*, 61: 16, September 7, 34–7.

Romer, Christina D. (2009), 'The lessons of 1937', *Economist*, 391: 8636, June 20–26, 73.

Roubini, Nouriel (2009), 'The risk of a double-dip recession is rising', *Financial Times*, August 23, <http://www.ft.com>

Samuelson, Robert J. (2009), 'Ducking the deficit issue', *Washington Post*, August 31, A15.

Scheiber, Noam (2009), 'How the stimulus boosted GDP, cont'd', *New Republic (The Stash)*, July 31, <http://blogs.tnr.com>

Schor, Juliet (1999), 'The new politics of consumption: why Americans want so much more than they need', *Boston Review*, Summer, <http://bostonreview.net>

Somerville, Glenn (2007), 'Bush says economy strong despite stock swings', *Washington Post*, August 8, <http://www.washingtonpost.com>

Stelzer, Irwin (2009a), 'Endless Obama deficits threaten dollar's power', *Sunday Times*, May 24, <http://business.timesonline.co.uk>

Stelzer, Irwin (2009b), 'Obama's cures may just kill any recovery', *Sunday Times* (Business), July 12, 4.

Stolberg, Sheryl Gay and Bill Vlasic (2009), 'President gives a short lifeline to carmakers', *New York Times*, March 30, <http://www.nytimes.com>

Summers, Lawrence H. (2009), *Rescuing and Rebuilding the US Economy: A Progress Report*, Peterson Institute for International Economics, July 17, <http://www.piie.com>

Tuna, Cari, Liz Rappaport and Julie Jargon (2009), 'Halting recovery divides America in two', *Wall Street Journal*, August 29–30, A1 and A10.

USA Today (2009), 'Deficits and taxes', August 27, 10A.

Washington Post (2008), 'Obama and McCain tax proposals', <http://www.washingtonpost.com>

Washington Times (2009), 'The $10 trillion deficit disaster' (Comment and Analysis), August 27, A22.

White House (2009a), *Remarks of President Barack Obama on the Economy*, January 28, <http://www.whitehouse.gov>

White House (2009b), *Prepared Remarks of President Barack Obama Weekly Address – Saturday, April 4, 2009*, <http://www.whitehouse.gov>

Whoriskey, Peter (2009), 'U.S. gets majority stake in new GM: firm's investors cry foul over bankruptcy plan', *Washington Post*, June 1, <http://www.washingtonpost.com>

Zakaria, Fareed (2008), *The Post-American World: And the Rise of the Rest*, London: Allen Lane.

Index